THE POLITICS OF ECONOMIC INTERDEPENDENCE

Also by Edmund Dell

POLITICAL RESPONSIBILITY AND INDUSTRY
THE REPORT ON EUROPEAN INSTITUTIONS
(*with B. Biesheuvel and R. Marjolin*)

The Politics of Economic Interdependence

Edmund Dell

MACMILLAN
PRESS

First published 1987

Published by
THE MACMILLAN PRESS LTD
Houndmills, Basingstoke, Hampshire RG21 2XS
and London
Companies and representatives
throughout the world

Typeset by Wessex Typesetters
(Division of The Eastern Press Ltd)
Frome, Somerset

Printed in Hong Kong

British Library Cataloguing in Publication Data
Dell, Edmund
The politics of economic interdependence.
1. International economic relations
I. Title
337   HF1411
ISBN 0-333-44037-4

To Susi

Contents

Contents

Preface

Two months after the IMF crisis of November/December 1976 I delivered the fifth Rita Hinden Memorial Lecture under the title *The Politics of Economic Interdependence*. I was then Secretary of State for Trade. The lecture gave frank expression to my frustration with British economic policy over the previous years. The lecture contained only the most perfunctory genuflexion in the direction of collective cabinet responsibility. In the aftermath of the IMF crisis which I had foreseen as the inevitable consequence of the policies we had been pursuing, I had a right to speak my mind without the disguise of coded words.

Commentators, such as Mr Samuel Brittan of *The Financial Times*, while applauding much that I had said, regretted that I had reached my conclusions not on the basis of free market economics but by the more homely route of national self-interest and national pride. Subsequent controversy had me condemned as a mercantilist by some, as a monetarist by others. In fact I am not an economic theorist of any kind. I do believe that a prime responsibility of government is for national economic security. When, in the late 1970s, I explained my views to liberal economists, they told me that the idea of national economic security was a false analogy with military security. They found further justification for their scepticism in the lack of published academic authority on the subject of national economic security. With this book I do the best that I, a former politician, can do to provide the authority for which they asked.

I am grateful to Sir Arthur Knight, Lord McFadzean of Kelvinside, and Sir Peter Thornton, formerly my Permanent Secretary at the Department of Trade, for having read earlier drafts. It is an honour to have had the comments of three such friends, each of them with a lifetime's practical experience of the matters with which I deal. I am also indebted to Alyson Bailes and Rodric Braithwaite. My wife, to whom I dedicate this book, has, as usual, been my severest critic. All responsibility remains mine. My personal computer has acted as my secretary. It has not complained once as the book went through its successive drafts. I could not have had a more attentive servant, ready at all times of day and night to register my thoughts.

A variant of Chapter 17 appeared in June 1986 in *The World Economy*, the journal of the Trade Policy Research Centre, under the title 'Of Free Trade and Reciprocity'. I have incorporated some material from my article 'Trade Policy: Retrospect and Prospect' which appeared in *International Affairs*, the journal of the Royal Institute of International Affairs, in Spring 1984.

EDMUND DELL

Part I
Harmony and Conflict in International Economic Relations

1 Introduction

In 1763, the Duc de Choiseul, Minister to Louis XV, wrote to the President of the Board of Trade, pleading that: '*pour l'amour de Dieu, ne laissons pas les querrelles de pêcheurs dégénérer en querrelles de nations*' (ed. Coleman, 1969, p. 80). During the intervening centuries progress in human civilisation has been so slow that the quarrels of fishermen continue to degenerate into quarrels between nations. These days, quarrels about fish have little economic significance though still a considerable political significance. But whether or not the competition between producers of different nationalities is in products of economic significance, it continues to generate rivalry between governments. Governments do not doubt that they have a role to play in support of their own producers. Governments believe that they should stimulate exports and discourage imports. Exports are good. Imports of manufactured goods are in part a measure of the failures of domestic industry, in part the reluctant price paid for the right to export. If the price can be reduced, so much the better. Choiseul's peaceful message has fallen on deaf ears.

Thirteen years after Choiseul wrote, Adam Smith published *The Wealth of Nations*, one of the most influential of the world's unread books. Governments were to be taught to behave better. There were, no doubt, some very few cases where government intervention in economic processes could be justified. But for the most part governments had misdirected themselves in believing that they should be players in the game of economic competition. Free trade was to rule. The freedom which any government gave to its merchants, to export and to import, was not to be conditional on any reciprocal action by foreign governments. The governments, and the peoples of the world, were to rely on an invisible hand. The invisible hand would convert self-interest into the general good and generate welfare for the people and harmony among nations.

Adam Smith was not the first writer to discover that free trade would generate a community of interest among nations. David Hume had in 1758 in his essay *Jealousy of Trade* written:

I shall therefore venture to acknowledge that, not only as a man, but as a British subject, I pray for the flourishing commerce of Germany, Spain, Italy and even France itself. I am at least certain that Great Britain, and all those nations, would flourish more did their sovereigns and ministers adopt such enlarged and benevolent sentiments towards each other   (Hume, 1955, p. 82).

For more than two hundred years liberal economists have been striving to persuade governments of the need for enlarged and benevolent sentiments. They have tried to convince them of the unwisdom of most of their interventions, interventions believed to have costs in welfare, and to be productive only of international conflict. The arguments of the liberals were reinforced after the Second World War. Economic competition supported by the power of the state had proved to be highly dangerous. It had led to wars. It may have had some part in the origins of the Second World War itself. It was important to diminish the influence of the state in trade competition, perhaps eventually to remove it altogether. Trade competition had to be civilised and the most important civilising action available was to leave it to businessmen. Businessmen could fight each other to their hearts' content. Their weapons would be their products, their prices, and their services. At least they would not usually be using guns, let alone nuclear weapons. Indeed, if the liberal economists were right, we would all be more prosperous as a result of greater competition.

Great as has been their influence, in this major respect the liberal economists have failed. For this there are good reasons as well as bad. Among the bad reasons may be simply that governments feel more comfortable in the possession of power. Power will not be easily sacrificed on the altar of liberal economic doctrines. There are, however, good reasons why governments continue to intervene and why they wish to retain a power to intervene effectively. The first is that they see that conflict, not harmony, is the norm of international economic relations. A second is that the state is a source of protection for national interests. A third is that the outcome of policy is uncertain and that the power of intervention may be needed to change course. The insights of economists do not provide a sufficiently persuasive basis for total commitment or for abandoning the power to change course. They cannot command total commitment from governments because they leave economic processes deeply shrouded in an indefinite number of veils. A fourth reason is that it may be necessary to protect citizens not just from the impact of unguided market forces but also from the guided missiles discharged by the interventionist policies of foreign governments. Always there, alongside the invisible hand, are the readily visible hands of interventionist governments attempting to rearrange in the national interest the panorama of international economic relations.

A fifth reason why governments intervene, and the last that will be given at this point, is that a nation's relative economic performance may not be good enough, thereby leaving it exposed to great perils. Governments are understandably concerned with the relative performance of their economies and not just with its absolute performance. They know that a reasonable performance by historic standards may yet leave their countries languishing relative to their competitors. That can have seriously debilitating effects. Governments reserve the right to intervene in an attempt to improve the relative performance of their economies. However poor the experience of some governments with their efforts to improve economic performance by intervention, they will not renounce the right to try.

But is there not a naturally occurring *balance* between nations? Does not the tide of events restore balance by pressing down on those who have risen too high, and raising up those who have fallen too low? The evidence, unfortunately, is against it. It is true that over long periods the balance of power changes. All the great empires have declined and fallen. It can happen even to the two superpowers that today dominate our affairs. But such changes occur over periods too long to give much satisfaction to those who, in the meantime, have to suffer on the downside of international relationships. The developing countries remain poor even though some are fighting through to greater prosperity. Even if OPEC now collapsed, the memory of years of deprivation exacerbated by high oil prices would remain. The USA will not lightly abandon policies that enable it to suck in the savings of Europe and Japan. There is no law of balance that will give the meek in their lifetime their turn to inherit the earth.

Economists may persuade themselves that the greatest wisdom reposes in that combination of policies that conduces to the most efficient deployment and use of world resources, and the maximisation of welfare internationally. Those policies include the greatest possible freedom for international trade. Governments have a narrower vision. They are primarily interested in national advantage. Moreover the more modest of them make no claim to know what is best for the world as a whole or how to achieve it. They doubt whether economists really know either. The arguments of economists are too uncertain to disturb a more natural intention to enhance the power of national economic defence even if it be at some cost to governments themselves, to their peoples, and to international relationships. If that more natural intention is to be changed there will have to be a more assured prospect of reciprocal benefits to compensate for whatever is thought to have been lost.

Economic liberalism requires that governments resist any supplication from industry for special help. That is the liberal norm. To give special help can only distort the world economy. The policy of governments departs from this liberal norm. The government norm is to help where it reasonably can. There may be good reason for not helping, such as the cost, the improbability of success, the existence of international agreements which it would be counter-productive to violate, the possibility of an unfavourable impact on current international negotiations, or even because a dose of foreign competition is thought likely to benefit the supplicant's industry. Thus assistance may be refused for a wide spectrum of practical reasons. But the inclination will be to respond to requests for assistance in the most helpful spirit possible, not to refuse on grounds of liberal principle.

With governments, these reasons for intervention have proved more persuasive than all the books and all the arguments of the liberals. Tendencies so deep-rooted in the conduct of nations demand more thorough enquiry than has yet been undertaken by economists of the liberal school. These days many liberal economists have first-hand experience of government. Their theories have, therefore, been exposed to the corrupting influence of participation in government. Confronted with actual problems, their intellectual vigour and curiosity has led them to recommend interventions in economic processes in order to remove market imperfections and reduce social tensions. They have come to believe that interventions of this kind are consistent with economic liberalism. These interventions are sanctified by the name of adjustment policies. Adjustment policies are presented as passing the liberal test because, although they are interventionist, they sound as though they are helping market processes. The idea of adjustment policies shows that something more is felt to be necessary than Adam Smith's invisible hand. The benefits of free trade and free exchanges are no longer seen as automatic. Indeed, it is argued, free markets need the support not just of adjustment policies but also of some measure of international economic policy coordination. Thus the pressure towards intervention is encouraged by the compromises of liberal economists as well as by the exigencies of government.

THE NEED FOR MULTIDISCIPLINARY STUDY

International economic relationships deserve and require the kind of multidisciplinary study directed these days to questions of defence. The problems are at least as difficult, and hardly less important. Economists claim to be more objective than politicians. The truth is that they are as much at the mercy of the conjuncture and of the pressures created by the conjuncture. There is no more a science of economics than there is a science of politics. A wider vision is required if the study of international economic relationships is to yield results usable by governments both in promoting national interests and in reconciling international economic conflicts. It is unlikely that such a study can lead to anything but a pragmatic response to a changing international scene. The pragmatism can be salted with as much liberalism as possible but governments must be expected to show a strong inclination to help their own side. A liberal slant to pragmatism is the most that can be expected from governments. A liberal slant implies that a high value is being placed on freedom, and that is unlikely to be wrong. Liberal pragmatism does not rule out intervention but ensures that liberalism is not unnecessarily sacrificed to intervention.

International economic relationships are, in part, relationships

between states. States are political institutions. Like other
political institutions they are self-protective. They will insist on
retaining the right to protect. States may have many common
interests, both political and economic. They may share a belief
in a particular economic system such as capitalism, and its
associated values. But states also have conflicting interests,
among them conflicting economic interests. Disagreements
between states arise not just from differences of interest but also
from differences in economic understanding. Differences in
economic understanding, and the resulting differences in
economic policy, cannot be avoided. All these conflicts and all
these differences of interest and understanding, emphasise to
the state the importance of a capacity for self-defence.

During the first half of the 1980s, the fate of the American
and world economies has been determined far more by political
decisions about the size of the American defence budget than
by any other single factor. There has been serious complaint
about the American budget deficit and American interest rates.
They are alleged to have held back European recovery. The
Americans are financing their deficits in part with resources
won from Europe by high rates of interest. To prevent an even
greater outflow of money, European governments have been
forced to raise their own interest rates to historically high levels.
Competition for resources has thus taken place at high rates of
interest between the strongest, and most politically secure,
economy in the world, and those who for purposes other than
economic are its closest allies. Developing countries with large
indebtedness feel themselves particularly severely damaged.
The servicing of their indebtedness, already a heavy burden,
becomes heavier with every increase in American interest rates.
The Americans, on the other hand, seemed for a long time
relatively relaxed. They could claim with some justification that
the policies of which their trading partners complained were in
fact acting as a locomotive drawing forward the economies of
the world.

More recently increasing concern has become apparent even
in the USA. Their federal budget deficit is now seen as
threatening to the future of the American economy. Indirectly
it can undermine political stability in the developing world.
Discussion is in progress in Congress to decide the most
acceptable methods of eliminating it by, say, 1991. It would be

optimistic to assume success. But even if there were success, the very fact that domestic American policy can produce such a major imbalance in the world economy, and that it can persist for so many years, makes it inevitable that countries should try to retain such levels of discretion in the formulation of their own policies as may be necessary to give the maximum possible protection against the excesses of others. The USA still seems to be able to get away for long periods with deficits in both its budget and its current account which would rapidly undermine the currency of any other country. For critics of American policy it is hardly a comfort that even the USA may not be able to get away with it indefinitely. There is the fear that it may then turn, as it did under President Nixon, to destabilising devices of another kind which will enable it to export its problems in its trading partners.

When nations find themselves in conflict they will attempt to resolve it by mutual accommodation. They will seek the maximum possible stability, the maximum possible agreement, and the maximum possible mutual understanding. In days gone by a failure to find an accommodation of interests could lead to war. These days the resolution of economic conflict and the conquest of markets by military force is not acceptable. Other means must be found of arriving at accommodations of interest. The normal way is the way of negotiation. Power, both economic and political, will be a determinant of where at the end of a negotiation the balance of advantage lies. The accommodation will necessarily take more account of relative power than of liberal economic principles. Interdependence improves the opportunities for turning economic success into economic power. Economic efficiency and the use of economic power are the acceptable and more peaceful methods of gaining advantage in a negotiation.

For those countries which, without being superpowers, have achieved economic leadership, this new situation has considerable attractions. For the nations ravaged by war such as Germany and Japan, but also France and Italy, freer trade has opened opportunities which they have exploited from their renewed industrial base and with their skills in production, marketing and research. Moreover while freer trade in industrial goods has opened to them such wealth-creating opportunities, they have been able to reserve from the free market areas of their economy which they were not yet ready to expose to it: agriculture and services in the case of Germany and almost everything in the case of Japan. In France, Colbertian principles are as much part of the ordinary modes of thought as free trade principles once were in the UK. France, operating in accordance with those principles, has been able to manage a transition from an agricultural society to an industrial society with remarkable success, without much by way of social dislocation, helped by the rigid protection given to its agricultural sector by the common agricultural policy of the European Community.

Germany and Japan have gained far more by their economic skills than they ever won by aggressive war. A new power structure is being created in the world, one based not on military power but on economic efficiency and technological expertise. If the USA has to buy from Japan what it cannot yet make for itself, that puts significant bargaining power in Japanese hands. This new economic power structure exists alongside that other power structure which is dependent on military force. Countries such as Germany and Japan may not be able to challenge the USA in its military power. But they can invade its domestic market with great effect. The USA can then defend itself only by those trade protective strategies which it overtly rejects, or by pleading for that consideration of its domestic political problems which the military leader of the Western Alliance so obviously thinks it deserves.

Not all countries can achieve the economic performance of a Germany or a Japan. Those countries that cannot achieve economic leadership will want as a minimum to be able to defend their own interests. The existence of economic excellence and efficiency in the hands of a competitor, is not a compulsively persuasive argument where the government of an importing country sees vital interests endangered. Governments can admire the merits of a competitor nation without being prepared to permit those merits uninhibited sway within their own territories. However undeserving their people, and however poor their economic performance, they will do their protective duties.

KEEPING THE TEMPERATURE DOWN

Relative economic power and competitiveness changes with time. In these days of advanced technology, comparative advantage can switch rapidly from place to place. International economic relationships are continuously in flux. They require a continuum of negotiation between states and between groups of states to find accommodation and to reduce tension. Such negotiations have not removed friction from international relationships. But they have so far, in the period since the Second World War, managed to keep friction from generating white heat.

The USA is not the easiest country with which to negotiate because of its tendency to manifest bad temper. The bad temper can sometimes spill over into threats. Threats are not the best way of sealing the cooperation of those who have a choice. Nevertheless while the rest of the non-communist world is so dependent on American strength for its defence, the USA is less to blame for allowing itself sometimes this undiplomatic luxury. And it has shown some genius in finding how to combine bad temper with sufficient restraint. Outbursts of frustration with its allies have not prevented its playing its part in keeping down the temperature of international economic relations. President Carter fought hard to defend the open international trading system. The tradition of Presidential support for the open trading system has been maintained by President Reagan, despite pressures from Congress and from industries adversely affected in their domestic and overseas markets by the rising dollar. Although frequently succumbing to these protectionist pressures, he has fought back where he could. 'We and our trading partners are in the same boat', he said in 1984 about protectionism, 'if one partner shoots a hole in the boat, it doesn't make sense for the other partner to shoot another. Some call that getting tough. I call it getting wet – all over' (*The Financial Times*, 25 July 84).

International political relations can be improved by agreements of different kinds negotiated between the major industrialised nations at economic summits. Whether the functioning of the international economic system is also improved is more questionable. Nevertheless if there is no natural harmony of interests, negotiation represents the next best alternative. Summit meetings between heads of government were an invention of the 1970s, called into existence to prevent excesses of economic nationalism in response to the unaccustomed problem of economic recession. Some government officials believed that there could be a better alternative to negotiation. There could be a power, created and installed by economic summits, which could resolve the problems of conflict by managing the world economy. Actual experience of summitry has proved wrong those who allowed their imaginations to soar so high. Management by a collective of nations requires agreement on policy, and there is no such agreement. Effective leadership would require firmness of purpose, and there is no such firmness. Firmness of purpose requires from leaders a collective conviction in the rightness of policy, and there is no such conviction. Even if there were sufficient conviction behind a firm agreement, there would be no international sovereign to enforce it against the will of contending parties. Nor, realistically, can there be expected to be such a sovereign in the future. The most that could have been hoped for is such a dominant partner as was the USA in the early years after the Second World War. But that moment of history has passed.

The fact that there is a problem by no means implies that there is a solution. The summits may be the best, even if very inadequate, answer in a situation in which there is no solution. There are rules which, in the aftermath of war, were established by international agreement to ease the process of accommodating conflict. Summits are particularly necessary when such rules are at a discount, as they are now because they are perceived by some countries as having failed adequately to protect their national interests.

Leaders of principal nations can do something to prevent that deepening hostility which can be so destructive of international relations. They can achieve temporary settlement by a process of accommodation if accommodation is possible. If accommodation is not possible, at least they can achieve greater understanding of each other's dilemmas. Probably even today there is more economic collaboration between nations than there was in the 1930s.

The search for accommodations of interest will go on. In the best circumstances such accommodations may lead to agreements which fashion a generation of peace and progress. In other cases the agreements in question may be narrowly focused on specific, if annoying, sources of friction. The post-war construction of the Bretton Woods system and of the open international trading system was of the first kind and resulted not from any natural harmony of economic interests but from negotiations conducted in particular political circumstances between states with particular negotiating strengths. The principal factor was American economic and political dominance combined with American leadership in defence.

Even in the 1970s, after the first oil shock, and after American economic dominance had declined, it proved possible to conclude successfully a further (Tokyo) round of multilateral trade negotiations. Commenced before the 1973 oil shock, the negotiations stumbled on for six years before completion in 1979. The success that was eventually achieved was primarily the success of avoiding failure. It was achieved mainly because the US Administration wanted it and what the US Administration wanted was still of great importance to its allies. President Carter and his special trade representative, Robert Strauss, took a modest political objective. In the midst of economic recession, they could not significantly liberalise the world trading system, and would not have wished to. But they wanted a success because they saw it as a means of deflecting protectionist pressures in Congress. For that purpose the process as well as the results was helpful. The process of negotiation may have a value quite apart from the specific agreements concluded. It provides an argument for deferring protectionist action. In the end, the specific agreements must be capable of being represented as a successful outcome to the negotiations. What would be regarded in Congress as a success was a judgement that Robert Strauss was superbly equipped to make. He judged it right. Although the Tokyo Round was not a great success in removing barriers to trade, it was a success in terms of the US administration's limited political objective. It is an example of a more narrowly focused agreement but narrowly focused agreements are all that is likely in the 1980s.

All these negotiations were undertaken and concluded successfully because the participant states considered success to be in their interests. They wished to find sufficient accommodation however different their predominant economic interests and the political and economic power that they could bring to bear. It is absurd to imagine that this search for accommodation, and the relationships thereby established, can be sufficiently understood without the most careful analysis of the political motivations that lie behind the actions of states. The study of economics is rendered nugatory if it cuts itself adrift from analysis of the whole complex of reasons why nations agree and disagree.

THE LAW OF INSTABILITY IN INTERNATIONAL ECONOMIC RELATIONS

Harmony, to the extent that it can be achieved, is the product of negotiation. It is not the natural order. In a world in which conflict is the norm, the first objective of the state must be the achievement of economic security. It is of the nature of the state that its principal responsibility, in economic matters as in military, should be self-defence. There is nothing in economic theory that could or should persuade a prudent government to abandon that priority. Certainly there are then the practical problems of making that priority effective and, if possible, of making it consistent with a generally liberal approach to international economic relationships.

One of the few reliable economic laws is the law of instability in international economic relations. Governments are in the business of protecting national interests. They may from time to time, or even often, perform their protective duties badly or even counter-productively. That does not remove the responsibility they have as governments. Governments will strive for national economic security. They will not be dissuaded by the thought that in an interdependent world such an objective can only be chimaerical. They will shrug off such defeatist teaching. They will do their duty and try.

2 The Instinct for National Economic Security

Governments are frequently guided by instinct. One of the strongest of these instincts is the instinct for national economic security.

SECURITY – THE FIRST OBJECTIVE

There was a time when military security was unquestionably the first objective of the state and the first concern of governments. Commitment to any other purposes than that of security was limited to the extent that they were perceived to conflict with security. Military security is sought to perpetuate the independence of the state. It preserves to the state some freedom of action to deal with its most fundamental concerns. In the world of superpowers, that freedom of action may be severely constrained. Many countries, by reason of their scant resources, can do very little to provide for their own military security. They may be dependent on their alliances or on whatever balance of forces exists in the world. The greater the power, the greater the security. But however great the power, absolute national security is not available.

Responsibility for military security cannot be located anywhere but with the state. But there are dangers. The power needed to resist external aggression can equally well be used against internal dissension. Governments have engaged in military adventures which, far from promoting security, have provoked powerful retaliation. Priority for security has therefore always in the end led to a demand for democratic control of the armed services and of decisions as to their use. Where the military has been successfully controlled through representative systems of government, the priority given to security has been qualified. The rise of democracy has emphasised the social responsibilities of the state. Expenditure on security is no longer unquestioned where it conflicts with other objectives seen also to be desirable. These can include the right to spend one's own money as one wishes, or the maintenance of a welfare state. A balance of objectives has replaced the absolute objective of security. Yet even in a democracy a deep sense of the priority the state must give to its security remains.

There is an economic dimension to military security. Military security benefits from economic strength. It benefits from an ability, financial and industrial, to sustain the burdens of defence. Military security may require the retention of industries particularly directed at military supply. Governments have always insisted on the right to operate this degree of protection. Even Adam Smith was prepared to concede it. That right will be claimed whatever the competitive situation internationally, even if the products of those industries could be bought more cheaply abroad. The American government will not abandon its steel industry even if steel can be imported more cheaply from Japan. Scandinavian countries have argued, with more questionable validity, that there is a limit to which they can accept the contraction of their textile industry, given strategic considerations. Modern advanced technologies are today essential to the operational effectiveness of armed forces. The ability of nations to defend themselves militarily could well be eroded by an inability to maintain a competitive capacity at the frontiers of technology. Capacity in the advanced technologies will therefore be protected and fostered by any major country. It will not be content simply to import. On the other hand, neither protection, nor subsidy, nor indeed competition, can guarantee that defence industries remain technologically competitive. But such is the military importance of technological leadership that the industries concerned will always be given a specially protected status, and will, if necessary, be defended against the market. Defence is more important than free trade.

AN ANALOGY

There is an analogy between military security and economic security. The value of the analogy is that it conveys warnings. Three such warnings are already clear. First, democratic governments may prejudice economic security by a failure to understand the power of the market. The market may retaliate. Governments must be on their guard. Secondly, power acquired by government for important and desirable purposes can be turned to other less acceptable purposes. The instinct for economic security can open the door to wasteful protectionism. Some means of defence must be found against the abuse of state power. Thirdly, power taken for economic purposes may be even less capable of achieving its supposed objectives. Not too much must be expected from the techniques of economic security if economic performance is lacking.

INTERDEPENDENCE COMPELS ATTENTION TO ECONOMIC SECURITY

The instinct for national economic security has been an influence throughout the history of the nation state. It was implicit in the writings of the mercantilists. It can be traced even in the writings of Adam Smith. But it is modern interdependence that has compelled national governments to identify economic security as a prime requirement of policy. The instinct for national economic security impels governments to seek to retain in their hands the greatest possible control of national economic destinies; so to conduct themselves in international negotiations as to retain the maximum of independent discretion in the formulation and implementation of economic policy. There are no economic laws which prescribe how these objectives can be secured. Nor does instinct provide any sure guide to governments how to manage their affairs in order to achieve these ends.

The working of economic processes is highly uncertain. There are many economic theories, but they do not have the compelling logic of the physical sciences. Acceptance of them involves risk, and governments will seek to reduce risk. In a competitive international environment there are gains and losses for companies and for countries. In some economic environments there will be a reasonable prospect that, for each individual country, the gains from a free market will exceed the losses. That happy out-turn is more likely when the world economy is expanding rapidly. But no one can be sure. Governments cannot rely on it. The instinct for economic security dictates that there be contingency plans against the failure of policy to yield the expected dividend.

Risk cannot be avoided. There is no friendly rule that provides an escape from risk. The greater the strength of the economy, the greater the risks that may be acceptable. The assessment of risk may depend on the ideology of the assessor. Conviction can convey a courage in risk-taking that may be absent in a pragmatist. It was no doubt a conviction politician who led the Gadarene swine. But the pragmatist may spend his time cowering before insubstantial fears. Interdependence and freer trade increase uncertainty and risk. There therefore has to be clear prospect of compensation for the additional exposure. The compensation does not necessarily have to be in economic terms. There may be forms of compensation available that are more certain than any economic benefit that can be promised from economic interdependence. The uncertainties confirm governments in seeking from economic interdependence benefits more calculable and more tangible than liberal economic policies can provide. In the early days after the war, those more calculable benefits were found primarily in the political advantages of acceding where possible to the exigencies of the USA as the dominant partner in the North Atlantic Alliance, and in the cohesion which the American policy of economic interdependence, as a result, lent to that Alliance. The need for cohesion within the Alliance is still a dominant factor in the survival of the interdependent system.

Interdependence is a threat to independence. But it is not a threat equally to all states. The tendency of international trade and of international financial exchanges is to rob the state of its power of decision. Those governments that feel themselves particularly exposed will be especially sensitive to the requirements of economic security. Their concern with economic security will increase as the dangers increase. Countries other than the most powerful can become intolerably constrained in their ability to make their own policy choices. More and more they do what they do through lack of choice. No state wishes to find itself so bound by international agreements, or by the force of circumstances, that it can decide nothing other than to obey. Explicitly or implicitly, there will be included on every serious agenda concerned with international economic relations, the key question, what independent discretion will the adoption of this proposed policy leave in our hands? Great determination is needed if national discretion in the formation of policy is to be retained. The powerful are under less pressure. Their power allows them more discretion. They will seek to maximise that discretion by attempts to influence or coerce the actions of foreign governments. But even the most powerful may at the end of an unwise course of policy be forced into making unwelcome decisions. Interdependence converts the instinct for economic security into an explicit tenet of policy.

INTERDEPENDENCE: SOLUTION OR ILLUSION

The proposition that governments have a prime, and inescapable, interest in national economic security, is not new. Though not new, it is still controversial. It is very easy to take the propaganda about interdependence as an indication of the real nature of interdependence. Those whose acquaintance with interdependence lies in the practice of government-to-government negotiation, or of international commercial exchanges, are less likely to be so deceived. For once, as we shall see, these practical men have been listening to that prince of defunct economists, John Maynard Keynes himself. They can tell the propaganda from the reality. They know that interdependence is not a mutual aid society but a power struggle. By some, interdependence is seen as a solution to world economic problems. More interdependence will solve more problems. One obstacle to the happy implementation of this message is that the drive for interdependence is in conflict with the instinct for economic security. Various questions therefore arise: is the instinct for economic security simply an expression of the self-interest of governments, can governments be persuaded to override it if they cannot just forget it, how far are extensions to interdependence politically practical given that governments probably will not forget it, and, of great importance today, whatever benefits interdependence may thus far have yielded, is more of it, in truth, the solution for which the world is searching?

These questions and their answers form the subject-matter of this book. To introduce that subject-matter, I shall start with three observations which provide something of the intellectual and political framework within which such a discussion needs to take place.

First, there is a group consisting of a residue of liberal economists who question the beliefs of the practical men engaged in the business of international economic diplomacy and international economic transactions who place economic security high on their agenda. The world of these liberal economists does not require the concept of economic security. They feel secure in another set of beliefs for which they have high authority. They are supported in them by a large corpus of learned literature. They are, it is true, professional economists rather than practical men of affairs. But unlike some who take part in these debates they are relatively free of vested interests, or at least their vested interests are the vested interests of scholars, not of those whose position and livelihoods may depend on their ability to influence governments. Those economists whose position and livelihood *do* depend on their ability to influence governments, have long since compromised their liberalism. The residue to which I am here referring believes that this is a world whose harmony is broken only by the self-interested and counter-productive interventions of government, and that if it is necessary to talk at all about any such concept as economic security, it can only be in order to provide some kind of shield or excuse for the protectionist and discriminatory actions of government. If international exchanges are inevitably, and for all participants, a *positive-sum game*, then any regard paid to the instinct for economic security is to be frighted by false fires. Any government that fails to disarm economically because it wishes to maintain its power and discretion in the formulation and implementation of policy is simply preserving its own prerogatives at the expense of its people. It is because such views are so firmly held by so respectable a body of men that it is necessary to press the point that concern for economic security is an influence that governments cannot deny.

Secondly, both thinkers and practitioners suffer from the lack of an adequate theory of international economic relations, and there is no prospect of agreeing one. What theory there is is weighted heavily with liberal optimism. As a result, 'solutions' are propounded by economists, and even advocated by some governments, which take no account of the imperatives of national economic security and of the impediments it necessarily places on international economic collaboration. There is exaggeration even amongst some practitioners of government of the possibilities of international economic management and international economic harmony. These failures of understanding are illustrated by the pressures exerted on Germany and Japan in the late 1970s to act as 'locomotives' to the world economy, pressures which culminated in the counter-productive Bonn Summit of 1978. They are illustrated in the late 1980s by the pressures to reflate being brought to bear on Germany and Japan by the USA. The US Administration evidently feels, as the British government did in the 1970s, that, as they cannot manage their own economy successfully themselves, Germany and Japan should abandon their habitual policy stance and loosen their reins in order to compensate for American failures. The lesson has not been sufficiently learnt that one country cannot be expected to take risks on behalf of another without clear compensation. Germany and Japan must be expected to consider themselves the best judges of where their economic security lies. They cannot be expected to prejudice their own economic security in the interests of the USA unless the USA can offer something substantial in return or exercise some effective coercion.

Thirdly, even if they provide inadequate analysis of the nature of international economic relations, the insights of liberal economics can be turned to a valuable purpose. They provide a base from which to criticise the unjustified use of government economic power, and the costs that arise from it. Pragmatism, the inevitable policy consequence of a concern for economic security, has its dangers, indeed quite serious dangers. It can lead simply to submission to vested interests. In a democratic state it can be rather easy for lobbies to exert successful pressure on governments. The activity even of a small minority may win out against the passivity of a majority. The misuse of the power to protect can be a serious matter. The banner of economic security may be misused by being raised to wave over protective actions that have little connection with it. Even if the liberal norm is abandoned as a standard of international conduct and is replaced by a more pragmatic approach, it can help to provide the necessary defence against the extravagances and distortions to which mere pragmatism can open the door.

A NARROWING VISION

In the great days of interdependence after the Second World War, it was regularly questioned whether Britain's governments were sufficiently committed to the requirements of economic security. They were believed to be so understanding of the demands of foreigners as to neglect British national interests. Samuel Brittan once wrote:

> A particular feature of Whitehall hampering economic policy has been the existence of what Mr. Roger Opie has christened the 'overseas lobby'. One does not need to have any truck with the more chauvinistic forms of patriotism to be mildly disturbed by the number of departments which approach economic problems primarily from the point of view of international negotiation, and how few are professionally concerned to put forward the interests of this country (Brittan, 1971, p. 470).

Brittan may no longer endorse these words but they expressed a fashionable criticism of the British civil service. Actually it is rather an attractive characteristic to be concerned with the problems of others. Possibly only the most powerful countries can now afford it. Life has certainly moved on. It is the pressures rather than the pleasures of interdependence that now dominate the minds of British civil servants. British governments fight their corner in international negotiations with a dedication equal to that of the most selfish of their contemporaries. The instinct for economic security has become explicit even in UK policy.

It may be, however, that because of its traditions, so different from those of Germany and Japan, because of the many international networks within which it operates – the Atlantic Alliance, the European Community, the monetary network based on the International Monetary Fund and the World Bank, the Commonwealth – the UK is still too much inclined to derive exaggerated expectations from international economic cooperation and coordination. Other countries with different traditions and narrower networks, may see more clearly that to base policy on a diminishing prospect of international economic cooperation gives too many hostages to fortune. It is also likely that the UK's inclination to see policy in terms of international economic coordination is strengthened by its poor economic performance. The illusion flourishes that the coordination route is the easier route, at a time when it is exceedingly doubtful whether it is any route at all.

KEYNES AGAINST ECONOMIC ENTANGLEMENTS

It is not only governments that have a concern for economic security. There are also economists who have perceived the dilemma confronting governments. It was a dilemma even before the high days of interdependence. Keynes wrote in a famous statement:

> I sympathise, therefore, with those who would minimise, rather than those who would maximise, economic entanglement among nations. Ideas, knowledge, science, hospitality, travel – these are things which should of their nature be international. But let goods be homespun whenever it is reasonably and conveniently possible, and, above all, let finance be primarily national (Keynes, June 1933).

Fashions change. One of the most worrying things about economics is the way fashions change. This quotation from Keynes has been called a 'statement of considerable irony, given that a major contributing factor to the Great Depression was a wholesale adoption by governments at the beginning of the 1930s of its policy message' (Blackhurst etc., 1977, p. 3). That protectionism was a major contributing factor towards the Great Depression is controversial. That was clearly not the view at the time of the governments either in the USA, or in the UK, or Germany. Their object was to reconstruct their national economies. The idea that the reconstruction of national economies came first, and that small faith could be placed in the curative properties of international trade until national economies were once more strong, was not at all absurd. Indeed, it influenced the policy of developed countries in the immediate aftermath of the Second World War. A period of protectionism, more or less authorised by the USA, preceded the growth of interdependence. It still influences both the policy of developing countries and the attitude of developed countries towards them.

Keynes was writing during the depression when his first concern was the cure of unemployment. Later, according to Roy Harrod, he reconsidered his earlier attitude. During his negotiations with the USA at the end of the Second World War, he formed the view that 'The Americans seemed to be as fully convinced as he that a nation should not be compelled by her open trading commitments to take action likely to lead to a domestic slump.' Therefore 'His mind reverted to Adam Smith and to the great truths which he preached. Of course they were truths; but for him they had been submerged in recent years by what seemed to be the more urgent problem of mass unemployment and trade depression' (Harrod, 1951, p. 609). These views are by no means a recantation of Keynes' earlier stand. On the contrary they show that he continued to see an incompatibility between the cure of mass unemployment and the extension of freer trade. The cure of mass unemployment had to come first.

After the Second World War all governments of major industrialised countries were committing themselves to full employment and believed that they knew how to deliver on their commitment. Keynes thought that he knew how to deliver on the commitment. He found that the Americans were then taking a helpful stand on the importance of full employment. That, he felt, should enable the world to give higher priority to the establishment of an open trading system and to the benefits of the international division of labour. New circumstances validate new measures. On the assumption that the commitment to full employment could be delivered, the new measures were fully consistent with his earlier views.

There was, however, a difficulty against which the instinct for economic security is not always a sufficient safeguard. There is the arrogance of economic theory even in the hands of such a pragmatist as Keynes. As Keynes should have realised, American policy is not carved in stone. American views could once more change. Circumstances would certainly change and with them the balance of advantage to be found in particular policies. Keynes, the pragmatist, would then once more try to change the balance of his views. But would it then be possible? Could weaker nations retreat from interdependence if American priorities or world circumstances changed drastically, or if the ability of governments to deliver on their commitment to full employment was, for whatever reason, undermined? The development of interdependence could make it very difficult indeed for some countries to take an independent stance on the relative importance of full employment on the one hand and of an open trading system on the other. This should have muted Keynes' enthusiasm for the economic benefits of free trade even if the Americans were for the moment exhibiting commitment to full employment.

More recently, other writers have questioned whether the cost in national autonomy is any longer justified by the gains from interdependence. They have suggested that the risks of interdependence have begun to outweigh the expected gains. They have noticed that interdependence has not provided any automatic answer to the problems of conflict and uncertainty, let alone unemployment. They have pointed to the dilemma that interdependence may require a degree of international regulation and management that is unattainable. Some have argued that an international code should permit protective actions where politically and socially sensitive situations are confronted. Such views suggest that those who hold them understand the signifiance of the instinct for economic security.

HOW INTERNATIONAL AGREEMENTS CAN BECOME COUNTER-PRODUCTIVE

International institutions or rules of conduct may, in some circumstances, neutralise the instinct for economic security. But they cannot eliminate its influence and, as a result, some elements in international agreements can become counter-productive.

Multilateral trade negotiations have been mainly concerned with the reduction of tariffs. Tariffs are now very low and, for the most part, are bound in the GATT. The reduction of tariffs has, however, been followed by the growth of protectionist industrial policies. There has been a development of what liberal economists have called 'the new protectionism', that is protectionism by all kinds of non-tariff barriers which are not controlled by the negotiated agreements. The irony is that the new protectionism is regarded as worse than the old. Better have tariffs, it is now said, than the new protectionism. 'Tariffs are instruments of the market economy.' They 'do not inhibit shifts in trade patterns in response to changes in comparative advantage that are reflected by changes in relative costs.' On the other hand,

> non-tariff measures interfere with the operation of the market mechanism by restricting consumer choice and limiting competition between domestic and foreign producers. The use of non-tariff measures also involves administrative discretion that introduces arbitrariness in the decision-making process (Balassa, 1979, p. 289).

No doubt this criticism of non-tariff measures has merit. But their development has been encouraged by the success of negotiations to reduce tariffs, negotiations partly motivated by economic liberalism. It might well have been better in the years after the war to negotiate a reduced but reasonable and continuing level of tariff protection rather than to provoke the escalation of non-tariff barriers, by a series of tariff-reducing rounds. Economists now weep about the distortions caused by this foreseeable consequence of tariff reductions. Economic liberalism has frequently demonstrated its tendency to degenerate into protectionism. If economists had a broader vision of human society they might more often avoid the pain of discovering that the body politic has this innate tendency to reject their implants and that the last situation can be worse than the first.

CONCLUSION

Free trade is an inspirational element in the rhetoric of governments. That rhetoric is 'like the hand on the highway that pointeth the way but walketh not therein itself.' Governments, generally, remain unpersuaded by their own rhetoric. The practice of governments is dominated by considerations of economic security. Assessment of risk, calculations of advantage, the availability of a defensive armoury, all this is the raw material of policy making in the field of international economic relations. This brings grave dangers. The search for security can lead, and in the past has led, to the narrowest possible interpretation of the interests of the nation and even to wars in the prosecution of those interests. Today the interest of nations lies in accommodation wherever it can be obtained. If accommodation cannot be reached, mutual understanding is the next best thing. The ways of reconciliation cannot ignore essential interests, including the interest in economic security. But the choice of reconciliation is made easier by the experience of economic progress in a liberal world after the war and because of the degree of interdependence then established. The attribution of special economic benefit to interdependence and liberalisation as compared to other possible international systems may be an illusion, but illusions too can have their influence on policy.

We have left the Age of Faith and re-entered an Age of Mercantilism. Yet, in its essentials, the system of freer trade between developed countries built up since the war survives. Its blessings have seemed a great deal less obvious than heretofore to governments obsessed by the current account of the balance of payments and to politicians confronted with mounting unemployment in their constituencies. It survives, though in every country strong protectionist pressure has continued now for at least twelve years. Fortunately there has been a willingness to understand the political problems of others, and to seek compromises and accommodations, and this has helped to surmount the intense pressures in the direction of outright protectionism. No single developed country has yet taken it upon itself to precipitate the collapse of the system by adopting restrictions of a kind that would force its trading partners into massive retaliation. Even the last Labour government, though it came near to the point of protectionist action, in the end rejected it and remained part of the international consensus that has brought the world through to this point, with the open trading system relatively unscathed.

Fear of the political consequences of major economic conflict between the members of the Western alliance has helped to keep the edifice of freer trade in place, crumbling here and there but at least not crashing to the ground. The common interest of military security within the Western alliance has so far triumphed over the divisive forces of economic competition and the pressures to take too narrow a view of the requirements of economic security. International economic summits may not have produced great successes, or any significant agreements about the way out of recession, but at least they have led to greater understanding and have helped to avoid breakdown. Concern about economic security continues but clearly so does the desire to keep in being the system of freer international exchanges.

Reconciliation of conflicting interests is made easier, not more difficult, if it is understood that account must be taken of the priority given to economic security. It is the part of statesmanship to seek the reconciliation, not the exacerbation, of conflict. It is not the part of wisdom to cry after formulae that will wish it out of existence.

3 The Hard Road to Economic Security

ECONOMIC SECURITY AND ECONOMIC STRENGTH

The most reliable route to economic security is through economic strength. If economic strength is there, there will be less worry about the current account of the balance of payments, or about the impact of foreign imports on domestic employment. If it is not there, it is not easy to be certain how to get it there. In the worst cases a high degree of dependence on international charity will follow. A government may reduce exposure to confidence factors by restrictive fiscal and monetary measures. It may thereby show a better face to the world's financial markets. But economic strength depends on economic performance. Economic performance is beyond the command of government because there is no economic theory that reliably prescribes the way of achieving it. The sources of economic growth are not well understood. There is no clear relationship between economic performance and government attitudes to free trade. The USA, Japan, Germany, France, Hong Kong, Korea, Singapore and Taiwan, all have different attitudes to foreign trade. Some have been relatively liberal. Some have been exceedingly protectionist. All have performed well. The UK has tried protection and it has tried relative openness. Neither has done much for its economic performance.

RESPONSIBLE ECONOMIC MANAGEMENT

There is a general requirement for responsible economic management. If the actions of government are not protective of the reputation of its economic management, and the value of its national currency, it is unlikely that anyone else will care much for either. Neither of these purposes necessarily requires that action be taken to protect a nation's industry. Indeed industrial protection may have exactly the opposite effect by confirming that the currency is overvalued and that economic management has failed. 'Protective' should not necessarily be taken to imply 'protectionist'. Protectionism is one form of protective action, to which recourse may sometimes be necessary, but it is certainly not the only form or by any means always the most appropriate. In a weak economy, highly exposed to movements in international confidence, responsible economic management may carry a heavy political price. The governments of countries with weak economies are likely to shuffle anxiously between responsible economic management and other political imperatives.

Governments may attempt to rationalise the actions which they take to protect their currency, to control the growth of their money supply, and to reduce their central borrowing requirements, in terms of some economic theory or other. Instead of allowing these defensive measures to be self-justifying and to stand on their own merits, they claim such things as that these measures will help to defeat inflation and that the defeat of inflation is a necessary prerequisite of economic growth. In fact governments have no deeper knowledge of the sources of economic growth than any other of the more or less qualified experts who pronounce on this and similar problems. The reason for their actions is protective. The rest is propaganda of the kind which promises a light at the end of the tunnel when the propagandist is not even sure that it is a tunnel he is in.

ECONOMIC SECURITY AND THE CURRENT ACCOUNT

A strong current account is for most countries the key index of national economic security. At the very least all countries will wish to have a current account which, when in deficit, can be comfortably financed without official assistance and at a price in interest rates that they are willing to pay. All countries know that a continuing large adverse balance may undermine their currency. Immune from such considerations as it sometimes seems, that danger can arise even in the USA.

At various times governments have been advised that they can ignore both the balance of payments and the current account. There are those who claim that a country's external payments must necessarily balance and that therefore there can be no problem with the current account. Any deficit will always be financed. Governments are ill-advised to show such complacency. There is mounting experience of the problems that can beset a country that relies on any such automaticity. International trade is an area of intense conflict and competition. The current account surpluses and deficits of the nations of the world must sum to zero. This is one respect in which international trade must be a zero sum game. If it is at all worrying to run a current account deficit, and many countries find it worrying, then the nations with such deficits have costs to set against any benefit from trade. The problem resolves itself into determining the best or least harmful way of ensuring a defensible current account, that is a current account in balance or in surplus or comfortably financeable if in deficit. But to the degree to which the problem is solved, there is an impact on other countries. Not every country can have a surplus on current account or, at a time of recession especially, a comfortably financeable deficit. The comfort of one country can be the discomfort of another. If the USA finances a deficit at high interest rates, it is likely to lead to complaint from other countries. It is the old mercantilist problem. Countries cannot benefit equally from international trade, and some may actually lose.

There is a long history of controversy among economists about the importance of the balance of payments and of the current account. Adam Smith declared that 'Nothing . . . can be more absurd than this whole doctrine of the balance of trade' (Smith, 1947, vol. 1, p. 431). The balance of trade is not, of course, the same thing as the current account. But in an age in which there were fewer services traded internationally, there was less difference between the two. It was this absurd doctrine that in Smith's view gave rise to restraints on trade and to almost all the other regulations of commerce. Indeed the very concept of the balance of payments is mercantilist in character.

These days the current account of the balance of payments means something even to liberal economists. They reject import controls as the preferred method of remedying a weak current account. They prefer devaluation or restrictions on the budget deficit. But they are as concerned with the current account as are those more prepared to impose trade restrictions at the frontier. Some liberal economists appear to base the whole case for liberal trade on the proposition that balance of payments equilibrium can be reliably achieved through the instrumentality of equilibrium exchange rates. Yet if equilibrium exchange rates cannot themselves be reliably achieved, this would appear to leave the case for liberal trade in tatters. By their concern for this problem of the balance of payments, liberal economists are led to share some of the anxieties of those governments whose approach to the problem is motivated by a recognition of the instinct for economic security.

Governments act in many ways to protect the balance of payments, ways which, contrary to liberal doctrine, have intentionally discriminatory effects. Exports are encouraged. Imports are discouraged. One method is action on the exchange rate. Governments, however, distrust the equilibrating influences of exchange rates. Other weapons therefore are rolled into action. These include government procurement, subsidies, and persuasions offered to potential foreign investors in the form of incentives to invest here rather than elsewhere. 'Payments imbalances are a convenient excuse for protectionism even though the use of import restrictions is an inefficient response to balance-of-payments problems' (Blackhurst *et al.*, 1977, p. 59). Inefficient they may be, but many governments have remained unpersuaded that these instruments are not the best, and most rapidly acting, of an inefficient bunch.

Interventions to restrict imports lead to conflicts between nations. So far as possible these conflicts are resolved through the machinery of the GATT, in other words through a form of international law. But the GATT has not much to say about protection by subsidy, except in the case of export subsidies. Frequently the conflicts are resolved through government-to-government negotiation or even industry to industry negotiation. The fact that these conflicts can often be resolved in these ways shows that governments understand each others' problems, and are prepared to act in a spirit of mutual accommodation.

Henderson says: 'Few of the protectionist moves of recent years are to be explained with reference to balance of payments difficulties, though there have been exceptions of which France is a leading recent instance' (Henderson, 1983, p. 12). Perhaps Henderson thinks that the British government did not have the balance of payments in mind in deciding to protect the textile industry or the motor car industry or the electronics industry. In the short term this may indeed be true. In the short term there is no evidence that selective import restrictions benefit the balance of payments. They may merely divert expenditure to other imported goods and absorb in the domestic market goods that would otherwise have been exported. But Henderson is unwise to neglect the possibility that in protecting the textile industry, the motor car industry or the electronics industry, the British government had in mind the desirability of retaining in the UK, and hopefully strengthening, industries which would in the future not merely compete with imports in the home market but also become important elements in future export performance.

In any case it would be wrong to take too simplistic a view of what constitutes protection. Protection does not only take place at the frontier. Industrial policy is the real new protectionism. Industrial policy, with all the subsidies that go with it, is the obverse of tariff reduction. As the tariffs come down, expenditure on industrial policy goes up. The expenditure includes subsidies direct and indirect, general and selective. It is intended to encourage both import substitution and export performance. Export performance may be assisted by subsidising interest rates on export credit. So well recognised is this that it is subject to an international agreement that is sometimes respected. All this is intended to influence the balance of payments.

Keynes understood the importance of the current account. He knew also that many of his fellow economists did not understand it. He wrote: 'we, the faculty of economists, have been guilty of presumptuous error in treating as a puerile obsession what for centuries has been a prime object of practical statecraft' (Keynes, 1947, p. 339). Governments, on the other hand, have seldom been prepared to treat the current account of the balance of payments with benign neglect. It is central to their feeling of economic security. They know that a current account deficit which is proving difficult to finance is a source of weakness. It is the kind of weakness that can place a government on the road to the IMF. If they have to take restrictive measures to correct an imbalance, they would prefer to be able to decide on them voluntarily and not under the pressure of conditional borrowing. If Keynes is right, it is perhaps fortunate that governments have been prepared over the centuries to rely more on their own instincts, and on what

Henderson in his 1985 Reith Lectures contemptuously describes as 'do-it-yourself economics', than on the advice of economists. The do-it-yourself boom in economic policy-making, as in the provision of other goods and services, derives from the high cost of professional services and the poor quality so often supplied.

STRENGTH THROUGH TECHNOLOGY

Technological success can alter the balance of power both economic and political. The economic and military power with which the USA dominates the world is based on technology. It is the technology of the microchip, of the delivery of nuclear weapons, of space adventure. A major input into the cost of American technological advance comes from the government under the headings of defence and space. The USA has proved that where there is an established and large market, for example a market provided by defence requirements or ambitions in space, then there can be major unplanned benefits from large government expenditures in industry. Vast government expenditures, of a size beyond the capacity of most powers other than the superpowers, can affect international power relationships. They affect not merely the relative military capacity of nations. They affect also their economic capacity to win markets overseas for civilian versions of products brought into existence for military purposes or for the purposes of space investigations. The result, in the case of these American expenditures, has been to make available to the civil market products of high quality, and of advanced characteristics, long before the market unassisted would have found resources sufficient to develop them.

The dependence of so many countries on American technology is a powerful negotiating weapon in the hands of the US administration. It encourages submission to American trade policy in order that the products of American technology can more easily become available to those who had not the means to pursue research that far. The technology becomes the property, or at least the instrument, of American multinational corporations. Government expenditures become an important weapon in the hands of companies whose existence strengthens American influence overseas. Similarly the denial of technology to a potential enemy becomes both an important concern and an important weapon of state policy. When power depends so much on technology, it makes those with a technological edge less ready to share even with their allies. The danger that advanced technology will be leaked to the Communist bloc is exploited by the Americans as a reason for denying that technology to potential competitors in the West.

The result, inevitably, is that national technological industries become a resource which governments crush to their nationalistic bosoms and try to defend against all comers. Certain companies are placed in a category of national importance. This importance is underlined by, but is not alone dependent on, their military significance. Market forces in the form of foreign takeover become unacceptable and provision is made to give companies special protection against such hazards. Powers were taken in the Labour Government's 1974 Industry Act for that purpose. Michael Howard MP, a Minister at the Department of Trade and Industry in Mrs Thatcher's government, announced that references to the Monopolies and Mergers Commission could take place, not just where a question of competition policy was involved in a proposed takeover or merger, but 'where the destiny of a vital national capability is at issue' (*The Financial Times*, 6 December 1985). As Europe does not wish to become the technological colony of America or Japan, and yet feels that the individual countries lack the resources with which to compete, attempts are made to organise a technological Europe in competition with these major rivals. The USA, for its part, becomes frightened that the Japanese semi-conductor industry, producing within a protected market, will overwhelm the American industry with its exports. The USA therefore pressurises Japan into an international semi-conductor cartel, an electronic OPEC, with perhaps a better chance of surviving competition because production is so much more concentrated.

STRENGTH THROUGH ALLIANCE

One way to greater economic strength may be through an alliance of some kind with other governments which see a common economic or political interest. There are many examples of such alliances, none of them perfect because national interests preclude perfection. An obvious example of an alliance, continuing, sometimes powerful, but stumbling in times of oil glut, is that of the Organisation of Petroleum Exporting Countries (OPEC). The developed, Organisation for Economic Cooperation and Development (OECD) countries, form an imperfect, and often shifting, alliance for the purpose of negotiating with the underdeveloped countries also imperfectly allied in the so-called Group of 77. The Soviet bloc constitutes a more perfect economic, as well as political, alliance but only under the control of Soviet power. Even there conflicts of national economic interest emerge in Comecon debates.

Two options for alliance have seemed open to British governments, one with Europe, the other with the USA. Europe was intended to be an alliance of equals. The problem with the European alliance is that it has involved the high costs of the common agricultural policy which Britain had to accept as a condition of entry; and that it may do little to help with one of the key conditions of economic strength, a sound current account. The European Community was intended to be the type of alliance in which the collective strength was greater than the sum of its parts. To some extent it is precisely that. It enables Europe to negotiate with the USA in trade matters on more equal terms, and to launch cooperative technological concepts such as Eureka for which resources might not be available on a national basis. But Europe is also an alliance of nation states. The full potential of its members is not mobilised because each government is responsible to its own people and is concerned to retain its own discretion. The stronger economies of the Community, such as the German, do not wish to exhaust their resources supporting the weaker economies, or their currencies. The governments of the weaker economies may not always agree with the prescriptions offered by their partners. They may prefer easier roads to recovery. Even the European Monetary System can have only a limited role in mobilising the strength of the European alliance. The development of common action is inhibited by the very pressures that bring the alliance into being.

The European Community was constructed under two complementary influences. The first was the intense desire in Europe after the Second World War to prevent any repetition of what had come to be thought of as European civil war. The second was the wish of the USA to strengthen Europe as an ally against the Soviet Union and to ensure by means of European economic recovery that it did not fall into the trap of communism. The USA believed that a common market within Europe would conduce to these purposes. For the sake of those purposes the USA was prepared to permit discrimination by Europe against its economic interests. The process of European unification began with the Coal and Steel Community constituted by the six original signatories of the Treaty of Paris. That Treaty contained a relatively high level of supranationalism. So far as supranationalism was concerned, the Treaty of Rome, the second stage in the construction of Europe, was a large step downhill. There followed the so-called Luxembourg compromise by which France signalled a major retreat from supranationalism, and its intention that the Community should be no more than an alliance of sovereign states.

In the 1980s there at first appeared to be a revival of enthusiasm for European political unity, or 'European Union' in the terminology of the federalist ideologues. This revival was stimulated by the sense of relative industrial decline in face of American and Japanese technological leadership, by fear of the consequences for Europe of American economic policy under President Reagan, and by dislike of the tone and manner of President Reagan's foreign policy. At first it appeared that supranationalism within Europe might regain lost ground and resume its onward march. It was not to be. At a meeting in Luxembourg in December 1985, modest reforms to Community procedures, to be embodied in an amended Treaty, were agreed. They fell far short of any fundamental change in the nature of the European Community as an alliance of sovereign states.

The USA has sometimes been thought to provide the UK with an option alternative to Europe if it wished to follow the road of economic strength through alliance. Britain's declining economy has frequently led British governments into looking for aid from the USA, whether from its government or from its bankers. There is a 'special relationship' that, at least on the British side, is taken to exist between the USA and the UK. It has sometimes been thought by British governments that Britain was attending appropriately to its own security by becoming increasingly dependent on the USA. The charity of a friend may have been thought of as an acceptable substitute for the more tiring alternative of one's own exertions. This could not be the kind of alliance between governments in which all the partners contribute something significant to its strength. The two countries are too unequal in their resources and the UK's economic performance has been too poor. For the UK, an alliance with the USA could not be anything other than a more or less disguised form of dependency. That is how it has turned out, dependence on one side and increasing boredom on the other.

FRENCH PRAGMATISM

Since the war, governments have been under great international pressure to open their markets, whatever confidence they may have felt in the ability of their industry to withstand foreign competition. The French have been among those countries which have most strongly resisted this pressure and, despite their commitments to the Treaty of Rome, have been prepared to use, nationalistically, the infant industry argument in defence of new and old industries alike. Raymond Barre, then Prime Minister of France, said:

when a country develops a sector that is indispensable to the structural equilibrium of its economy but unable to meet normal competition until it reaches a sufficient size, that country may rightfully take such steps as are necessary to protect this activity from being destroyed while it is vulnerable.

He added:

France cannot allow international competition to develop under conditions that would throw its economic structures into confusion, bring about the sudden collapse of whole sections of its industry or agriculture, put thousands of workers out of work, and jeopardise its independence by eliminating essential activities (Balassa, 1979, p. 288n).

More recently Barre has repeated this view:

When a large group with a fundamental role in the economy is threatened, a government should not allow it to collapse. But the Government should ensure that a solution is found which allows the company durably to get back on its feet (*The Financial Times*, 19 November 1984).

The excuse for the intervention is always the durability of the solution. But French political and social attitudes are likely to impel intervention whatever the long-term prospects of the patient.

THE SEARCH FOR ECONOMIC SECURITY CANNOT BE ABANDONED SIMPLY BECAUSE GOVERNMENTS ARE NOT INVARIABLY WISE AND BRAVE

A concept such as economic security can be used to justify the cowardice of governments in the face of pressure groups, or at least the inability of governments to control pressure groups in the general interest. The temptation to use any excuse for capitulating to pressures for protection is very great. Politicians too often give in to pressures which they should resist. On the other hand the fact that governments are often cowardly should not lead critics to assume that any protective step, or any other intervention in the interests of economic security, is necessarily simply a capitulation to pressure from vested interests. Brock and Magee have written:

> International economists are careful to avoid explicit consideration of the political process in their analysis of international commercial policy. This behaviour is understandable since international economists do not have a comparative advantage in politics (Brock and Magee, 1980, pp. 1–2).

From this one learns that these international economists, having no expertise in the matter, and not wishing to acquire any, are careful to avoid explicit consideration of a key element in international commercial relationships. But how can economists prescribe if their vision is so narrow? Who do they think they are helping if they ignore so large a part of the problem? Economists are very ready to engage in oversimplifications of economic processes. It is understandable, therefore, that they feel unable to contemplate the complexities of the political process. But in that case, their words are fit only for textbooks. Governments may legitimately take account of considerations other than those in the study of which economists have a comparative advantage. Finding accommodation among various pressures can be a legitimate object of statesmanship. Defence of social peace may justify costs in welfare.

The search for economic security embarrasses a government with uncertainties. It can make no assumption that its actions will always prove to have been in the interests of itself or its people. It can have no assurance that the policy option it has chosen is best. By definition, there is no certainty. At best there is a balance of probabilities, but one which may itself turn out to be mistaken. There can be no presumption that there is a single national interest or that society is so homogeneous that no interest group will ever see its interests sacrificed or endangered by state action. The fact that it is the first objective of any state to endeavour to protect its own security, and that of its citizens, does not imply that any action it takes to that end will necessarily be wise or successful. It does not guarantee that any action that it claims to be motivated by the instinct for economic security has not in truth some other baser, and less presentable, motivation. The search for economic security cannot be dependent for its validity on any claim for the wisdom, knowledge or foresight of governments. That may make the exercise of discretion by governments more worrying for those subject to it. It does not affect the importance, or the strength, of the instinct for economic security. It is, however, a reason to look for safeguards.

THE RULE OF LAW?

If governments cannot be relied on to act with wisdom, should they not be allowed only the minimum possible discretion? Should not their actions be governed by law? Too much discretion does have its dangers as it involves a degree of trust which governments frequently betray. To that extent it will be a matter of congratulation for those whose faith is in law or in market forces that, in the modern international economic environment, severe constraints operate. These constraints limit the possibilities for excessive government discretion. Some will feel injustice in the fact that the constraints act more powerfully on the weak than on the strong. But the fact that there are dangers in discretion will not prevent governments striving to preserve it. Nor, despite the risks of malefaction, should they refrain. In democratic countries laws protect many human freedoms. In the international arena there are agreements about rules of conduct which are sometimes respected. Such laws and such rules are a great aid to civilised living. But there are many areas of economic policy that cannot be governed by laws or rules, or in which it has proved too difficult to negotiate or enforce laws or rules. Uncertainty as to the outcome of policy is too great. One reason why the instinct for economic security is a powerful influence on the actions of governments is precisely because there are so many areas of international policy, and these the most crucial, in which it would be inappropriate to give ultimate obedience to any man-made laws or rules. However good the rules and the laws in those areas of policy where it is appropriate to enact them, in many areas of policy we will still find overselves dependent on good governments and good men if we can find them.

4 The Costs of Economic Security

INTRODUCTION

For a strong economy the costs of economic security may be small. The strength of the economy already implies security. For a Japan, the costs of protection may be small precisely because of the efficiency of domestic production. For a weak economy the problem is more difficult and the costs will be greater. Costs may arise in various ways. There are the costs that are inherent in policy. In the case of economic security the inherent costs are those that are likely to arise from defending the current account and the value of the currency. There are the costs that arise from mistakes in the application of policy. Among these are the costs that will arise from the application of policies that are, by their very nature, accident prone. Such a policy is industrial policy. Where industrial intervention becomes a major ingredient of policy, it is likely to be accident-prone. But these days it is seen that even *laissez-faire* has costs. Under the guise of 'benign neglect', it has won praise from those who have won its dividends but blame from those who have paid its costs.

THE COST TO INTERNATIONAL COLLABORATION

Concern for economic security makes it more difficult to negotiate international collaborative arrangements intended to raise the level of world economic activity. A cooperative solution to a hazardous economic conjuncture may seem to many economists and some governments better than any available national solution. They will argue that countries overly concerned to protect their own current account will thereby myopically accept a low level equilibrium instead of a high level equilibrium which might be available from more outgoing policies. But such cooperative solutions depend for their own viability on a long-term commitment to agreed action and even

41

to rules intended to bind to such agreements. The search for economic security, on the other hand, will leave countries determined at best to give no more than conditional adherence to such rules. Such a lukewarm approach to international collaboration undoubtedly undermines the more extravagant dreams of economic salvation through collaboration. Governments are ill-advised to waste too much sleep on such unborn children. They should question both the prospects for, and the likely effects of, such collaboration. They should note that concern for economic security motivates the economically strong, such as Germany and Japan, and, therefore, should also motivate the economically weak such as the UK. The strong will refuse to exhaust their strength in defence of the weak, and the weak should know better than to depend on the strong. Commonsense and hard experience should deter governments from chasing phantoms.

INDUSTRIAL POLICY

Concern for economic security is these days frequently associated with those policies gathered together under the collective name of 'industrial policy'. Great benefits have been claimed for a well-considered industrial policy. Experience suggests that there are some problems in justifying those claims. Moreover, once the door is opened to industrial policy, it is very difficult to establish limits. What is commenced with the best intentions may end in gross extravagance. In principle there is no reason why the good sense that defines the circumstances of permissible intervention should not also define its limits. The difficulty is not that there cannot be sensible interventions. It is rather that once interventionism is permitted there will be much room for debate about the limits. Political pressures can be relied on to push the limits further. It can easily be agreed that stupid things should not be done in the name of industrial policy. The problem will be to avoid it.

Perhaps the best protection against the worst excesses of industrial policy will be a government's understanding of the costs and failures of past interventions. But even if its critical faculties lead to the conclusion that many past interventions have been costly failures, that will not be the end of the matter.

It will not exclude the continuation of past interventions of a kind believed to have been beneficial, or new ideas for intervention expected to be beneficial. Thus it is as well to assume that where industrial intervention is most looked to for major contributions to economic security, it will be most costly.

It is also protectionist. Sometimes industrial policy is called 'adjustment policy' implying some harmless cushioning of the process of adaptation to foreign competition. In a liberal age in which protection or 'mercantilism' is spurned by all right-thinking persons, the name 'industrial policy' or 'adjustment policy' is designed to give respectability to protection by calling it something else. For some economists 'industrial policy' is bad, implying protection in transparent disguise, but 'adjustment policy' is good, implying respect for market forces. In practice it is not often possible to tell the difference. In an attempt to mitigate its protectionist character, the OECD guidelines on industrial policy emphasise the importance of markets open to international competition, warn about its restrictive aspects and call for it to be, so far as possible, temporary, digressive, transparent and general as well as encouraging to adjustment. Industrial policies have not proved to be either temporary or digressive. Even where they are transparent and general, they are still protectionist.

There is a more optimistic approach to industrial policy which does not see it as a denial of market forces. On the contrary, it is argued, industrial policy should work with the grain of the market and should incorporate the idea of competition. Unfortunately the idea that industrial policy can always be made to work with the grain of market forces, and thereby actually facilitate the working of market forces, assumes too great insight, and foresight, in the managers of industrial policy. If they have the level of success in identifying the direction of market forces implied by this approach, they are very exceptional people for whom massive rewards should be available in the market place.

One example of industrial policy working in the grain of market forces might be where it operated to take people out of declining 'sunset' industries and to redeploy them in progressive 'sunrise' industries. Unfortunately industrial policy has been poor in identifying declining industries in advance of obvious problems with competition. When it has, belatedly, identified such industries it has usually slowed adjustment rather than speeded it. It has acted in the role of social policy, to reduce social tensions by wiping the fevered brow of declining industries with subsidies. Nor has industrial policy been particularly successful in identifying the progressive industries to which people should be transferred. When their identity *has* been established, the problem has been to make them competitive.

There has been international collaboration to take redundant capital out of production. This may be cited as an example of industrial policy working in the grain of market forces. The European Community acted to restructure the European steel industry. Such policies have certainly reduced costs by taking out of production capacity that had been kept in operation only by subsidy. But such internationally agreed policies pay more regard to reciprocity than they do to comparative advantage. And from a purely economic point of view the situation would almost certainly have been better if industrial policy had not encouraged the introduction of the subsidies in the first place, and simply let market forces operate.

To call industrial policy protectionist should not necessarily be to condemn it. Industrial policies deserve to be considered on their merits. There have been successes as well as failures. The managers of industrial policy will no doubt try to reduce the costs. The ways of doing so will have to be consistent with the social and political objectives of intervening in the first place. It may not always be possible, consistent with those objectives, to reduce the costs. They will not, in any case, be susceptible to exact calculation. Industrial policy works best, and costs least, in those economic environments that need it least. It works worst, and costs most, in those economic environments which require from it curative powers beyond its capacity to deliver. Industrial policy may enhance good economic performance. It is unlikely to do much to rescue poor economic performance. Where, therefore, industrial policy is used as a cure for poor economic performance, it is likely that the purely economic costs will exceed the purely economic benefits. This should not be taken to mean that the costs, net of benefits, will necessarily be large.

But, large or small, these are costs which governments have been willing to accept. They accept them without really knowing what they are. They guess that they are less than the benefits even if not always in balance sheet terms. The first of these benefits is the sense of greater economic security. A second benefit may be a reduction in social tensions. This is a perfectly reputable objective for governments. They may, however, exaggerate the dangers of social tension as an excuse for implementing politically convenient interventions under the splendid banner of industrial policy. Governments console themselves with the thought that by accepting one set of costs they are reducing another set of costs that would otherwise fall on their people. This other set of costs is that which would arise from the unimpeded impact of market forces and of other countries' measures of industrial policy. Again, they have no real way of knowing. But there will be great pressure on them to accept the argument that they must respond reciprocally to the actions of other governments. If other countries subsidise, they must subsidise. There is no argument of economic theory sufficiently persuasive to lead them to resist such pressures. The only persuasive argument may be that the cost of calculable subsidies in the national budget is becoming excessive.

VESTED INTERESTS

The strengthening of vested interests is liable to be one of the most important costs of economic security. 'The political effects of this system favour neither the rich nor the poor but the established and the organised.' Because vested interests are strengthened and listened to, it becomes difficult to defend truthfully some of the decisions that governments make.

> The proper criticism of the system is not that its political decisions are discretionary but that they are arbitrary. They are made beyond the reach of public opinion and discussion – in part because, in a proper discussion, the decisions could not be defended. . . . Government is now universally believed to be there to be lobbied (Tumlir, 1984, pp. 17–18).

It is, unfortunately, an illusion to imagine that there is some constitutional or legal device which will set democratic governments beyond the influence of lobbies, if such governments see political advantage in coming within the influence of lobbies. Jan Tumlir thought that the Treaty of Rome, properly enforced, would provide the constitutional answer for the UK. He deceived himself. There is no way other than the determination of governments themselves to take decisions on their merits. They can be assisted in that course by informed public criticism, and by clear warnings as to the consequences of corrupt submissions. There are, however, certain ways of avoiding the influence of vested interests that should be placed firmly out of court. Deepak Lal advises us that 'A courageous, ruthless and perhaps undemocratic government is required to ride roughshod over these newly-created special interest groups' (Lal, 1983, p. 33). Evidently we need a new injunction to recommend to the followers of Adam Smith, that democracy is more important than opulence.

Nevertheless Tumlir's warning is entirely appropriate. If governments become the instrument of vested interests, the ability of a nation to accommodate itself to new competition and to seize new wealth-creating opportunities will be reduced. It can become a way to fossilise society. It will be those nations whose economic performance is already poor that will face this dilemma, and there may be no answer. They may find themselves in a vicious circle of decline. Every defensive move, even if it relieves one problem, will exacerbate another. A principal advantage of freer trade can be that it helps to deny to vested interests an entrenched position from which they can resist change. If a government is capable of resisting vested interests without the assistance of freer trade, and if society is sufficiently in tune with the requirements of industrial progress, the arguments for free trade lose a great deal of their force. In these circumstances the economic costs of protectionism would probably be a good deal less than qualitative statements about the advantages of international competition may suggest. In any event the costs are not likely to be of such a size as themselves to be the determining factor of decline.

WELFARE

Welfare is likely, to some degree, to be a sacrifice to the search for security whether it be military or economic. If security comes first, welfare comes somewhere later. It is the most naïve of errors to imagine that states, in selecting policies, invariably put the welfare of their citizens, or even of some class of their citizens, first. Economists may be concerned with welfare. States are concerned with security. Here I differ from Keohane and Nye. In the course of discussing the premises necessary in the formulation of 'an economic process model of regime change', they say:

> governments will be highly responsive to domestic demands for a rising standard of living. National economic welfare will usually be the dominant political goal, and a rising gross national product will be a critical political indicator (Keohane and Nye, 1977, p. 41).

There can be no doubt about the political importance for governments of a rising standard of living. However it is probable that in all those situations in which a conscious choice has to be made between national economic security and an increase in welfare, the choice, no doubt after prolonged and uneasy debate, will be for security. That choice is likely to be made even on narrow political grounds. A government perceived to have placed security in peril even in the search for an increase in welfare is likely to prejudice the support of its electorate. Nevertheless the pursuit of economic security and of welfare are certainly not always in conflict. On the contrary, although welfare may be second to security, it may sometimes be a key component of economic security.

ENERGY

In the pursuit of economic security, states in recent years have sought to make themselves less dependent on OPEC supplies of oil. Security requires stable supplies of energy. So does welfare. The costs that arise may, therefore, be attributable to welfare as much as to security. The costs have been high but in the circumstances have been accepted. OPEC has seemed not just a cartel, not just potentially unreliable as a supplier, but has been known overtly to bargain oil against influence in matters political and economic. The conversion of shortage into glut has, for the time being, reduced the influence OPEC countries can exert in international affairs. Despite the present glut, prudence and the desire for greater economic security are likely to dictate the development, under national control, of alternative sources of energy even at higher costs, though not, of course, at any cost. A return to shortage, or a greater concentration of supply capability in a few Middle Eastern countries, would not merely raise the price once again. It could revive ambitions to barter oil against political influence. Nations prefer to make up their own minds about the great issues of the day. They do not wish the chance location of large quantities of oil beneath the Arabian desert to be a more persuasive argument than it need be.

Part of the higher cost of alternative sources of energy may be attributable to vested interests at home that exploit the instinct for economic security. British miners have raised the cry of energy self-sufficiency. They have tried to make it as potent a weapon in their hands as the cry for agricultural self-sufficiency has been in the hands of the agricultural interest. A government which hopes to escape from foreign influence in the determination of its policies may simply find itself subjected to as heavy pressure from domestic groupings which are quite as self-interested. It is possible that governments will supinely submit to the domestic pressures at the very moment that they are heroically resisting the foreign pressures. They must ensure that the legitimate desire for economic security is not mercilessly exploited by domestic pressure groups. Coal can, after all, be imported, a discovery made by the Thatcher government when it most needed it.

In future, energy costs may prove to be a decisive determinant of the competitiveness of the products of industry, or at least of those products with high energy intensity. Products from countries with low energy costs may find themselves in competition with products from countries whose much higher energy costs have derived in part from a desire to avoid too great a dependence on OPEC supplies. Governments have accepted the additional vulnerability this could create for their manufacturing industry. Should that become a major factor in international trade, they assume that some means of protection for their new energy sources and for the products of their disadvantaged industry would be found even if it involved some disruption in the open trading system. Action to protect high cost sources of energy and the products which that high cost energy helps to produce could have the most profound implications for international economic relations. The effects on the international trading system may be even more difficult to accommodate than have been the effects on it arising from the protection of agriculture.

AGRICULTURAL POLICY

In most countries there is a tradition of agricultural protection, partly for social reasons, partly because the agricultural interest has always been very powerful, and partly in the interests of security. Agricultural production provides, apart from energy, the most obvious example of comparative advantage. But agriculture is the industry in which the force of the comparative advantage logic is most determinedly rejected by almost every government. Governments accept on behalf of their peoples enormous resource costs in defence of their own agricultural industry. The Common Agricultural Policy of the European Community is a particularly expensive example of this refusal to accept the logic of comparative advantage.

It is now sometimes argued that the interests of security no longer require the protection of high-cost European agriculture. It is certainly true that Europe, without undue risk, could agree to much larger imports of food. Its resistance to this must be attributed to political pressures rather than to any considerations of economic security. However, even a prudent liberal government might wish to deny free trade in agricultural products in the interests of keeping a secure base of domestic food supplies. It is easy to recommend free trade in agriculture, less easy to take the risk of implementing it. Even the most friendly foreign suppliers are not always totally reliable, the USA among them. Any of them would be only too ready to exploit a strong market position. It is better to deny them the opportunity.

The protection of agriculture also carries indirect costs. There can be little doubt about the advantage in temperate food production of the North American plains, and of Australia and New Zealand, as compared with the European Community. By the time of the Kennedy Round the Americans had come to the conclusion that they had a decisive competitive edge in agricultural trade and were determined to exploit it to the full.

The fact that the European Community will not concede either to the USA or to all those other countries that possess a comparative advantage in agriculture, the full prize, or at least a fuller prize, from their endowment, is a continuing provocation in international trade. It threatens advances towards freer trade in manufactured goods and services. Yet even the USA is prepared to adopt quite modest negotiating objectives by way of greater opportunities for its agricultural products within the European Community. No doubt it is constrained in its demands by an assessment of what is practicable politically within Europe, and by the realisation that as the Europeans show few signs of acting unilaterally to liberalise the CAP, it would need to pay for any European concessions in some kind of reciprocal currency. American pressure on Europe may also be restrained by the thought that its own agricultural policy will not bear rational examination. To subsidise grain exports to the Soviet Union, in competition with other Western suppliers, is an ironic demonstration of the superiority of capitalist production.

QUESTIONING THE COSTS

The fact that governments are willing to pay the costs of economic security underlines its importance to them. By no means all these costs are justified by the objective. It is right, therefore, to subject the costs accepted in the supposed cause of economic security to critical examination. Unfortunately there is a great obstacle on the road to a scientific determination of these matters. Estimates of cost require complex calculations of a kind which undermines confidence in the result. The cost and benefit of a particular policy may not in fact be measurable, or there may be controversy over the respective valuations of cost and benefit. It is political judgement that inevitably will prevail. Nevertheless the uncertainties of economic analysis and forecasting do not justify accepting demonstrable costs which yield no return or a totally inadequate return. The return may sometimes be political but there must be some benefit that can be justified in public discussion. Alongside the instinct for economic security should go another instinct, one that questions government actions that are clearly costly to welfare in order to determine who benefits and whether it is worth it. Elsewhere I have described this as the *laissez-faire* instinct (Dell, 1973, p. 24). Investigating the cost may change the policy.

5 The Limits of Economic Interdependence

Interdependence should not be allowed to dictate the surrender of national economic defences. On the contrary, defences should be kept sufficiently intact.

In principle it would be right to try to define the word 'interdependence'. To attempt too much at this point would be to fall into a trap, the trap of believing that in international economic diplomacy, words mean what the dictionary says they mean. The word 'interdependence' is used to describe the post-war system of economic relations between Western developed countries created under American leadership. Sometimes it is extended to include relationships with developing countries, but their commitment to it is far less even than that of developed countries. It is a word from the diplomatic dictionary full of overtones and nuances. Something of its real nature will be uncovered as this chapter progresses.

INTERDEPENDENCE UNDER AMERICAN LEADERSHIP

The first twenty-five years after the Second World War was a period of economic disarmament leading to much greater interdependence among the nations of the developed world. There was nothing inevitable about this process. Export markets were more difficult than domestic markets, prices were lower, competition was keener. It was only gradually that international trade came to be seen as 'the motor of economic growth' (Shonfield, 1982, p. 14). That was a turning point. At a time of rapid economic expansion it is easier to sustain, and for governments to accept, the argument for freer international trade. Booming exports created a constituency for freer trade in every developed country. For a time it might have seemed that nations had forgotten the need to retain their own capability for economic self-defence. But practical enthusiasm for freer trade was never very great. Even in the most prosperous periods, the process of economic disarmament found governments doubtful and reluctant. The instinct for economic security may have been dormant. It was not dead.

Leadership by the USA was essential to the process of economic disarmament. If the USA had not put its weight behind it, the post-war movement towards economic interdependence would at the very least have been even more halting. There might have been more by way of *ad hoc* cooperation and less by way of what American scholars call 'international regimes'. There might have been less commitment to a form of cooperation which allowed the USA particular privileges. American leadership determined the path that was chosen. Yet the USA was incurring many fewer risks than were its partners. Its political and economic power was essential to the drive towards interdependence but interdependence was not to be allowed to prejudice that political and economic power. The USA disarmed economically less than did its partners. This was not because it did not enter into reciprocal agreements for economic disarmament. The reason was that for the USA there was always a safeguard for its independence which its partners possessed only to a much smaller degree. Once its partners in interdependence had committed themselves to the path of economic disarmament, withdrawal would be for them very difficult and very costly. It would be a great deal less costly for the USA. Its economic power made the option of withdrawal one that would always be open. For its partners, interdependence placed a question mark against their economic sovereignty. The USA could be confident that its sovereignty would in no practical way by impaired.

The USA had many reasons for being willing to lead a drive to interdependence. It foresaw political dangers in a divided world, and regarded interdependence as a means of uniting the West. It began to see that interdependence was consistent with its own economic interests. Europe and Japan, for their part, were willing to accept American leadership if it eased the political problems of recovery from the war. For its European partners, to do what the USA wanted had a certain inevitability in the immediate post-war years. Their economies were in ruins. They perceived an increasing political and military threat from the East. They were looking for aid and for a powerful ally. For America's European allies, interdependence was bound, at the outset, to be a form of dependence glorified by a high-sounding name.

Keohane has argued that while

> hegemonic powers may help to create international regimes ... cooperation can develop among egoists without a hegemon. .... Whether a hegemon exists or not, international regimes depend on the existence of patterns of common or complementary interests that are perceived or capable of being perceived by political actors (Keohane, 1984, p. 78).

Part of the evidence for this proposition is that certain international regimes survived the decline of American economic hegemony. It is equally true that the Bretton Woods *regime* did not survive the decline of American economic hegemony, even though the Bretton Woods *institutions* have survived. It is unquestionable that common or complementary interests contribute to the creation of international regimes. The problem arises when the common or complementary interests are more than counterbalanced by conflicting interests. If they are, the power of a hegemon may be necessary to weight the balance in favour of cooperation. The continuance of certain international regimes has been secured by the fact that even though American economic hegemony may have declined, its key role in the defence of the West has remained.

MONETARY POLICY

American leadership after the war can be seen in both the monetary and the trade areas. The new international monetary system could not have been created at Bretton Woods without the backing of American power, and could not have operated successfully without a large outflow of American capital to the rest of the world. The Bretton Woods agreements derived from an attempt to supplement market forces by human ingenuity. The international community felt dissatisfied with the economic record of the inter-war years. The USA, together with the UK, therefore attempted to create and manage a regime that would safeguard mankind from poverty and war. The key word in monetary policy as in trade policy was 'non-discrimination'. The agreements were based on a concept of fixed, if adjustable, exchange rates together with convertibility of currencies. The concern for fixed, if adjustable, exchange rates derived from a perception of the inter-war years during which, it was thought, competitive devaluations had led to protectionism. If exchange rates were fixed at appropriate levels then, presumably, no country would find itself incommoded by an unfavourable current account. Therefore, devaluation was made subject to agreement by the International Monetary Fund, in principle a grave derogation of national sovereignty. If, on the other hand, particular countries did have trouble with their balance of payments, they were expected, with the agreement of the IMF, to take action to correct the disequilibrium. The IMF was created to give some assistance to this process of adjustment. But IMF money was to be available only on terms of ever stiffer conditionality.

In practice, post-war reconstruction proved more difficult than anticipated, and Bretton Woods proved unequal to its tasks. The resources available to the IMF were inadequate. The UK's dash to convertibility under cover of a large American loan of US$3.5bn proved a dramatic failure. The USA felt compelled to step in and to act unilaterally through the Marshall Plan to help restore the economies of its allies. The situation was in the end relieved by a number of unplanned developments. Through aid in various forms, and through military expenditures overseas, for example in Korea, the USA created a dollar standard. At the time the dollar, widely circulated in international transactions of every kind, was a unit of currency of unquestionable value. It was convertible into gold at US$35 per fine ounce, it could finance investment and development among America's allies, it could be used internationally as a reserve and trading currency, and it could be regarded when in national reserves as a reliable store of value. The USA learnt to accept that it was necessary for the time being for its allies to discriminate against it. That could not be avoided during the period of reconstruction. They could not earn enough dollars not to discriminate. Thus for the time being the goal of convertibility was abandoned, and the Europeans, with American encouragement and with the help of some American funds, established their own convertibility system through the European Payments Union. The ambition of non-discrimination was suspended in the interests of recovery.

The American motivation in thus easing the problems of recovery among its allies was largely political. The object had been to find the road to recovery most consistent with the maintenance of American leadership, with the survival of democratic political systems, and with the defence of the West against the emerging threat of Soviet imperialism.

The recovery was a guarantee against the spread of communism. The methods chosen, while certainly a demonstration of American generosity, and often involving discrimination against American interests, helped to preserve American power and influence. The fact that American policies appeared to work in the general interest was a strong defence when it was argued that those policies were also, at whatever apparent sacrifice, in American interests. It is by no means clear that no other route to recovery was available, other that is than the route opened by generous American assistance. But other, more independent, routes which America's allies might have chosen, or in the absence of American assistance been forced to choose, might well have encountered greater political hazards along the way.

By the end of the 1950s, Japanese and European recovery was well in train, and the USA would have liked to see its own balance of payments restored and the outflow of capital reversed. One form of discrimination against the dollar was reduced when European currencies became more freely convertible in 1958. The USA sought the ending or reduction of other forms of discrimination through the Dillon and Kennedy rounds of multilateral trade negotiations. It was hoped that success with these rounds might help with the American balance of payments. The IMF, which had had little part to play during the earlier period of American leadership and management, now began to assume its role of helping to finance the balance of payments deficits of countries such as the UK during their periods of adjustment. But the IMF's resources were limited, and might be unequal to its tasks in this new era. Ten leading countries agreed in December 1961 on the General Arrangements to Borrow. The object was to provide additional support for the international monetary system. However the funds were to be under the control of the contributors, not of the IMF. They would be contributed to the IMF but only if the Group of Ten agreed collectively to do so. The spirit of internationalism was not to be allowed too free a sway over the self-interest of the major industrialised nations.

Yet the system of interdependence was becoming more genuinely interdependent in the real sense of that word. This culmination of post-war experience was marked by the creation of the Special Drawing Right, a new internationally-created reserve asset. The USA was no longer the sole support of interdependence. Other countries were making their contribution. However, once this condition of greater equality among the major industrialised nations was reached, tensions emerged which led eventually to the breakdown of the system. The USA could still pay for goods and services in dollars, even though their value had become questionable. The USA could thus more easily avoid the consequences for domestic economic policy of its balance of payments deficit, and conduct a war in Vietnam which many considered to be ill-advised if not actually immoral. The UK had found that a reserve currency which is not above suspicion is a reserve currency in peril. Would the same be true of the dollar? Or would it be protected in its role of reserve currency by the lack of any credible alternative?

The suspicion that the dollar was overvalued was confirmed by the USA's deteriorating trade performance. The mounting flow of American overseas investment, buying up companies and goods in dollars increasingly believed not to be worth their fixed exchange value, brought about a political reaction. The economic and political privileges which the USA possessed as the generator of a reserve currency caused resentment. The flow of internationally mobile dollars began to undermine the weaker currencies of the developed world, and the economic policies of their home governments. It became increasingly difficult to defend fixed exchange rates, the corner-stone of the interdependent system. The idea of protecting national autonomy by reverting to a floating rate system began to emerge. In the end it was the USA itself that pulled the plug on interdependence. On 15 August 1971, with the USA in balance of trade deficit for the first time in the twentieth century, and without any consultation with his allies, President Nixon suspended the convertibility of the dollar and imposed an import surcharge. The most powerful nation on earth had decided that there must be limits to interdependence.

Thus in monetary affairs since the Second World War there

has been a period of *de facto* American management followed by a period in which a more genuine interdependence led to the crisis of the autumn of 1971. The decline of American dominance had made interdependence unmanageable. By its ultimatum of 15 August 1971, the USA tried to force its partners into cooperation on its own terms. It failed to do so. The balance of concern and the balance of power were no longer sufficiently in the USA's favour. The December 1971 conference at the Smithsonian brought the USA back into the system but without providing a means of managing interdependence. In June 1972, the UK floated sterling. By March 1973 all the major world currencies were floating. A Committee of Twenty was constituted to agree on means of reforming the international monetary system. Its deliberations revealed that each party to the discussion was devoted only to its own remedies, those which it took to be in its own interests. Inflation finally spelt the death of fixed but adjustable exchange rates. The 1973–4 oil shock was a final blow to any attempt to manage an interdependent monetary system.

Floating rates have proved to have certain virtues, some of a negative kind. They have not prevented the growth of international trade and investment. They have accommodated the shocks to the world economic system constituted by high and differential rates of inflation and by the oil price hikes. It is inconceivable that a fixed rate system could have done as well. However, the virtues of floating rates are relative. Neither the fixed rate system, in its time, nor floating rates since, have provided the solution which the world wanted to the problems of monetary interdependence. Neither have proved adequate to the task of so balancing the affairs of nations that none feels under threat. Floating rates had at first been seen as a merciful release from the restraints imposed on national autonomy and domestic economic policy by the fixed rate system. They were found to be neither a merciful release nor a substitute for the international management of an interdependent monetary system which even with fixed rates had proved unattainable. It was merely that one set of constraints on economic autonomy had been replaced by another. International monetary flows increased yet further. Contrary to some expectations, it was discovered that floating rates did not even eliminate balance of payments problems. In 1978, and again in 1979, the USA was compelled by severe international pressures to amend its domestic economic policies to safeguard the value of a declining dollar. No longer, it appeared, could the USA ignore international monetary concerns in formulating its domestic economic policy. These humiliating experiences were among the factors that in 1980 cost President Carter the Presidency.

There is much room for retrospective discussion whether policies have proved to be in the interests even of the countries that advocated them. The USA has firmly refused to consider a return to a fixed rate system, despite strong pressure at various times particularly from the French (Putnam and Bayne, 1984, pp. 30–3). The European Monetary System (EMS) was created in 1979 to constitute 'a zone of monetary stability' among the closely knit economies of the European Community. The EMS has not been able to avoid exchange rate adjustments. The UK has, under successive governments, refused to join the exchange rate mechanism of the EMS. It has preferred that sterling should float unilaterally. The critics of UK membership have been unable to see how the EMS exchange rate system could accommodate the effect on sterling of monetary flows influenced, sometimes in contrary directions, by a combination of oil prices, domestic economic policy, and UK economic performance. The Germans would have to be exceedingly generous and exceedingly patient to buy and sell sterling, in accordance with UK interests, in all the varying situations sterling might face.

The USA, whose leadership and aid was such an important constituent of economic recovery in the first phase after the Second World War, is now regarded as a rogue elephant whose actions, even when by accident beneficial to world economic growth, are totally self-regarding. The final result of its extraordinary combination of Keynesianism and monetarism cannot be foreseen. American policy may once again reach a watershed. It may lead to the imposition of even narrower limits on interdependence.

TRADE POLICY

During the post-war years a system of trade relationships has been constructed which has shown itself capable of surviving great pressures. The system was created with the help of the powerful influence for liberalisation deriving from the USA. The USA was overwhelmingly dominant in the world economy. It was giving large scale aid to the reconstruction of Europe and other parts of the world. In return it wanted allies and markets for its goods. That there could be some conflict between the desire for allies and the desire for markets was then already apparent but less worrying. The USA, rich, powerful, and benevolent, could manage all. For the benefit of its allies it was at first ready to accept some loss of trade opportunities. In the end, however, the USA became as jealous of its trading interests as were any of its partners. Friction then developed even among close friends.

For the USA, to give leadership in trade liberalisation was much more difficult than in monetary policy. Trade policy is more directly political than international monetary policy. It entrenches more obviously on domestic vested interests. Members of the US Congress are intimately linked with these vested interests in their various districts. Congress has always felt it necessary to exercise control over what it has perceived as the excessive liberalism of successive Presidents. Presidents, it seems, may be diverted from a sufficiently narrow perception of American interests by the broader requirements of American foreign policy. Every American President has had to buy from Congress permission to liberalise with payments in the form of some concessions to specific protectionist pressures.

Congress has experienced a longer learning curve than any President. It is a continuing body possessed of an historic memory. Presidents and members of their Administrations have little memory. They come in and they go out. They lack, to advise them, any such body as the British civil service with its store of experience of hazards met and avoided. Experience, as well as vested interest, leads Congress to be more protectionist than the President. In the early years after the war Congress felt instinctively that the fact that the USA was then economically predominant did not mean that things could not change. A power to protect, free of too much international surveillance, might be valuable hereafter. Congress's instinct for economic security was very strong, stronger than that of the over-confident Administration. The threat of a Congressional veto has always been an invaluable weapon in the hands of American negotiators. They do not need to reply to argument.

It is enough to say that Congress would never agree. The European Community had to be invented to provide European negotiators, now the Commission of the European Communities, with an equivalent negotiating tool – the threat of a veto by the Council of Ministers.

The UK's intellectual contribution to the cause of economic interdependence has been preeminent. During the War the UK put to the American Administration a proposal based on James Meade's project for a Commercial Union. The Commercial Union would reduce trade barriers by substantial specified amounts; establish an agreed code of international trading conduct; provide machinery for safeguarding the balance of payments and for dealing with complaints of infringements; and carry out research for, and supply information to, member states (Curzon and Curzon, 1976, p. 145). This idea was rejected by the USA on the grounds that Congress would never agree to large linear cuts in tariffs even if spaced over many years. All that could be expected, it was said, was the renewal of the Reciprocal Trade Agreements Act of 1934. There was, after the Second World War, no generally held presumption among governments that freer trade would lead to economic expansion. The idea that free trade and economic prosperity were in some way connected was a slow growth. The economic boom preceded, it did not follow, the major free trade advances. It was to reduce discrimination against its trade that, after much initial hesitation, the USA became the leader of the free trade movement.

After the war the US Administration attempted to create an International Trade Organisation. In 1947 it negotiated the Havana Charter for an International Trade Organisation with its trading partners. It was 'a mere shadow of James Meade's Commercial Union' (Curzon and Curzon, 1976, p. 145). Even at that time, and under those conditions, there were conflicts of approach and of interest among participant nations. The proposals as originally formulated did not neglect American interests as the Truman Administration saw them. But the concessions which the USA was forced to make to get agreement made the negotiated document less attractive from an American point of view. The concession of imperial preference to the British was a blow to the American cause of non-discrimination. By these concessions, the administration lost friends in

Congress. The enemies of liberalisation on the other hand are always there. Yet the Charter, and the idea of an International Trade Organisation, had been pressed on the initiative of the US Administration and enough survived of the original principles to leave the US Administration wishing to proceed. To withdraw would be a defeat for American leadership and for American liberalism. It soon, however, became clear that the USA would not submit its own right of self-determination to the proposed International Trade Organisation. Congress would not have it. In 1950, the US Administration was forced to decide not to submit the Havana Charter to Congress because it would inevitably be defeated.

THE GATT

The General Agreement on Tariffs and Trade had been drawn up in 1947, pending the ratification of the Havana Charter. It had been adopted on a 'provisional' basis. It embodied much, though by no means all, of the Havana Charter. A provisional GATT would suffice for all the purposes the USA had in view and would leave untouched its final right of self-determination. It was the GATT that became the operative document so far as international trade was concerned. It was the GATT that emerged out of the defeat of the administration's first great liberal impulse. The GATT, with its own bureaucracy and its own Director General, remains and continues provisional.

The key note of the GATT was non-discrimination although even that commitment was highly diluted. There was no strong suggestion in the GATT that free trade was the way to economic expansion. At British insistence, the GATT recognised the Keynesian doctrine that full employment came before unrestricted trade. The USA made sure that the GATT contained no clear obligation to reduce tariffs. The idea that the object of the GATT was the substantial reduction of tariffs and other barriers to trade was only added to the Agreement in 1955 as a vague statement of intent. In 1958, at last, the contracting parties to the GATT embarked on a 'Programme of action directed towards an expansion of international trade'. This was to be a 'co-ordinated programme of action directed to a substantial advance towards the attainment of the objectives of the General Agreement through the further reduction of barriers to the expansion of international trade.' The Curzons' judgement is that the GATT could have developed either way and that it was because of the economic boom that the GATT's outward-looking philosophy was able to prevail over its inward-looking philosophy (Curzon and Curzon, 1976, p. 149). It was not because governments had suddenly experienced a rush of liberal economic doctrines to their heads.

Thus, to start with, the GATT was ambivalent about the reduction of barriers to trade. It had a 'very lukewarm commitment to freer trade' (Curzon and Curzon, 1976, p. 148). If it had not been so lukewarm, it would have been more concerned, as Baldwin has pointed out, with consumer interests rather than producer interests. The GATT has a 'pro-government and pro-business (as opposed to pro-consumer) bias'. 'The producer bias of the agreement manifests itself in such areas as dumping and subsidisation' (Baldwin, 1979, pp. 25–6). Unlike the Havana Charter of the International Trade Organisation, the GATT does not include any rules concerning restrictive business practices, an omission which in retrospect is hard to justify in view of the rapid growth of multinational enterprises.

A typical misconception about the GATT is illustrated in a book written on behalf of the developing countries which found themselves victims of the Multi-Fibre Arrangement: 'if the GATT system has any meaning, access to markets should be a natural right for those who possess a comparative advantage and are capable of production at competitive prices.' There is no possible reading of the GATT that could justify the idea that there is a natural right to export to foreign countries. It is a negotiated right, and thereby subject to all the perils of negotiation, interpretation and retraction (Choi *et al.*, 1985, p. 20).

The GATT was an agreement negotiated between governments with very different aims. If those aims were imperfectly reconciled, then the GATT is not so different in that respect from the treaties produced by other international negotiations. The GATT, the ark of the covenant of post-war free trade, was constructed not out of the doctrines of liberal economics, but in the long-practised mercantilist way of bargaining one interest against another. However even such compromises would not have been achieved if it had not been for the pressure that the US Administration exerted, even though it was handicapped by Congressional constraints. The pressure for freer trade was successful in the 1950s and 1960s because, at a time of economic boom, the reduction of tariffs appeared to be an act of economic disarmament which developed countries could well risk. In any case tariffs were not the only, and possibly not even the most effective, means of protection. And, if all else failed, new protective policies could be invented. The GATT itself was not lacking in escape clauses. The GATT is an ambivalent, fundamentally mercantilist, document. It was assumed that, other things being equal, lower tariffs and more trade were more conducive to prosperity than higher tariffs and less trade. But other things were not necessarily equal. The ability to protect must remain.

TO REDUCE DISCRIMINATION IN TRADE

As with monetary policy, the USA, in the 1950s, was prepared to accept discrimination against its exports in order to help rebuild the European and Japanese economies. By the early 1950s quotas on trade between members of the Organisation for European Economic Cooperation had been removed. The European Payments Union was coupled with this elimination of most quantitative import restrictions on intra-European trade. This made possible multilateralism within Europe but strengthened discrimination against the USA. Discrimination was permitted to its partners even at a time when the USA was negotiating tariff reductions on a supposedly reciprocal basis. The effect of the exchange controls operated by the Europeans and Japanese was to deprive the USA of a major part of the gains it might otherwise have expected from the trade negotiations.

The protectionism which the USA˙ was, in the late 1940s and 1950s, prepared to permit to its allies in both monetary and trade policies, was regarded as strengthening their prospects of recovery from the destruction of war, not weakening them. Pragmatists in government were not prepared to live by the principle that monetary interdependence and free trade are in all circumstances the best way of promoting economic recovery. American restraint in face of European protectionism may be explained, and possibly correctly, as a farsighted contribution to the eventual establishment of a multilateral world economy. As such, it was moderately successful. The time would come when the USA would drag a reluctant multilateralism out of its allies. It is, however, clear that it was not multilateralism but protectionism that was seen as the cure for Europe's post-war economic problems. Only when cured was Europe to be expected to stand up to the full blast of a multilateralism that included American competition. And even then a new form of discrimination against the USA was invented in the form of the European Economic Community.

1955 was a year of some importance in international trade history. Japan was admitted to the GATT. But at the same time Japan's success as an exporter of textiles was becoming a matter of some concern both in the USA and in the UK. Methods both inside and outside the GATT regime were being sought to restrain Japan's vigorous onslaught. It was an early example of the fact that to be free, trade had to be thought to be 'fair' by the nation that was to be the lucky recipient of the cheap imports. In other words, exports had not to be too cheap. The threat of a multiplicity of unilateral restrictive actions against Japan, by GATT members but outside the GATT, alerted the USA to the need for action to avert a re-growth of protectionism. Protection against Japan and the developing countries was one thing. This was the permissible exception. It must not be allowed to spread further.

Indeed, by the late 1950s, the time had come when the USA, in trade policy as in monetary policy, was looking for some return for its earlier sacrifices. The economies of its allies had recovered. Their discrimination against the USA was no longer acceptable. For the USA freer trade became the answer to the gathering regional discrimination against its exports of which the European Community was the prime example. Lower tariffs were expected to mean less discrimination. It was at this point that the USA learnt the wisdom of the Marquis of Halifax's observation that gratitude is a lively sense of favours yet to come. Even in those days of rapidly expanding international trade, its allies proved less ready to return its favours than they had been to receive them. It took a series of hard-fought multilateral negotiating rounds in which concessions were exchanged reciprocally, to achieve the substantial reduction in tariffs which were then bound in the

GATT. Step by step, through one negotiating round after another, an exchange of mutually acceptable concessions opened Western markets. American names were, appropriately, attached to the more important of the earlier of these negotiating rounds – Dillon, Kennedy. But no favours were voluntarily conceded to the USA. No ground was given in recognition of past American generosity.

The Kennedy Round of the 1960s was the high point. It was the American instrument for reducing discrimination and consolidating the Western economic and political system. Even though the Round concluded in agreement among negotiators, it failed to solve the mounting economic problems of the USA. Protectionist sentiment in the USA, and in the American Congress, remained unsatisfied that at least as much had been obtained as had been conceded. Neither President Johnson nor President Nixon were able to obtain Congressional approval for the abolition of the American selling price non-tariff barrier to the import of chemical products, nor were they able to obtain even minimal powers to conclude further international trade agreements. For some years the President of the USA did not have Congressional authority for negotiating trade agreements. The pressure was all the other way, towards the imposition by the USA of voluntary export agreements, limiting exports to the USA of Japanese and European goods. For the moment at least, the drive had gone out of American pressure for an ever more open trading system. Then, in 1973, with a touch of irony as well as of hope, Tokyo was chosen as the host for an international conference to launch a further GATT negotiating round. The Tokyo Round was not to be completed until 1979.

Gradually a more open trading system had been created though the openness was largely confined to manufactured goods. Yet even during the Kennedy Round negotiations, it was not unusual to see attempts made to compensate for the reduction in protective tariffs by the development of various kinds of non-tariff barrier. Protection of European agriculture remained inviolate. And as the relative importance of the European Community and of Japan in the world economy increased, as the American trade balance and confidence in American economic leadership declined, as the USA's own motivation was increasingly questioned, negotiations for the reduction of barriers to trade became tougher and the outcome of the negotiations became less significant.

THE MULTI-FIBRE ARRANGEMENTS

Contemporary with these steps towards more open international trade generally, had gone the effort to control trade in textiles specifically. The American and UK textile industries were in the lead clamouring for protection, at first against a resurgent Japan and then against Hong Kong and other developing countries. In the early years after the Second World War there was a shortage of textile products. The textile industries of the USA and UK found world markets anxious for their supplies. It did not last long. Soon both the American and the British industries were fighting for survival even within their own domestic markets. Both the British and American governments discovered a need to control textile imports.

The UK industry and government felt that owing to the Commonwealth connection, the penetration of the UK market by developing country textile exports substantially exceeded that experienced by other developed countries. They thought that the other developed countries, including the USA, should be required to import a good deal more before the UK was required to import any more. What the UK felt about the developed world as a whole, the USA thought about the EEC. The EEC had succeeded in keeping imports to a relatively low level. The EEC was not, however, given to sentimentality. The situation complained of was one the UK and USA had brought on themselves. The USA and UK had admitted large quantities of textile imports on free trade principles. They now expected to be allowed to pass part of the resulting problem to others on mercantilist principles.

The negotiated solution to this conundrum consisted of bilateral agreements within a multilateral framework. The proclaimed object of the multilateral framework has not been to deny the developing country suppliers increasing markets in developed countries. It has been to regulate the flow. It was also intended to confine the disease of developed country protectionism to their textile imports from developing countries.

The bilateral agreements between exporting and importing countries were the cutting edge of the arrangement and were intended to deal with the actual problem of excessive imports. Bilateral agreements, by their nature, threaten the principle of non-discrimination. But that was a secondary consideration compared with the desire to control textile imports and in a way which made possible favours to client states.

Over the years, *force majeure* produced agreement on a succession of multilateral arrangements within which bilaterals could be separately negotiated with separate suppliers. At first they dealt only with cotton goods but from 1973 the Multi-Fibre Arrangements (MFAs) have covered most textile fibres. These Arrangements have continued up to the present day. All these Arrangements departed from GATT in various important respects. They introduced the concept of market disruption in place of the GATT concept of serious injury. They imposed quantitative restrictions without serious injury to domestic producers being proved and without compensation to exporters. Increasingly they left the judgement as to the need for action solely in the hands of powerful importing countries which were not content to be bound by inconvenient rules. They were discriminatory in effect, discriminating both between developed and developing countries and between developing countries themselves. At the very time when the USA was exerting pressure on its allies to reduce barriers to trade, partly so that there should be less discrimination against its own exporters, there was brought into existence what has become a permanent scheme for the discriminatory regulation of textile trade.

By 1977 two new factors were operating, the deepening recession and a relative reduction in American power within the international textile market. The EEC had become the principal world importer of textiles consequent on the equalising process on which the USA had earlier insisted, and on UK membership. The European Community, under pressure from the UK and France, was becoming increasingly protectionist, not least where textiles were concerned. It saw that it could never get multilateral agreement to an MFA which was as explicitly protectionist as it wanted. It was not prepared to renew the MFA unaltered unless it was permitted such 'reasonable departures' as were necessary to enable it to achieve the limits on imports previously agreed in the Council of

Ministers. The method would be by means of bilateral negotiations. There was no definition of 'reasonable', nor of the extent of the 'departures'. The bilateral agreements negotiated by the EEC with supplying countries became, so far as the EEC was concerned, the real MFA. What was done was not merely in volation of the GATT. It was at odds also with the Treaty of Rome. Country quotas for textiles, such as were negotiated by the EEC under the 1977 renewal of the MFA, were inconsistent with the common market which had, supposedly, been established under that Treaty.

The multilateral framework for textile trade was decaying. In 1977 and 1981, the Europeans led the protectionist drive. By 1986, with the Europeans marginally more liberal, the USA took over the protectionist lead. In each case it was through the bilaterals that the restrictions were primarily imposed. The value to developing countries of a multilateral framework had always depended principally on its being relatively liberal. The developed countries of the world were becoming increasingly protectionist and were prepared to have their way by one means or another whatever the multilateral framework. The MFA as renewed in 1977, and again in 1981 and 1986, could be defended only as somewhat better than the alternative. The alternative would have been no multilateral framework at all. Developed countries would have been left free to impose unilateral restrictions. Apparently developing countries felt, after long debate and despite every provocation, that the multilateral framework still had some value for them.

The history of the MFA exemplifies the insistence of national governments on remaining judges in their own cause whenever they have the power. The USA has always been careful to ensure that its sovereign right to determine when market disruption was taking place should not be prejudiced by any form of international judgement. The EEC rapidly gained the self-confidence to take the same view. The history of the MFA shows the value of alliances in establishing limits to economic interdependence, especially in the case of middle-sized powers. Even the USA had to take notice of the negotiating power of the European Community. The EEC had become the key consumer of developing country textile imports. No renewed MFA could have worked without EEC adherence to it. The UK and France, acting together, were able to exploit that power by turning the EEC on to a more protectionist course, even though that was contrary to the wishes of a major member, Germany, and also of Denmark. Germany accepted that its trade links with developing countries might be damaged by its consent to EEC policy in the MFA negotiations. For the sake of unity within the Community, it made the sacrifice. In this case, France and the UK were the beneficiaries of the alliance, Germany was the loser. Germany, however, realised that its overall interests lay in the unity of the European Alliance even at some sacrifice. For its part the European Commission was glad to perform its protectionist role. The Commission was not highly regarded among member states. Its representative role in the MFA negotiations confirmed its prerogative to act on trade policy matters on behalf of the Community as a whole. Its success in this role was one positive factor in its generally weakening balance sheet of prestige.

The exercise of sovereign rights need not stop with one particular group of products. The action taken in the case of textiles underlined a principle. That principle clearly is that there is a right to take exceptional action, action at best distantly related to the GATT, to refuse entry to imports claimed to be disruptive. A principle established in the case of textiles could not be denied if other product groups came under comparable threat. In the view of governments, even though free trade may be a contributor to prosperity, it carries too many risks to be allowed to run unchecked. International trade is not a right but a concession. If the concession becomes politically inconvenient, it will be withdrawn or at least modified. If the risk is seen in advance, the precautions will be taken in advance. Above all, power, and the freedom to use it, is not to be lightly, or irrevocably, prejudiced.

THE NIXON MEASURES, 15 AUGUST 1971

On 15 August 1971 President Nixon imposed an import surcharge and made the dollar inconvertible. He then demanded, as the price for returning the USA to full participation in the international economic system, that the other OECD countries should take steps which would bring about a major improvement in the American balance of payments. There was a further demand that the EEC should drop its negotiations for a free trade area with EFTA, thus breaking the agreement on which the negotiations with the UK, Norway, and Denmark, for entry into the EEC, were based. The USA wanted the discrimination against it constituted by the existence of the EEC to be reduced not increased. It did not want the area of discrimination to be extended to include the residue of EFTA after the new members joined the EEC. There were indeed signs in the USA of diminished enthusiasm for British entry into the EEC though British entry had long been promoted by the USA. Finally the EEC was instructed to change the rules of the Common Agricultural Policy.

These were terms for settlement amounting to capitulation. Even the USA could not enforce them. There was a severe deterioration in the political climate between the USA and its allies. The USA found it politically advisable to settle on terms well short of those it had originally demanded. There was a realignment of currencies at the conference at the Smithsonian Institute in December 1971. The dollar was devalued and the import surcharge was withdrawn. The realignment quite rapidly transformed the American balance of payments by making the dollar more competitive. The USA thus achieved a great deal of what it had wanted but by no means all. There had been a compromise. The existence of the NATO Alliance was the principal stabilising force in the international economic scene in 1971 as it has been during recent years of recession and economic strife. Nevertheless the action taken by the USA in August 1971 served, or should have served, as a warning that the post-war economic settlement was in danger, that the flow of American benevolence was at an end, and that life would be more difficult thereafter.

OPEC FIRES ITS SHOT

In the autumn of 1973 came the oil shock. The price of oil was quadrupled in the course of a year. In 1979 the price of oil was doubled. It was difficult to perceive these actions other than as the exercise of uncontrolled monopoly power. In developed countries there were those liberals who were able the more stoically to contemplate the effect of all this on their country's current account and their consumers' standard of living because of the certainty of retribution to come. OPEC would shortly collapse. In fact it took thirteen years before OPEC's power over the oil market was shaken, at least temporarily. In the meantime, a great deal of money had passed into the coffers of OPEC members. But the vindication of a liberal principle is worth waiting for even if it takes a little time and costs a great deal of money.

It appears that it is possible for a group of nations to act against the interests of the rest, to exact a tax which consumers have little choice but to pay, and to get away with it at least for a time. By 1986 the price of oil was at last collapsing. Life without OPEC could begin again. But the relief was mixed and the joy half-hearted. What would happen to deeply indebted Mexico? What would happen to an American banking system worryingly exposed to the risk of default? Above all, when would market power return to Saudi Arabia and its neighbours in the Gulf, and how would they use that power when the decline of non-OPEC sources of oil placed the initiative once more in their hands?

GERMANY AND JAPAN

Germany and Japan are two countries which have so far combined an understanding of the need to look after themselves with a remarkable ability actually to do it. The effect of the 1973 oil shock was to separate the men from the boys, the strong from the weak. The Federal Republic of Germany kept its current account surplus throughout the subsequent crisis. Japan fell momentarily into deficit but also rapidly succeeded in returning to larger and larger current account surplus. Germany and Japan make a current account surplus a major object of policy. Increasingly massive currency flows across the exchanges confirm them in this policy. Some thought that two such strong economies could afford to be helpful to the struggling economies of so much of the world by running a current account deficit. They could do more to expand domestic demand. Because of their history, because of a continuing sense of separateness, because of their dependence on imports of raw materials, above all because of their understanding of a mercantilist world as it is, they are determined to avoid the exposure to confidence factors that the financing of a current account deficit involves. Whatever pressure their trading partners bring upon them for less self-regarding policies, on that point they will stand firm.

Japan is frequently accused of acting unfairly. Trade, the Japanese are told, must be not just free but fair. Yet they supply good products at good prices and the world wants to buy them. To whom then are they being unfair? If their unfairness arises from their failure to buy what they do not want to buy, they can legitimately claim that they have not come across that definition in the economic textbooks. They wait to be taught that they are under any such obligation. If the world wants to persuade them of a concept so foreign to the theory of free trade, it will have to turn to persuaders that it has, as yet, shrunk from using. If other countries feel themselves disadvantaged by the successes of Japan, it can only be because they do not believe in the theory of free trade. But Japan could impose no greater humiliation on those Western countries that prate so eloquently about their devotion to free trade, than to compel them to admit that they do not, and never have, believed in it. Even the Japanese might take pause before committing so unpardonable an offence.

THE USA REVIVED

The USA has shown great powers of recuperation. The USA whose vast oil imports had provided OPEC with the lever that made the oil shock possible, and whose economic dominance had seemed to be in decline, succeeded to a remarkable extent in reversing that decline. It was the USA that took the lead both in the establishment of the large, internationally subscribed, capital fund intended to provide something of a safety net for any of the Western nations that fell into serious balance of payments difficulties, and in the creation of the scheme for sharing oil supplies in case of another emergency. The USA did not ignore the predicaments of its allies. The political imperatives of the USA demanded that it do what it could to safeguard the economies of its weaker allies. The paradox of American power is that the USA has felt unable to enjoy it alone. It has never felt able to ignore the consequences for the economic and political strength of its allies of disruptive economic and political conjunctures. It has therefore supported allies who have thereupon regained confidence enough to niggle about its policies. There is no ingratitude greater than political ingratitude.

In one respect the power of the USA had never declined. During the most difficult economic conjunctures, its role in the defence of the West had remained paramount, and the dependence of its allies on American strength had remained. Even if its dominant role in economic affairs has been diluted, the onset of crisis turns eyes toward Washington seeking for leadership. Without the USA exerting a leadership role there can be no leadership among the countries of the Western Alliance or in international economic policy. Even with the USA exerting such a role there may be no leadership in economic policy because its lead may no longer be automatically followed. There is the additional problem that its leadership, even where supported by its allies, may no longer determine events. The market in the form of immense sums of mobile money, is there ready to dispose of any solution proposed that ignores its power and its criteria.

THE UK's EXPERIENCE OF AN INTERDEPENDENT WORLD

The UK's disabling area of weakness has, for many decades, been its economic performance. The UK has sought every means of restoring competitiveness to British industry other than by devaluing the pound sterling, hence cutting the standard of living of the British people and stimulating inflation. Even when fundamental disequilibrium was only too apparent, UK governments resisted the option of devaluation. In the fixed rate years, devaluation was a defeat for economic policy, a defeat played out before the world as a whole and, more particularly, before the UK electorate. The political constraints have receded since sterling was floated. The fall in the value of the currency was never in the end prevented, and whether from a fixed rate or a floating rate, there have been the same costs. Devaluation has brought short-term gains but no permament change in the secular process of relative industrial decline. The country of Keynes found that Keynesian economics in the fixed-rate years provided relief but no cure. Perhaps even the relief was won at an unacceptable price in inflation and myopia in face of fundamental problems. The failures of macroeconomic policies have led UK governments to the use of a variety of devices. These have ranged from defiance in the form of import controls to supplication in the form of appeals to friendly governments for money and for the adoption by them of economic policies helpful to the solution of UK dilemmas.

The GATT has always permitted import controls for balance of payments reasons. This is one illustration of the caution with which member nations entered into the GATT. However during a period of rapid economic expansion, it was seldom necessary to have recourse to general import controls. There was increasing reluctance to do so combined with increasing questioning as to their utility for the purpose of correcting balance of payments deficits. In 1964, the UK, with a new government faced by what was considered to be an insupportable balance of payments deficit, introduced a 15 per cent import surcharge. The import surcharge was criticised for endangering the whole free trade system. Protection for balance of payments reasons might, in law, be GATT-worthy. Yet if a country like the UK took such steps, others might follow. In the view of its critics, the UK should instead have chosen deflation, a policy hardly attractive to a newly-elected government with a small majority contemplating a further election. Under international pressure the surcharge was cut the following year to 10 per cent. It was abolished one year later. But that followed an election victory which gave the government a substantial majority in Parliament. Thus the import surcharge lasted only two years. Its withdrawal left the basic economic problems of the UK unresolved. One year later there followed the devaluation of November 1967. All this happened to a major industrialised country during an era of economic expansion years before the Nixon measures of 15 August 1971 or the oil shock of the autumn of 1973.

The history of the UK import surcharge, and of the further import restrictions adopted by the UK in 1969, teaches two lessons. First, they illustrate the fact that the measures of economic disarmament adopted during the hey day of the post-war economic expansion were, to a degree, tentative. They were capable of being recalled if necessity required and internationally acceptable ways could be found. The second lesson, however, is that when a country like the UK adopts a policy of overt, widely-based, protectionism, it subjects itself to intolerable international pressures which in the end force the abandonment of the policy. Other OECD countries which have adopted general import controls for balance of payments reasons have found it difficult to sustain them. In almost every case they have been abandoned within two years.

At the time, the book solution for a fundamental disequilibrium in the balance of payments was devaluation combined with deflation of domestic demand. The disrepute of import controls arises in part from academic studies. But it is not any academic study of the relative merits of devaluation on the one hand and import surcharges or quantitative import restrictions on the other, that has forced major countries to withdraw from general import controls. It is the result of the exercise of power by those countries with power to use, countries which consider it inconsistent with their interests that the free trade system should be endangered. There may seem to be some illogicality in this situation. General import controls are intended to have the same effect on imports as does devaluation. Indeed in some respects devaluation may be regarded as a more aggressive move. It serves not merely to reduce imports but equally to promote exports. Yet the introduction of general import controls by a major trading nation has always been seen post-war as representing a graver danger to the future of the open trading system than has devaluation.

In 1974 a new British government was elected. The government lacked a majority in Parliament, and the country faced both a crippling miners' strike and a large current account deficit. The government made a costly settlement of the strike, costly in political as well as in economic terms. Thereafter it attempted to persuade the rest of the developed world that the course of conduct appropriate for it to follow in the wake of the oil price hike was one carefully designed to relieve the problems of the UK. The UK's advice to the world was in tune with recommendations from Keynesian economists. The strong economies of the world, specifically the USA, Germany and Japan, were to act as locomotives. They would draw the rest of the world out of recession by compensating for the contractionary effects of the oil price hike. Otherwise, it was argued, the UK could not be expected to resist mounting protectionist pressures.

This advocacy, though eloquent, was greeted with some scepticism. No other country took too much notice of the UK's advice. The UK did not appear to be the most obvious country to which to look for economic advice. That advice was seen simply as a reflection of policies which had damaged the UK's economic performance over the years and which had taken it into the world recession economically weaker than almost any other developed country. In their recommendations these economists neglected too much that part of the Keynesian heritage that understood the instinct for economic security. Certainly the major countries to which they appealed were very influenced in their policies by that instinct and their example left little alternative to the more prudent of their contemporaries. Germany and Japan saw the requirements of the time as defensive, look after your balance of payments, look after your public expenditure, look after your borrowing, look after your inflation, do not on any account increase your dependence on the goodwill of other countries. Other developed countries understood perfectly well, or, if at first they did not, were made to understand, that the first responsibility of governments was to toughen defensive policies, not soften them. A little later the control of the money supply, seen by some as a means by which inflation could be controlled, became part of the inevitable defensive armoury. Monetarism had arrived.

British policy between March 1974 and autumn 1976 was a combination of fiscal excitement and dangerous thoughts. Protectionism by one means or another was very much on the agenda. The government, feeling its well-meant advice scorned by its trading partners, sank into a mood in which pulling down the temple of free trade was an option by no means to be ignored. In fact it was not a realistic option. In the end it was realised that such policies were more likely to bring down the British government than the temple of free trade. The government came to the conclusion that the UK had to live in the world, not attempt to get off it. The crunch came during the IMF negotiations in November and December 1976. The *literati* and the left in the Labour Cabinet had still not come to grips with the realities of international relations. But the realists, inevitably in a crisis, triumphed, thereby saving the government.

The new UK government had grossly overestimated both the UK's influence, whether that influence was exercised by argument, or by supplication, or by threat, and the degree to which countries saw common interests in tackling the crisis. A developed country that falls on evil times is in a worse case even than a developing country. It exercises little influence on the international economic environment, and it cannot even muster international sympathy in its support. The new government had overestimated the devotion of its friends, whether President Ford's America or Chancellor Helmut Schmidt's Germany. Both, not inappropriately, were concerned to teach the UK that, as Trollope had put it, 'It is very well to have friends to lean upon, but it is not always well to lean upon one's friends' (Trollope, 1985, vol. 2, p. 106). The episode showed that the UK could expect to have no friend better than itself. If there could not be self-discipline, the discipline would have to be externally imposed. The UK government suffered a humiliating but educational experience. But there could be no other realistic expectation than that it would be rebuffed when it hawked its begging bowl round the capitals of the world and attempted to borrow with menaces.

THE BONN SUMMIT, 1978

There was, of course, the Bonn Summit of 1978. This was the high point of post-1973 international summitry. As so often with policies of economic stimulation, by the time they came they were too much and too late, giving untimely encouragement to those in OPEC who were only waiting for Western recovery to give another twist to the oil price spiral, and thereby place a further tax on the world's economy.

Bonn had been preceded by the unsuccessful London Summit of 1977, the first attended by President Carter. The USA under President Carter seemed prepared to make its contribution to world economic regeneration. The Carter Administration had been influenced in these policies by Keynesian economists as well as by the political pressures brought about by recession in the USA. But in the USA there were also strong counter-pressures from those who felt that, for the USA as for other countries, there were great dangers in expansionary policies. Nevertheless in the US Administration at least, the UK now had a powerful ally in its advocacy of the locomotive thesis. Prime Minister Callaghan and other British Ministers returned from visits to Washington persuaded of President Carter's wisdom and political insight and, above all, of his desire to help the UK. At last there was prospect of an international response to the UK's economic prayers. At the London Summit, Germany and Japan strongly resisted. The most they would do was to commit themselves to growth targets they had already established. But it was rapidly apparent that their existing targets were beyond the potential of their existing policies. At the time of the summit, Japan was forecasting that it would be going into deficit on current account during 1977. Instead it ended the year with a massive surplus. The London Summit failed to achieve the UK's objective of a coordinated expansion.

With the UK continuing to murmur threateningly about protectionism, attention began to concentrate on the next summit to be held in Bonn. The Bonn Summit would, it was hoped, at last prove that the way forward lay not in myopic nationalism but in international collaboration. Governments were to show that they could retain charge over their national destinies and their independence without the mutually destructive consequence of competitive deflation. In the end, despite much trumpeting that a great success had been achieved, the Bonn Summit promised only to deceive.

It did at least appear to promise. But in the end it was found that the promise had a great deal more of clever presentation than of redrawn policy. Germany came under intense international pressure. But what it did, it had almost certainly decided it could afford to do anyhow. A combination of considerations led the German government in 1978 to decide that there was room, consistent with its defensive posture, for some stimulation to the German economy. One consideration was that inflation was low and that the growth out-turn had been slower than expected. Another consideration was that, by careful tactics, the German government could force its partners to pay a price in terms of trade policy for what it in any case intended to do by way of fiscal policy. Another was the desire of the German government to extract from the US Administration a pledge to remove its oil price controls. The key fact, certainly, was that the German government and the Bundesbank had concluded that some expansion could be undertaken safely (Putnam and Bayne, 1984, pp. 86–9). No action was taken which was considered inconsistent with a proper defensive posture.

Japan was coming under very strong American pressure to do something effective about its trade surplus. It wished to appear cooperative. It broke through the rigid ceiling hitherto fixed on the size of its budget deficit. But again it could be comfortable with what it was doing. There was, it was believed, no unacceptable exposure as a response to international pressures. Even Britain, in its spring budget, had thought itself capable of making some contribution to the rising euphoria. Given that nothing was asked of any country at the Bonn Summit that it could not, in the opinion of its government, comfortably do, there was no reason why there should be disagreement or a refusal to participate in what was conceived and publicised as a relaunching of the world economy.

In fact, what was done was not as safe as it appeared at the time. New events intervened. The Bonn plan for international coordination of economic policies, was prematurely cut short by the further oil shock of 1979. Its results would in any case have been affected by the fact that until this further oil shock the USA was moving from longstanding current account deficit into visible and substantial surplus. But in the circumstances of the 1979 oil shock, self-defence was reinforced as the dominant policy motivation of all countries that felt themselves exposed and whose governments had the necessary domestic political muscle. In retrospect the Bonn Summit acquired a bad reputation for having done exactly what Helmut Schmidt believed he had most carefully avoided. By authorising coordinated expansion it had exposed his own country and other participant countries to grave dangers. After the 1979 oil shock, Germany moved briefly into current account deficit, an experience it had avoided even after 1973. Japan, which had gone into current account deficit after the 1973 oil shock, repeated the experience after the second oil shock. For both Germany and Japan all this was very worrying and, no doubt, reinforced their concern to avoid adventures in future. Before the end of his term, President Carter was appointing Paul

Volcker as Chairman of the Federal Reserve Board as a way of restoring confidence in the American dollar.

In 1979, a new government was elected in Britain. Whether justly or not, it was called 'monetarist'. Whether because it was monetarist or because it saw the needs of self-defence, and that Britain was in no position to stand out alone in an interdependent world, it placed Britain in a defensive posture. In doing so it was greatly helped by self-sufficiency in oil. In the period after the 1979 oil price hike, oil self-sufficiency gave an unaccustomed tinge of strength to Britain's economy. There was, however, a price to be paid. Since 1979 unemployment, already high by post-war standards, has soared. A combination of pressures, arising from political constraints and continuing poor economic performance, weakened the resolve even of the Thatcher government. Economic strength remains a difficult objective for the most resolute government when economic performance is poor even with the advantage of oil self-sufficiency. With a weakening oil price and a level of inflation too high by the standards of the USA, Germany and Japan, international doubts about the British economy leave it exposed to flurries on the international exchanges. The best that the market will do is to reserve judgement.

AFTER THE OIL SHOCK – NORM OR ABERRATION?

Secular trends had long been emphasising to the countries of the world the need for greater self-reliance. Then came the oil shock. A key characteristic of the post-war world had been the availability of oil at low and stable prices. It had come to be thought of as a law of nature that cheap oil would be everlastingly available, guaranteed by the might of the USA and by the mainly American oil majors. Now the OPEC cartel had wrenched oil free of American dominance. It had decided, in alliance, to take charge of its principal resource. It, thereby, dealt a severe blow to American power and leadership, but it also created a conjuncture in which American leadership could once more become acceptable to its allies, other than France.

There was much debate as to whether the new, and much more competitive, world after the oil shock was to be regarded as the new norm or as an unfortunate, and temporary, aberration in the period of steady growth and stable relationships which the world had experienced in the first twenty-five years after the Second World War. Whatever the answer to that question, the immediate pressures where obvious enough. Charity was to begin at home. Charity was to be available to foreigners only on stiff conditions. It was a time for some new thinking, or perhaps for some old thinking. Self-dependence rather than interdependence.

Defensive policies had their costs. There was slower growth of trade, an exacerbation of trade rivalries, protectionism followed by emulation and retaliation, departure after departure from well-established rules of conduct in international economic relations, and a heightened concern about social stability in circumstances in which unemployment was rising to levels which Keynesian optimism had made unthinkable. Had someone blundered? For twenty-five years things had really gone rather well. But did twenty-five years of relative international cooperation undermine the lessons of centuries of economic conflict between states? Twenty-five years is a short moment in human history. The world had now retrogressed to conflict and to a predisposition to export social problems which it was no longer possible to solve at home. Experience had once more demonstrated that there have to be limits to economic interdependence. Governments must look after their own.

CONCLUSION

The USA has accumulated both a large budget deficit and a large deficit in its current account. In so far as any country has acted as a locomotive drawing the economies of the rest of the world into economic growth and prosperity, it is the USA. The final irony is that surplus nations call upon the USA to balance its current account even though that would stop the main locomotive economy of the world in its tracks, and though meanwhile they refuse to supply any compensating stimulus themselves. The USA has achieved its own growth despite high interest rates and against a recent background of a depreciating dollar. The world watches the USA, uncertain whether it would rather cope with a collapse in the dollar or with a strong dollar sustained by high interest rates; whether it prefers to be drawn out of recession by a large American current account deficit or to be cast back into recession by a resilient US economy taking itself out of deficit through the instrumentality of a cheaper dollar.

The world of economic relations is dominated by competition, competition for orders, for supplies, for resources. It is only an hypothesis that economic competition between states is always of mutual benefit and never simply a zero-sum game. This hypothesis has seldom been seen by governments under pressure to be an acceptable basis for policy. At all times, and especially at times of recession, states will do everything that they feel they can to maintain their freedom of action and, when opportunity offers, to extend its boundaries. The desire for greater coordination of policies between major nations is unfulfilled due to conflicting interests and conflicting perceptions. It is a liberal illusion that departures from the liberal norm only harm, or necessarily harm, the country that practices them. In an interdependent world, just as in a world of traditionally independent and sovereign states, one country can impose costs on another. Inevitably, therefore, countries will seek to protect themselves. They will not, if they can avoid it, meekly accept the costs imposed upon them by others. There is in this nothing necessarily inconsistent with the survival of an open trading system. But those nations will be most devoted to that objective which in their international economic relations have reason to feel most secure.

There is no lack of evidence that in recent years a state's powers of independent decision-making, in the economic as in the military field, have become greatly constrained. Providing for effective self-defence can be a task of some difficulty. There may not be too many options available. Many kinds of action which, in the past, may have seemed appropriate to a balance of payments problem may now carry unacceptable costs. Direct action on the balance of payments may be very hazardous. There may be a high risk of retaliation. There may be other unforeseeable economic and political consequences. Economic interdependence has made any calculation of the costs and benefits of independent action very uncertain. The free floating of currencies which was expected to enhance independence as compared with the fixed parities of the Bretton Woods era, has not had that effect. The exposure of sterling to large international money flows has substantially confined the ability of British governments to conduct reflationary policies of a Keynesian kind.

The need to maintain confidence is not a catch word. Whatever are the nostrums of the market at any particular time will become matters of serious concern for any Minister of Finance who wishes to challenge them. Ideas, or ideologies, become more important than facts or objective analysis. But then what are the facts and where is the objective analysis? Where there is as little science as there is in economic policy-making, it is not surprising that sentiment rules, however ill-informed it may sometimes seem to governments. Governments should not blame others for being ruled by sentiment when they are ruled by it to so large an extent themselves. In the end restrictive fiscal and monetary policies may be found to be the only viable option.

Economic strength is the key factor in international economic relations. It is defined by the degree of independence a nation can command in an interdependent world. It is a star by which all countries will steer if their navigators are sufficiently clear sighted, which means if their vision is not blurred by the wishfulfilment of economic liberalism. In a world in which so much is uncertain, and where governments make their own judgements of the national interest, it is both natural and forgiveable that it should be by the exercise of power, more than by the exercise of persuasion, that the international economic environment is fashioned. Major economies have a major impact, for good or ill, on the environment within which the rest of the world operates. Their governments will decide policy according to their own lights and in the interests, as they see them, of their own people. Their defensive postures will frequently react unfavourably on others. The most one can hope is that they will not set out deliberately to do harm.

6 The Limits of International Economic Commitment

RULEMAKING IN A WORLD OF CONFLICTING INTERESTS

A collectively agreed framework of rules intended to govern certain important aspects of international economic relations exists. The framework has been established around certain international institutions, especially the GATT, the IMF and the World Bank. These institutions have played their part in reconciling the conflicting interests of nations, and in finding ways of cooperation that are consistent both with their own mandate and with the state's insistence on the right of self-determination.

A liberal economic philosophy is not an essential ingredient of a rule-making approach to the resolution of international economic conflicts. Pragmatism would suggest the value of rules. Whatever the conflicts and uncertainties of international economic relations, a framework of rules can still have its advantages. Concern for national economic security can enhance rather than reduce the value of a framework of rules. Competition there will be. But at least there can be an accepted approach to the regulation of competition. Conflict, there will be. But at least there can be an accepted approach to the resolution of conflict. Rules may make the actions of other governments more predictable. Most states will be reluctant, at least on the first occasion, to break rules by which they are formally bound. Rules can constrain the power of large countries and of the larger economies. They may to some degree constrain the power of the three large trading blocs, the USA, the EEC and Japan, in dealing with each other and with the Third World.

Rules simplify the management of international conflict. It would be exhausting, and even impossible, if all disputes had to be dealt with on an *ad hoc* basis without benefit of rules. Rules

85

act as an influence towards agreement where agreement is possible. They reduce the administrative burden on small countries. They avoid the need for countries with small resources to enter into a series of bilateral agreements that would strain their capacity to negotiate, and, in their proliferation, might endanger the world trading system as a whole. Once an international agreement such as the GATT exists, there can be advantage to other countries in joining so that they have a seat at the negotiating table. In seeking a seat at the negotiating table, such countries will be aware that collective action between nations can be as much of a restrictive practice as collective action between companies. It can lead to conspiracies by some nations against the interests of others. It is better to be part of the action and to see what is going on.

THE OPTION OF DRAWING BACK

The actions of the state in handling its international economic relationships, or in mitigating the social effects of international economic competition, may be constrained by international agreements. As these agreements have been devised by politicians and government officials rather than by economists, every attempt has been made to ensure that countries are not left unnecessarily exposed. States signatory to such agreements will normally endeavour to live faithfully by them. Such agreements, and the obligations they embody, are not lightly cast aside. Nevertheless not all international agreements will be regarded as equally binding. There are certain agreements which, by their nature, are irreversible. The UK could not withdraw the concession of independence to Zimbabwe. Such agreements are easily identifiable. Among agreements which, in principle, are reversible, there will be degrees of commitment. A political agreement such as the Treaty of Rome, embodied in domestic law, will be at the highest point of the hierarchy of commitment. Even here, the commitment is not absolute. A defence agreement such as the North Atlantic Treaty Alliance will also carry a high level of commitment.

Agreements governing international economic relations, such as the GATT, have never carried the same degree of commitment. Even if a state or government, on the best economic advice available, perceives a particular course of economic conduct as the best, it cannot place ultimate reliance on it. It must always seek to leave to itself the option of drawing back. It was Shonfield's view that 'the whole thrust of the story up to the early 1970s has been away from the conception of enforceable laws which underlay the thinking of those who originally constructed the Bretton Woods system and its ancillary arrangements' (Shonfield, 1976, p. 83). Hudec has written that the GATT legal system can only be understood 'as an instrument of diplomacy'. He has also observed that: 'In one situation after another the rules could not be enforced and were put aside. . . . Before long GATT found itself operating with a formal legal structure containing a significant number of inoperative rules.' Nothing has, in this respect, changed since the early 1970s except that the movement away from the concept of enforceable laws has become even more pronounced (Hudec, 1975, p. 10).

Treaties can become legally enforceable through domestic legislation. If states wished to be strongly bound by the international commitments into which they enter, they might make those commitments the subject of their constitutional provisions or of their domestic legislation. Even constitutions and domestic legislation can be changed but the commitment would at least be stronger than it can be simply by reason of an international treaty. In fact states do not typically embody their international commitments in constitutions or in domestic legislation. Even in the case of the Treaty of Rome which *is* the subject of domestic legislation and where there is a Court charged to guarantee the operations of the Treaty according to law, commitments are not invariably respected or enforced.

Sometimes situations of conflict and disagreement are met by multilaterally negotiated revisions of treaties. This may be done because a treaty has worked out unsatisfactorily for all or most parties. Another reason may be that the treaty in question is frequently breached and has proved unenforceable. The choice may then lie between revising the treaty on the one hand, and, on the other, leaving certain or all of its provisions unenforceable and unenforced. It can happen, as in the case of the Nixon measures of August 1971, that a very powerful country will by its actions attempt to force the renegotiation of international agreements. Where treaties are breached and unenforced, the guilty will normally seek revision because they prefer to live by their international commitments. But it will not usually be a very strong preference if national interests point in a different direction. It will not be regarded as an intolerable burden on the national conscience if certain commitments into which a state has entered are then ignored.

There is in all international treaties between sovereign states, other than the irreversible kind, an implied clause which reserves to the participants the right to opt out if there is inadequate enforcement or if circumstances change significantly. That right exists even if the treaty is of unlimited duration. It exists because it cannot be denied. It does not have to be explicitly stated. It is covered by the state's inherent right of self-defence. In denying the ultimate degree of commitment to such engagements, a state is not acting dishonourably, for its partners are in the identical situation. All will endeavour to make the agreement work for their own benefit and, hopefully, to the benefit of all the participants. But if it does not work, each will have to balance its interests against any sanctions available to its partners, and the likelihood that they will use them. A state may be bound by its own helplessness. It cannot be bound simply by the terms of a treaty.

Keohane argues that a county's concern for its reputation will bind it to international agreements even contrary to its short-term interests. Loss of reputation will have adverse effects on its ability to enter into future agreements because it will not be trusted, and that is a cost which states will be reluctant to contemplate (Keohane, 1984, pp. 105–6). There is no doubt that the moral pressure of an agreement, more felt by some countries than by others, may suffice to persuade some countries to act, for some time, contrary to their perception of their own interests. However, breaches of international agreements, often minor, occasionally major, are rather frequent. States enter into agreements with their partners, and foreign companies enter into agreements with states, not because the parties are regarded as more than usually trustworthy but because the agreement is seen to be in their mutual interest at least for the foreseeable future. The parties to the agreement then watch each other like hawks for any breach. Although states will naturally calculate the costs of breaking any agreement, including the cost to their reputation, they will certainly not treat loss of reputation more seriously than international custom makes necessary, and they will not consent to submit to the seriously harmful consequences of an agreement into which they have entered unless there are very strong arguments for doing so, stronger that is than damage to reputation. Governments would be wrong, if they can avoid it, to allow serious costs to be imposed on their citizens purely because they had entered into an agreement that had turn out unfortunately. Where an international agreement has turned out unfortunately for one or more participants, the other participants may be prepared to accept that the best way of dealing with the situation in the interests of future relationships is either to permit or overlook any breach, or to enter into an agreed revision of the original agreement.

Shonfield attributes this view of the conditionality of international agreements in its most extreme form to the French:

> Equally traditional was the French view that states were in practice bound to seek their exclusive national advantage in any international encounter, and that an adversary relationship was the natural one; treaties simply disguised this fact and should therefore be interpreted in the narrowest possible way in order to minimise the constraints they imposed on national freedom of manoeuvre (Shonfield, 1976, p. 60)

Certainly the French understand the meaning and importance of economic security. But though the French, like other countries, seek their national advantage in international encounters, it underestimates them to imagine that they believe that an adversary relationship is invariably the natural base from which to start. The French understand perfectly well that international collaboration can have value and they seek agreements with other powers. They are simply franker than some other countries in the expression of their objectives. But it was the France of General de Gaulle rather than the UK that sought and achieved the historic reconciliation with Germany. It was the France of President Giscard d'Estaing which was especially anxious, in the 1970s, to establish agreement on international monetary collaboration.

STATES AND COMPANIES

States may resile from their agreements with companies, whether domestic or foreign, if those agreements turn out disadvantageously. This may happen, for example, if an agreement for the exploitation of a raw material resource leaves the state with an income from that exploitation smaller than that to which it feels itself entitled. After the oil price shock of 1973–4, the UK Parliament passed a Petroleum Revenue Tax in order to recoup for the government a larger part of the enhanced profit which the oil companies could be expected to make as a result of the greatly increased price of oil. The author, as Paymaster General, introduced the Petroleum Revenue Tax. No mention had been made by any UK government previously of the possibility of such a tax. Its introduction was considered by some to be both retrospective in effect and a breach of international law. However such arguments did not deter the government, nor did their rejection by the government in fact disillusion the oil companies. It was widely recognised that, in the changed circumstances, the UK government had to act to win for itself a greater share in the proceeds from the North Sea. Any other position would have been politically impossible. The government was bound, in its own interests, to act reasonably. It could not fail to act.

The exploitation of a key raw material such as oil has led other developed countries, such as Denmark, to move to change the rules in midstream. When there are such drastic changes in the surrounding circumstances as followed the 1973–4 oil shock, it is very difficult even for those adversely affected to deny the appropriateness of government action, at least in principle. But it is developing countries that are more frequently cited for the offence of retrospection, or of renegotiation, in their dealings with companies, especially foreign companies. There can be no doubt of their sovereign right so to do. Whether it is wise to act in this way is a question for judgement in the light of the circumstances. Recusant countries, normally, get away with it because in a competitive world there always seem to be other foreign companies willing to rush in to fill a vacuum caused by the indignant departure of one of their number. Indignation at ill-treatment can be an expensive luxury in which even the largest companies can seldom afford to indulge. As long as the renegotiated terms are anything like reasonable, sovereign rights will be accepted with a sigh and a shrug. But if there is too much of it, the penalty extracted will be a decline in the enthusiasm of multinational companies for foreign investment in developing countries. During the 1970s there developed a marked lack of enthusiasm for investment in commodities in developing countries. Investment in commodities moved to reliable developed countries and away from unreliable developing countries. Thus there can be penalties to be paid as retribution for the unreasonable exercise of sovereign rights.

Some nations act in an international context like a bull in a china shop. They throw off their obligations without grace, without courtesy, and without apology. They use their power to create mischief as yet one more negotiating weapon. Most developed nations cannot afford the cost of the broken crockery. They have to approach their objective with diplomacy, and with a greater sensitivity to the reactions of their trading partners and of the companies with which they deal.

SHOULD THE CLAIMS OF INTERNATIONAL ORDER BE ABSOLUTE?

Tumlir summarised the claims of international order thus:

> The rules of the international order define the legitimate rights of all constituent states. It follows that a national objective that could not be attained except through the infringement of these rules could not be considered legitimate. . . . There are ways of pursuing national objectives which are at the same time efficient and proof against protest from abroad. The international order cannot be deemed to be costly because it constrains countries to use policies that are best from the national viewpoint (Tumlir, 1979, pp. 257–8).

Of course no nation should lightly break an international agreement to which it is party. But one needs a very high degree of confidence in the laws of liberal economics, and in the ability to foresee and treat all manner of economic conjunctures, to make or accept statements that a national objective which can be obtained only through the infringement of rule is thereby necessarily illegitimate, and that there are invariably ways of pursuing national objectives that are at the same time efficient and proof against protest from abroad. This confidence is today shown by few governments. It is not a statement that anyone with responsibility for handling economic conjunctures is at all likely to make or accept.

Tomasso Padoa-Schioppa has claimed that 'there is no theoretical reason why the world should not be given the same kind of economic organisation as economists consider desirable for nations', a statement that points only to the laughable inadequacy of his theories. He wants to establish 'an effective and binding procedure for consultation and decision-making at the multi-country level', a proposal which in the nature of national sovereignties and conflicting economic perceptions and interests will be impossible to achieve. Similarly Willem Buiter believes that achieving credibility means restricting one's own freedom of action, and one's future capacity for reneging on earlier commitments. Yet there is no prospect of denying to those nations with the power to do so, the ability to renege on a commitment if things turn out seriously differently from expected, as they often will (Catalyst, Spring 1985). In international economic relations, the most one can hope for at any one time is a negotiated and temporary reconciliation of conflicting interests, not a solution to world economic dilemmas. The next 'round' will always be necessary in an attempt to defend the gains of the last.

HOW ABSOLUTE COMMITMENTS COULD BECOME A BARRIER TO INTERNATIONAL AGREEMENT

Agreement between states should not be made impossible by the utopian objective of absolute commitment. Absolute claims for the rules of international order are actually a barrier to progress towards more civilised international relationships. If governments were to be absolutely bound, they would deny all avoidable international commitments.

The earlier multilateral textile regimes limiting the import of textile products to developed countries helped the cause of liberalism by preventing rather more illiberal, unilaterally enforced, restrictions. There is much truth in the statement that

'In whatever areas the LDCs have developed the capacity to export manufactures that are highly competitive with the products of developed countries, the response has been towards protectionism' (Aggarwal, 1985, p. 200). It may be of little comfort to developing countries that protectionism has operated not just against developing countries, but between developed countries also, the principal victim being Japan. Yet the fact that the USA, and indeed other developed countries, have over the last decade been able to negotiate voluntary export restraints and other protective agreements covering such products as steel, cars, and colour television, has certainly helped the survival of the open trading system and of the GATT. The ability to negotiate voluntary export restraints has weakened the protectionist drive and diverted it from an attack on the open trading system as a whole.

Shonfield gives the Anglo-Japanese trade agreement of 1962 as an example of the value of limited commitment. Japan became a member of the GATT in 1955 following strong American pressure on its European allies. The USA had seen powerful political reasons for admitting Japan to the GATT. But the UK and other European countries, had, at first, strongly opposed the admission. In April 1955, the UK, France, and twelve other countries carried out their threat and invoked Article 35 of the GATT which permitted members to withhold most favoured nation treatment from new entrants. Then, in 1962, the UK made a treaty with Japan according Japan full GATT treatment. Shonfield observes:

> Thus the Anglo-Japanese trade agreement of 1962 according Japan full GATT treatment (Britain surrendering its right to discriminate against Japanese goods under Article 35) was conditional on the stated understanding that, if Britain ever failed to live up to its undertaking in any particular instance, the Japanese would not make use of their rights as a GATT member to pursue a complaint through that organisation. In this way Japan induced Britain to adopt a new and more liberal commercial policy by removing the British Government's anxiety that Japan might, possibly in awkward circumstances, try to use the GATT to enforce its rights (Shonfield, 1976, p. 78).

The USA did not use Article 35 against Japan. When it felt

under pressure from imports, it simply forced voluntary export agreements on Japan, contrary to its commitment to the GATT. Indeed, the first post-war voluntary export restraint agreement was exacted by the USA from Japan at about the same time as the USA was pressing its European allies to admit Japan to the GATT. It dealt with textile exports from Japan to the USA. Japan is highly dependent on the USA both for its defence and for its markets. It has a highly developed preference to conciliate the USA where possible. But Japan seems, in later years, to have learned how far it can provoke the USA without suffering retaliation. It has become cool enough, even at moments of crisis in its relations with the USA, to calculate rather accurately how far the USA will in fact be prepared to go.

THE 'RATHER CLOUDY LEGAL STATUS' OF THE GATT

The fate of the International Trade Organisation (the Havana Charter) after the Second World War showed that the United States Congress would not accept anything that appeared to give an international organisation enforceable supervision over American policies. Recourse was therefore had to a 'provisional' agreement, the GATT. It is provisional from the point of view of the USA and of the other contracting parties. In the USA, it is simply an 'executive agreement' made by the President without the advice and consent of the Senate under powers delegated to him by Congress. In other words, it was not ratified by the Senate, and hence is not legally binding on the Congress of the USA even though it is to Congress that the United States Constitution gives the power to levy tariffs and regulate foreign commerce.

Hudec has given an account of the decline in respect for GATT rules as countries began to claim or perceive that those rules were no longer comprehensive or properly balanced in the obligations they created. He himself is in favour of a reform of GATT adjudication procedures in order to avoid undermining its regulatory influence. After all one advantage of rules, however uncertain their binding force, is to enable willing politicians who wish to conduct a liberal trade policy to use them against domestic protectionist pressure groups by claiming that they are binding or, at least, have strong moral force. However Hudec also points out that 'the GATT has never felt it necessary or desirable to assert the binding status of these rules under formal international law'; that 'an unbending concept of obligation would be too brittle for the realities of trade policy affairs'; that 'GATT legal obligations had no self-executing legal force in the domestic law of the defendant country. The force behind panel decisions was dependent on whatever coercive pressure the GATT itself could generate'; and that 'It is illogical to expect governments to agree to stronger enforcement procedures for rules which they regard as invalid or inequitable' (Hudec, 1978, pp. 31, 30, 10, 23–4). He also emphasises that 'Governments were willing to adopt a fairly comprehensive and moderately demanding set of [GATT] rules, but only on the basis of a rather cloudy legal status called "provisional application", and on the basis of enforcement procedures that had considerable "flexibility"' (Hudec, 1978, pp. 53, 86).

A consequence of the cloudy legal status of the GATT is that powerful countries ignore it when they find it convenient so to do, or alternatively dominate it against the interests of other, less powerful, members. This is true, for example, of the USA and the European Community. These two trading blocs, together with Japan, in effect settled the Tokyo Round of multilateral trade negotiations between them. They introduced controls on textile trade of doubtful conformity to GATT principles. They frequently negotiate, outside the GATT, bilateral settlements of their own disputes. They ignore GATT panel findings when they are inconvenient. On the other hand it is also true that these powerful trade blocs would not be in the GATT if it attempted to tie their hands too tightly, and the other participants therefore have to decide which they prefer, to have the USA and the European Community within the GATT and under some, if loose, discipline, or to break up the organisation.

THE GATT AND THE FACILITATING VALUE OF ESCAPE CLAUSES

To make international agreements more consistent with the

obligations of the state to preserve its own security, there are very frequently escape clauses which attempt to define circumstances in which the force of the agreement may be relaxed. Such escape clauses can facilitate agreement and ratification by national governments and parliaments. Even an expurgated version of the Havana Charter, such as the GATT, would not have been accepted by the USA as an executive agreement if it had not contained numerous escape clauses, some of them tailored to the requirements of the renewed US Reciprocal Trade Agreements Act, both to protect existing vested interests and to provide against foreseeable dangers in which effective international supervision would be the last thing signatory states actually wanted. Congress, for example, required reassurance that trade agreements into which the USA entered would be negotiated on a strict basis of reciprocity and would not damage any existing American industry.

The UK ensured that all preferential agreements which existed prior to the establishment of the GATT were excluded from the obligations of the most favoured nation principle. Thus, for the time being, British imperial preference was safeguarded even though its abolition was a prime American target. The formation of customs unions and of free trade areas was permitted. This further exception to the most favoured nation principle had the effect of authorising future preferential areas such as the European Community. This was a wise provision because the European Community would certainly have been formed in any case, if necessary in despite of the GATT. Quantitative restrictions on imports remained permissible if balance of payments reasons could be argued in their support. Article 12 permitted it and European countries in the early days imposed Article 12 restrictions on much of their trade. Article 19 provided a safeguard against disruption caused by imports and it did not even say explicitly that its use had to be non-discriminatory. Article 25 permitted the 'waiver' of any GATT obligation 'in exceptional circumstances not elsewhere provided for in this agreement'.

An agreement with such escape clauses was a great deal easier to accept. The existence of escape routes did not make the agreement valueless. The escape routes existed by way of exception. The essential structure remained in being, eroded, scarred, but still extant. In international economic negotiations one takes what one can get. The hope is that it will be productive rather than counter-productive; that even if an agreement is not exactly a rock on which one can safely build a house, yet it will provide foundations of a certain solidity, and that, in due course, it will act as a base for future construction. There is the road of progress through compromises such as this, or there is despair. Those who mould the phrases, and draft the language, to accommodate the widely divergent intentions and ambitions of contracting powers, are serving a positive purpose after all.

THE SOVEREIGN RIGHT NOT TO PAY DEBTS

There is a sovereign right to default on debt repayment. The whole concept of 'sovereign debt' acknowledges not just the possibility of default, that possibility exists with any lending, but the special status of a loan to a 'sovereign', that is that his obligations cannot be enforced against him in any court. A sovereign cannot be forced into liquidation. His goods may be seized in a foreign country but their value may not come near the indebtedness and such action may provoke the sovereign debtor into outright repudiation of his debt, a consequence that may be considered worse than 'non-performance'.

Moreover the concept of sovereign debt implicitly recognises that for a sovereign, considerations other than financial respectability may determine policy. That policy may lead to a demand for rescheduling if the burden of servicing debt becomes politically or economically insupportable. Such countries are not as disadvantaged in a negotiation for rescheduling of debt and interest as might be thought. To begin with, they will demand the respect and consideration which any large debtor expects from his bank or banks, particularly from banks fearful of their credit rating. If, despite that expectation, the repayment terms are made intolerable they may well feel that default is the better option. They would prefer not to default because default may deprive them for some future period of access to international capital markets. Just as there is a sovereign right to default, there is a right of retaliation and reprisal. But they will do it if they feel forced to do it. Defaulting countries are not without negotiating weapons.

Developing countries have one way of avoiding default which, these days, would be conceded only with extreme reluctance to a developed country. They are not expected to deny themselves the benefits of general import controls and of export subsidies. Benefits they would be seen to be, despite all the arguments of the economic liberals. They might even have encouragement from the World Bank. Commercial banks, too, are likely to prefer direct action on the current account to the extreme action of default. Solvency is more important than free trade.

THE HOSTAGE RELATIONSHIP

Interdependence creates hostages to fortune. Interdependence can create a high degree of dependence. That dependence can become a factor in negotiations of many kinds, not limited to trade matters. It was not to secure any advantage in trade relations that France threatened to use the trade weapon against New Zealand in the Greenpeace *Rainbow Warrior* affair. Dependence can only be comfortably accepted if there is a reasonable degree of confidence that rules will not be lightly or precipitately broken, and that the threat of breach of rules is not used as a negotiating weapon. The lack of any such confidence is an impediment to the development of greater interdependence. But there would be no justification for any great confidence. The record of adherence to trade rules over the last ten years is not of a kind to make nations confident that the hostage relationship will never be used against them. This uncertainty must act as a restraint on the growth of world trade. But it is a factor which is not negotiable.

Suppliers become hostages to the willingness of major importing countries to continue reasonable adherence to the rules. As a major importing country, the USA's considerable discretion in formulating trade policy is a potential threat to its suppliers. If policy changes adversely, they have little recourse, the power equation being so strongly weighted against them. The USA and the EEC are very powerful in international trade, and much therefore turns on their conduct. The USA has frequently exploited trade relationships, and the dependence created by them, for purposes connected with its foreign policy. Such use is inconsistent with the principles of economic interdependence. It is not here a question whether the USA has been justified in doing so. Defence is more important than economic interdependence. But there can be no question that such actions have been, and continue to be, an impediment to the growth of economic interdependence.

These obstacles to the development of economic interdependence can take other, even less acceptable, forms. Interdependence gives hostages to countries whose courts of law and political institutions may prove unreliable as a protection to foreign interests. Both people and investments may be endangered in the course of quarrels with which the investing companies have nothing to do. Lack of respect for law and the subordination of courts to political pressures give governments a freedom of action which they can use against those of whom they find it convenient to disapprove. The UK is an ex-imperial power with quite a high profile in international affairs. Consequently the UK is particularly exposed in the hostage relationship. It is also particularly defenceless as its industrial weakness means that it has little to sell which its customers could not get from other sources. The USA is also somewhat exposed, and has suffered some humiliations, but at least it has the bargaining power which arises from great military strength, and from the fact that it markets a range of products which are not so easily obtainable elsewhere. The strength of an economy could be defined in terms of its ability to withstand boycotts. The USA has legislated to prevent its companies submitting to the Arab boycott. The UK deplores the Arab boycott in its public statements but has in practice submitted to it by leaving the decision whether or not to respect it to the commercial judgement of its companies.

The competitive instinct of developed countries, and of their entrepreneurs, may deny much comfort to those whose companies, citizens or investments become hostage to some extraneous political or economic pressure. Too often the instinct among developed countries is not to collaborate to defend their common interests but to seek a competitive advantage by exploiting each others' difficulties. Japan has shown itself especially adept at exploiting such advantages. Nevertheless the fear of giving hostages in the form of people or investments to unstable and vindictive governments has been a deterrent to the development of economic relationships. It is not surprising that this fear should have exerted a cautionary influence on trade and investment.

LIMITED COMMITMENT AND THE EUROPEAN COMMUNITY

The European Community is an alliance for economic security though of a particularly intimate kind given the constitutional implications of the Treaty of Rome. Sovereign powers, members of the Community, have engaged that for certain purposes the laws of an international entity, the European Community, will run. Britain has accepted, through the European Communites Act, 1972, that the laws of the European Community should be part of the laws of Britain. The object of creating the Community has been in part political, in part economic, to create some counterbalance, especially in the field of international economic relations, to the still dominating power of the USA and the rising economic power of Japan. But if it was found that the prosecution of these objectives had come into conflict with different and more important objectives, the whole alliance could be unwound. Thus even within the Community the national will is not submerged. Unwise as it might be, any member could secede. Or, more probably, it could accept banishment to an outer tier of European collaboration in which much that the other members had agreed to be binding on them, would not be binding on it.

The formation of the European Community is an example of the way limited commitment can ease the road towards agreement. Members did not have to open their markets all at once. It was to be a gradual process, protected in some areas by national vetoes and in others by the need for majority votes. They did not have to sacrifice their final sovereignty. They could feel the way forward, testing it at each stage against the willingness of their peoples to take the next step. In recent years progress towards the Common Market has been delayed by the onset of severe economic problems and high unemployment. European Governments have felt more protective and less ready to open their markets. Perhaps, in the end, all barriers will be removed. But the fact that there have been barriers, and that it has been possible to retain barriers, has made possible steps towards unity which, in other circumstances, could not have been taken.

THE LUXEMBOURG COMPROMISE

States may enter into commitments for joint action with other states in the hope that this will conduce to greater economic security. But in doing so they will limit the binding power of the commitments into which they do enter. If a commitment goes badly wrong it will have to be changed. An interesting case study of the conditional nature of international agreements is provided by the invention of the so-called Luxembourg Compromise.

The Treaty of Rome requires that certain matters foreseen as being by their nature very important should be resolved in the Council of Ministers by unanimity. On the other hand the Treaty provides that many other matters can be resolved by a qualified majority within the Council of Ministers. It soon became clear that even certain of the matters referred by the Treaty to a qualified majority could involve questions of major national interest for the member countries. It became the practice, therefore, to require unanimity within the Council except on budgetary matters. This practice was eventually confirmed by the so-called 'Luxembourg Compromise'. The France of General de Gaulle insisted on a right of veto. For some months it left vacant its seat within the Council of Ministers. Not until that right was *de facto* granted by the Luxembourg Compromise did the General agree to France reoccupying its seat.

The Luxembourg Compromise accepted the reality that voting could not, without causing a grave crisis in inter-Community relations, be used to override individual states on matters which they genuinely regarded as involving very important interests. The agreement at the Luxembourg summit in December 1985 on amendments to the Treaty of Rome has left member governments with a right of veto hardly at all diminished by comparison with the Luxembourg compromise. Thus even within the European Community national interest remains the essential determinant in the operation of a constitution created by a Treaty that binds all members. The right to defend important national interests by exercising a veto was seen as the pre-condition for the survival of the Community. Despite the terms of the Treaty, political realities have forced consent to procedures which must be especially objectionable to the more federalistically minded countries, and which seriously impede the decision-making mechanisms of the Community.

CONCLUSION

Limited commitment to international agreements has not been an entirely negative factor either in the creation or in the operation of an interdependent economic system. Only the imperfection of limited commitment has secured from nations the degree of commitment on which an interdependent world depends. If the norms laid down for national behaviour in international economic relations are too far from realism, it becomes easier to flout them. It is better if the norms run close to real expectations of decent international behaviour. The threat of reprisal and retaliation will be one consideration tending towards a disciplined acceptance of the burdens of interdependence, particularly among developed countries. But in the end developed countries as well as developing countries will have to be persuaded of the continuing benefits if they are to remain participants in interdependence and loyal adherents of the treaties and agreements they have signed. Experience shows that this is a task not without difficulty.

Shonfield concluded from his examination of international economic relations that 'The chief lesson that emerges is that international economic institutions in their present form can do no more than reinforce the processes of economic diplomacy' (Shonfield, 1976, p. 85). Given the erosion, during the recession of the 1970s and subsequently, of the rule of such laws of international economic behaviour as were previously respected, greater and greater recourse has necessarily been had to economic diplomacy. This diplomacy has taken place at all levels up to the highest. Economic summits have become a regular feature of international economic relations. They have not served to cure the world of its sickness. They *have* helped to prevent the worst outbreaks of economic nationalism and to preserve civilised behaviour even in the course of conflict. It would be wrong to regard them as having failed. They have helped to maintain economic peace, even if an uneasy peace. But their frequency has emphasised the difficulties which confront heads of government in fulfilling that vital responsibility.

7 Economic Security and the Free Movement of Capital

The liberal programme requires for its accomplishment the free movement of all the factors of production, including labour and capital. The free movement of labour is considered by governments incompatible with social stability, and restrictions are imposed on immigration by almost all countries. Most governments are thereby placed at odds with the liberal ideal. The free movement of capital may be subjected to restrictions, on emigration as well as on immigration. The objective of such restrictions is greater economic security. In 1979, UK exchange controls were abolished. They were abolished at a time when a current account surplus derived largely from the fortunate discovery of North Sea oil seemed to make it safe to do so. But the move had merit in that it was pointless to operate devices designed to keep sterling high when the probable consequence of North Sea oil was that it would move too high.

Since then destabilising flows of currency, triggered electronically, already large, have become even larger. As far back as 1978, Nobel Laureate Professor James Tobin of Yale University was suggesting throwing some sand in the wheels of what he even then regarded as excessively efficient money markets. He wanted a worldwide uniform tax on all spot currency conversions. The free movement of capital, previously questioned for its effect on jobs and domestic investment, is now questioned for its effect in destabilising the world economy. Some economists are trying to find ways of closing the stable door even though the horse has fled. A large American deficit is being financed at high rates of interest by flows of foreign currency, with the inevitable effect on rates of interest in the rest of the world and on the cost to the rest of the world of financing any indebtedness. Only the USA could create by its budget deficit this new justification for restriction, that the rest of the world might question why a priority use of its capital should be funding the American budget deficit. Yet governments of developed and developing countries alike may well wonder whether there is anything at all they can do.

THE IMPORT OF CAPITAL

Direct inward investment brings jobs, new technologies, new exporting industries, new management techniques. Yet there are many cases in which governments have thought it right to impose restrictions. Developing countries particularly have been worried about its political implications for their independence of action and about their ability to negotiate on equal terms with powerful companies with longstanding international experience. Foreign investment in indigenous raw materials has been frequently frowned upon. Even developed countries have been infected by this nationalistic virus. The UK found it sensible to involve foreign, mainly American, oil companies in the exploitation of North Sea oil and gas. Their involvement speeded the development of a resource seen to be essential to the prosperity of the UK. But the UK has wished to retain firm control over the activities of the oil companies. It has operated a licensing system for the allocation of territory for exploration, thus making it possible to give preference to British companies. It has encouraged the use of British equipment, required that the hydrocarbons be landed in the UK, and insisted, when the crisis of 1973–4 made apparent the insecurity of OPEC oil supplies, that 'participation' by a national oil company be retrospectively conceded. Beyond this, the government of the UK, while privatising, or partially privatising, its interests in state oil companies, has given those companies special protection against foreign takeover.

The UK has not limited its controls on the immigration of capital to cases where raw materials are involved. It has laid a comforting hand on certain companies which it regards as important from either a technological or a defence point of view, and has said, in effect, that these the foreigners shall not have. The Americans also have shown themselves sensitive to foreign incursions which threaten national ownership of key companies. It is unlikely that any foreign company would have the resources to bid for IBM. But if it did, and it tried, it would be likely to be ordered off the sidewalk by the federal government. The government of Jacques Chirac in France was concerned, in its privatisation programme, to ensure that the foreign takeover of key French enterprises was not thereby made easy, and yet M. Chirac was not able to persuade

President Mitterrand that the safeguards he proposed were sufficient.

There has been particular anxiety in Canada where domination of all aspects of economic life by American investment has been especially marked. This domination has been the subject of many political speeches and led under Prime Minister Trudeau to the elaboration of a highly protectionist energy policy. Such attitudes were, however, condemned in advance by the late Professor H. G. Johnson, himself a Canadian. A note in my possession, probably dating from 1963, reports that Professor Harry Johnson of the University of Chicago had spoken at Toronto on the 'spurious problem' of increasing American domination of the Canadian economy: 'a piece of hypocrisy perpetrated by commercial greed aiming to exploit the Canadian inferiority complex under the guise of patriotism.'

THE STRATEGY AND TACTICS OF INTERNATIONAL TRADE AND INVESTMENT: THE EXPERIENCE OF JAPAN

Economic liberalism is often regarded as the norm, and departures from it as regrettable exceptions made necessary by the sinfulness of mankind and of nations. In that context, Japan's attitudes to the free movement of capital stand out by reason of their singularity. The Japanese have in recent years been ready to exploit opportunities for direct overseas investment. They have seen it as a way of jumping obstacles to their exports, as creating new opportunities for their industries, and as helping to defend established positions of strength. Due to a combination of cultural, legal, and other obstacles, direct investment into Japan has not flourished anything like comparably. Much of what there has been by way of inward investment has been in partnership with indigenous Japanese firms. Japan's approach to international economic relations has been strategic in the sense that it has combined a high degree of planning of its export effort, whether that planning has been at government or at industry level, with a high degree of concern for the imperatives of national economic security. Japan has seen advantages in the export of capital. However, Japan has regarded inward investment as being inconsistent with its political and economic aims. Under pressure it has liberalised its regulations governing direct inward investment. But inward investment into Japan remains small.

Where international trade is regarded not as an exchange of benefits but as a form of warfare, a government is likely to be chary of permitting unrestrained inward investment. Inward investment gives the enemy status behind the barricades. If that is the philosophy, anything that is done by way of liberalisation will be done only as a result of pressure that it is thought wiser not to resist. With the emergence of Japan as a major competitor in the computer market, the question arises to what extent their ability to compete with American domination in this field is due to the impenetrability of Japan's home market both for trade and for investment. When the strategists and tacticians of industrial life argue for the opening of Japan's market they are arguing not just for an opportunity to sell and to invest but for an opportunity to do to them what they do to us. If they have the ability to disrupt our market, we want to be able to disrupt theirs.

THE FRENCH SEE IT THE JAPANESE WAY

In a memorandum submitted to the Athens meeting of the European Council in September 1983, the French argued from the Japanese analogy. In the advanced technologies, the Americans and the Japanese had moved far ahead of Europe. If Europe was to catch up, the internal barriers to trade within Europe must be removed so as to create a sufficiently large market within which European technological companies could flourish. But to make this possible more would be needed than a large internal market. It would also be necessary to give Europe a measure of protection both against imports and against inward investment. On inward investment there would have to be criteria defining when direct investment into the Community by third countries was acceptable. The view of the French administration was that member states should not invite investment which would increase production capacity in industries where there was already excess capacity. The protection against imports would be temporary but would safeguard the infant technological industries until they were sturdy adults. The protection against inward investment would ensure that the large European market remained available to European companies and that they would not be compelled to share it with locally based but foreign-owned multinationals. The French supported their proposition with the argument that it would actually be damaging to free trade and would be politically and economically undesirable if, simply by being first in the market, a company could then exercise an effective monopoly, swamping potential competition.

Many aspects of the French memorandum proved unacceptable to other member states. The British and Germans accepted that European collaboration was desirable where companies saw it as being in their interests and the competitive situation in national markets was not imperilled. Nevertheless, they believed that cooperation with American and Japanese companies could sometimes or even often be a more prospective route to technological development than confrontation with them. Britain and Germany, perhaps, thought that they had a better chance of attracting inward American and Japanese investment than did France. Britain and Germany might also have had some reason for scepticism as to whether the establishment of barriers against inward investment, and temporary protection against some imports, would in fact assist the process of removing internal barriers within Europe.

They claimed to be uneasy about the idea of temporary protection. As likely as not, protection intended to be temporary would be very difficult to phase out. Infant industries, backed by massive political commitment, tend to remain infant well into old age, and their European customers would be compelled for that long period to pay higher than international prices for essential components and equipment. Temporary protection for one set of industries would certainly lead to pressure for temporary protection for another set of industries. And in this case in addition there was the eternal question, what would the USA say about so confrontational a policy operated by its European NATO allies? It should not be thought that these arguments against temporary protection were insincere merely because both Britain and Germany already operate supposedly temporary protection for long lists of other industries. Ministers of all governments are profoundly sorry when they depart from the high principles that they so frequently profess. They are often so profoundly sorry that the thought escapes them that what they are doing may be right even if it departs from the professed principles.

There were, thus, many reasons why a European attempt to ape the Japanese was unlikely to be practical. Europe cannot behave like the Japanese because it starts from a different historical and social tradition and stands in a different relationship to the USA. The European Community consists of different countries, each with their own balance of payments, each with their own embarrassingly high levels of unemployment, and each with their own political problems. It consists of countries which are competing and not just cooperating. Among other things, they are competing for inward investment. This does not mean that the French were wrong. It is not untypical with the French, that their ideas should be superficially persuasive but politically impractical (Pearce *et al.*, 1985, Chapter 6).

THE FREE MOVEMENT OF CAPITAL DEGENERATES INTO PROTECTIONISM

The rejection of these French proposals does not imply that the British and Germans are unreservedly devoted to liberal policies. Rather does it indicate that in pursuit of their own policies and objectives, they do not want their hands unnecessarily tied. In the interest of those policies and objectives, they are quite prepared to employ protectionist methods. Like so many liberal freedoms, the free movement of capital degenerates into protectionism. Mobile capital is a valuable resource. Some forms of it, for example those intimately associated with American advanced technology, are viewed by many countries as an outstandingly valuable resource. The result is intense competition among countries for mobile capital. To conduct the battle for mobile capital successfully requires a number of devices, particularly protectionist devices. Even within the European Community it is not enough for any member country that mobile investment is attracted to Europe. The objective must be to attract it to a particular member country. The European Commission will attempt to prevent member countries outbidding one another. But this will only modify, it will not prevent, the offer of attractive protectionist morsels by way of bait. Thus there is a strong temptation to use national devices to win mobile investment, offering access to the European internal market as one of the attractions.

There is a dilemma here for governments. Are they, with the interests of their people at heart, and conscious of the claimed benefits of inward investment, to be blamed for competing with whatever weapons are available to them, to induce multinational corporations to locate their investments in their territories rather than in those of others? All this is part of the process whereby liberalism degenerates into protectionism. Everything becomes subject to a process of political negotiation in which the option of protection is one of a number of shots in the national locker.

HOW TO COMPETE FOR INWARD INVESTMENT

Developing countries often offer overt protection, protection at the frontier, as a way of achieving the important objective of attracting inward manufacturing investment. Foreign companies that accept these inducements then become a principal support for the highly protectionist regimes within which they operate. Developed countries find it difficult to offer protection at the frontier as an incentive. It would be too blatant a breach of their commitments to the GATT and to OECD. But they can offer subsidies, infrastructure improvements, or the support of government purchasing policies. The provision of such inducements is defended as necessary in a competitive market, any other behaviour being simply naïve. And the acceptance of such inducements by multinationals is defended by one of the arguments used to justify the export of capital, that it helps to defend markets otherwise under threat, in this case from the competitive investments of other multinationals.

Protectionist methods are not used only to attract mobile investment. They are used also to get the greatest national advantage out of it once it has arrived. The UK, relatively open though it has always been to inward investment, has been prepared under governments dedicated to respect for market forces, to press multinational companies to increase the UK content in their output. Such pressure has been brought not just on Japanese companies investing in Britain, but even-handedly on such an American company as General Motors in respect of its Vauxhall car subsidiary.

TWO WAYS IN WHICH AMERICAN ADVANCED TECHNOLOGY PROVOKES PROTECTIONISM

American multinationals are often the carriers of an advanced technological capacity that they owe to the American defence and space programmes. They are the means whereby, under their own strict control, this technology can be transferred to friendly foreign countries. Despite the strict control, American multinationals are therefore welcomed by countries that hope for a source of advanced technology products on their own soil. Not merely are they welcomed. Protectionist inducements are held out to attract them. Yet there is thereby created a form of industrial dependence which has great dangers. The USA has fertilised the world with its capital and its technology. But, at times, both have been switched off. It is like the stream of food aid that ruins domestic agriculture and then, with a bad harvest back home, suddenly dries up. Inward investment can become a drug of dependence. To start with it may fill a need. Later it may prevent indigenous growth. Moreover American investment overseas can become an instrument of American foreign policy. The US Administration, in an exercise of extraterritorial powers, may attempt to control the actions of American-owned subsidiaries in defiance of the law, policy, and sovereignty of those foreign countries in which they have invested. If governments are reluctant to become entirely dependent on American technology, it is not simply for illiberal reasons. Their reluctance to become dependent does not, of course, provide them with a reliable route to independence of American technology. But at least they will feel tempted to try what government subsidy can do to build a successful indigenous industry. Thus protectionism flourishes as a way of attracting American investment. It then flourishes as a way of competing with American technology.

THE NEED TO CONTROL INWARD INVESTMENT

Governments feel a need to control the actions of foreign companies active in their country. A large proportion of direct investment overseas is undertaken by those companies which have acquired the various descriptions, 'international', 'multinational', 'transnational'. Such descriptions could have been designed to obscure the fact that these companies have a national origin. One of the dilemmas for multinational companies when they invest abroad, as for the governments of their host countries, is precisely how they can be both foreign and national. Such companies feel themselves at risk if they are believed to be controlled from abroad, and yet have some problems in presenting themselves as genuinely naturalised when their ownership so clearly is foreign. The policies of the US Administration not infrequently make it particularly difficult for American multinationals to establish a non-American identity.

Host countries have power that can be used to supervise multinationals. Developed countries such as Canada and Australia have imposed heavy conditions on inward investment. The conditions have been designed to strengthen national control and national participation. It will often happen however, especially in less developed countries, and even in developed countries which wish to see advanced indigenous technological development, that, whatever conditions governments seek to impose, they will lack real alternatives if they really want the kind of investment under offer. In cases where domestic investment does not provide a credible alternative, their choice will be between having or not having a particular kind of investment in their country.

The result of this desire to regulate is that the decisions of multinational companies can become bound up in the politics of their host countries. They can be forced into making decisions that are more politically than industrially motivated. They thereby lose some of the benefit which they would otherwise try to gain by achieving the most advantageous international division of labour within their own companies. Having once invested on a substantial scale in a foreign country, their flexibility in respect of future investment decisions is reduced by their need to protect what they have already done against nationalistic political pressures.

CONCLUSION

To compete with the power of American advanced technology is a formidable task. Yet there is little point in crying out against the realities of the situation. Multinational competition may be hard for domestic industrial competitors. It is magnificent for consumers whether domestic or industrial. There is little evidence, other than from Japan, that protection against it would stimulate indigenous technological industries capable of equivalent performance in the advanced technologies. Ignorant of what they can really do for the best, most governments will incline to permit the continued inward investment while enforcing such conditions as they believe not to be counter-productive and giving such encouragement as they can to competitive domestic activity even though they are supposed not to discriminate. Fortunately not all technological development is in the so-called advanced technologies. There are vast areas of industrial activity where the negotiating position of governments will be much stronger.

From the liberal doctrine have been plucked elements, such as the free movement of capital, which sound fine and which can be turned to advantage by those with the power to do so. But these elements are purposively employed in a world which takes national advantage, not liberalism, as the criterion of conduct. The irony then is that in taking that criterion of conduct, nations face calculations of impossible complexity and dilemmas which they cannot really resolve.

The free movement of capital, and the operations of multinational companies, create dilemmas both for the companies themselves and for the governments of the home and the host countries. The dilemmas for governments include questions both of military and of economic security. Questions of power are involved as well as of welfare. In agreeing, as far as has been done, to the free movement of capital, some countries have simply given way to American pressure. It is always more comfortable to give way to American pressure than to resist it. Is that a good enough reason for conceding to pressure a decision which should be the result of calculation? But if the considerations are so complex that calculation may be defeated, from what firm ground can the pressure be opposed? Empirical studies, such as they are, have confirmed the widespread impression that the overall economic effect of inward investment has been beneficial. There are costs but they are usually of a kind impossible to measure and therefore impossible to set off against the almost equally incalculable benefits that are claimed. Such complex questions are in the end very likely indeed to be decided by pressure or inertia rather than by calculation. Most governments have been content to act as though this is just another of those questions where the best approach is not to think about it too much, to hope for the best, and to reserve the right to intervene when the balance of advantage in any particular major proposal for inward or outward investment seems substantially adverse. After all, in general, things seem to have gone quite well. The main problems have been in developing countries rather than developed, and that for political rather than economic reasons. It is probably too late to turn back now but it is never too late to learn how to get the best out of an uncertain situation. The UK needs inward investment. But it also needs its own strategic arm in the form of strong British multinationals.

8 Economic Security and the War of Two Worlds

Harmony is not the most obvious characteristic of relations between the developed and developing worlds. The common interests of which so much is spoken and so little done do not appear to lead to significant levels of cooperation. The developing world is anxious to secure a share in power which the developed world is as anxious to deny. As the developed world has most of the cards, there is little prospect of the developing world going away satisfied from any negotiation. Fortunately for the developing world it has on its side an intense sense of guilt felt in many influential quarters in the North. Without that, they would leave the negotiating table with even emptier hands. They might do better if their proposals were better thought out. The following chapter on the Common Fund illustrates three facts about North–South relations. The first is that a great deal of time is wasted on inadequately considered proposals.

The second is that so sensitive is the conscience of the North that a hearing can be found there even for inadequately considered, and indeed counter-productive, proposals. The third is that the governments of the developing world do not act as though their exclusive interest was in the fate of their own, only too numerous, poor.

AT THE MERCY OF FORTUNE

Since the Second World War there has emerged a Third World consisting of poor nations, many of them previously colonies, with their own interests to defend, and their own demands on the world community. The dilemmas of developing countries, already great, are increased by the actions of the developed world. They have suffered from the protective and protectionist policies of developed countries. The protective policies have taken a deflationary form and are therefore criticised for having reduced the economic prospects of the Third World. The

115

protectionist policies have deprived the Third World of some part of their export opportunities. The Third World has found that it cannot rely on the developed world or on world market forces for a solution to its problems of economic growth. It is being forced to greater dependence on internal sources of growth. For that purpose they are prepared to use many methods including protectionist methods. But those sources are frequently incapable of providing a rate of growth sufficient to satisfy clamant social demands.

DEVELOPING COUNTRIES ALSO WANT ECONOMIC SECURITY

The world community has no government to levy taxes for the purpose of providing nations with the economic security they desire for their peoples. There is no system of redistributive taxation. There is however a common humanity and a degree of common interest. There is also a desire to exercise influence and a readiness to pay for influence if it can be bought. In particular there is a desire to prevent developing countries falling under Soviet influence. Therefore aid is provided both bilaterally and multilaterally. The multilateral fallback arrangements created at Bretton Woods after the war are a source of help by which the necessities of nations facing economic emergencies can be relieved. The benefits of an internationally-financed adjustment mechanism planned to ease the accommodation of developed countries to new realities, could hardly be denied to developing countries with even greater problems.

The responsibility of the IMF and World Bank includes redress for the needs of those countries in the developing world which require assistance. Their need might arise from force of circumstances or from a failure of will. Thus has been provided some shelter for those least successful in looking after themselves in this uncertain world in which the power of the market is so often greater than the power of governments.

In recent years many developing countries have been forced to turn rather frequently to the IMF or World Bank. Developing countries are insistent that the provision of 'social security' at the discretion of the major developed countries, and particularly of the USA, is not acceptable as a method or sufficient in amount to relieve their necessities. They believed that they have a claim as of right. They demand that the world, or specifically the developed world, provides them as of right with guarantees of economic security through the medium of what has been called the New International Economic Order. The contradiction in this position is only too obvious. If they have a right, they should be able to take it as a right. They should not need to come clamouring to the developed world to give them what they have by right.

Developed countries are not alone in their wish to preserve their own discretion in formulating policy. Developing countries as well as developed countries feel bound to retain as far as they can such powers as will enable them to oppose unacceptable foreign interventions in their economic and political life. They may not altogether succeed. The circumstances and the pressures may be too much for them, particularly in a conjuncture such as the economic crisis of the 1970s and 1980s. But they will certainly try and, within the limits imposed by their own social and political situations, they will accept the costs of so trying, costs that may be heavy. For a developing country the costs of economic security include all those costs which an economic liberal would foresee. Significant among these costs are the costs of industrial development protected against imports by high barriers. 'These included capital intensity, low value added at international prices. . ., loss of scale, lack of competition, and the growth of 'inessential' production behind barriers to trade' (Little, 1979, p. 266). These costs can be to the economy as a whole and to particular sections of the economy. The protection of industry imposes costs on the rural population. Important among the costs is the creation of strong vested interests with the political power to demand protection even where their production is totally uncompetitive with foreign supplies, and which can therefore delay changes of policy in a liberal direction even where these are at last seen to be desirable. These vested interests have had the strong weapon of nationalism in their portfolio of persuaders.

CONDITIONALITY

The IMF and the World Bank discharge their responsibilities in their different ways. But a key feature has been 'conditionality'. Assistance has been provided conditionality on certain economic policies being followed by recipient governments. The conditionality tends to grow harsher as the need for aid increases. The point of the conditionality is simply to ensure, by making the alternative rather more unpleasant, that even the most profligate nation is forced to resist domestic political pressures and take seriously its responsibilities as a debtor. One effect of conditionality may be, and sometimes has been, to drive developing countries in the direction of deeper protection.

Multilateral aid, conditionally supplied, has had a two-fold objective. The objective of helping those disinclined to take on the whole burden of helping themselves is longstanding. More recently there has been the further objective, to protect private banks from the consequences of overlending. The OPEC surpluses created in the 1970s were recycled through the developed world banking system. It was hoped, thereby, to ensure that lending would be governed by prudential private sector principles. The recycling appeared, and not only to the banks, as a commonsense reaction to the accumulation of vast resources in the hands of a few oil-rich Arab countries. This process was seen at the time to be risky. Large short-term deposits were being lent long. It is now seen in retrospect to have been very risky indeed.

The huge indebtedness of certain Latin American countries has caused anxiety not just to them but to the governments and banking systems of the USA, the UK, and other major industrialised countries. The fact that anxiety has been caused on both sides of the divide between North and South has given developing countries some negotiating strength. They could threaten to default though the cost to them too of such an action might prove to be unacceptably high. They could strive to create or increase a current account surplus by a combination of import controls and export subsidies. They might thus place themselves in a position at least to meet the interest due on their indebtedness, or at any rate to provide something like a credible basis for rescheduling. The developed countries frequently complain both about the export subsidies and the import controls. They question developing country criticism of protectionism when developing countries themselves become ever more protectionist.

In the end, the protectionism of heavily indebted developing countries is accepted, even if with reluctance, because the alternative of default on indebtedness might appear even worse. It then has to be recognised that free trade policies are not invariably the preferred option. However, the cost to a poor country of being compelled to run a current account surplus in order to repay debt, can be serious. It can itself lead to political and social disruption. The process of improving the current account requires, in most cases, a severe cutback in growth and even declines in output. It is very much a matter of political judgement in such circumstances as to how much additional austerity can be accepted by people whose life, by Northern standards, is already austere in the extreme.

Tough conditionality has aroused bitter opposition in developing countries. The terms have often been politically unacceptable, and the indebted have used their indebtedness as a negotiating ploy against the lenders. In the negotiations with Argentina, Brazil and Mexico, the negotiating power has not been all on one side. For political reasons the US administration has had to step in to ease the burden of IMF conditionality on these countries. The 1986 'growth-oriented' agreement between Mexico and the IMF is a tribute to the negotiating power an impoverished debtor can deploy.

BILATERAL AID

The separate governments of the developed world have also established bilateral aid programmes. Bilateral aid has been much criticised. It creates an opportunity for the exercise of influence and has certainly been used in this way at various times by all the major donors. The USA has statutory backing for the use of aid in this way. The Hickenlooper amendment to the Foreign Assistance Act provides that US aid should be withheld where there is nationalisation or expropriation without prompt, adequate and effective compensation. The influence which a powerful country like the USA may attempt to exercise through the instrument of aid is not limited to economic purposes or the defence of American property. Aid can be used for political purposes, such as support for a government sympathetic to American aims in the East–West conflict. On the other hand there is a reluctance among some donor countries to give any handle to those who see aid as the instrument of a new imperialism. They do not wish to be caught out in the overt use of aid for the exercise of influence. They fear even to use too heavy a hand in supervising the use of their aid. For this reason developing countries sometimes prefer bilateral aid to that coming from a multilateral institution with fewer inhibitions.

Thus the most powerful nations of the world have provided a safety net to their less fortunate, or less competent, contemporaries. They do so while believing that aid cannot be anything other than secondary in the struggle for development. And they do so on condition and, so far as possible, at their own discretion and through agencies which they have established and which they control. These agencies and the nations that support them refuse to try to re-model the world to provide costless economic security to all its constituent nations. They may transfer resources but they will not transfer power. They will have as little as they can to do with such propositions as that of a New International Economic Order. They may, however, from time to time, see political, and even economic, reasons for being somewhat more forthcoming than a determined reliance on the pure milk of conditionality would suggest as appropriate.

When South–North relations become particularly confrontational, the response of the North is likely to become particularly resistant. In taking such action as it does, the developed world is making a calculation which is not simply humanitarian. It is assessing the political risks of not assisting. In addition, it is taking account of the impracticability of indebted developing countries really repaying in full the real value of the money lent to them. Naturally these calculations tend to direct assistance primarily to those developing countries whose political position is most sensitive and whose indebtedness most clearly threatens the private banking system of the developed world. Other developing countries have much more difficulty in making their case for help in their difficulties. But the key consideration is always that the developed world, and particularly the USA, should retain its discretion, and that, in order to maintain the spirit of conditionality, obligations should in general not be cancelled but, where necessary, postponed.

THE PREBISCH ANALYSIS

Developing countries were encouraged in their demands on developed countries by the ideas of Raul Prebisch, first Secretary General of The United Nations Conference on Trade and Development (UNCTAD). Prebisch had the insight to observe that as little could be achieved by a demand for rights, it might be better to proceed by way of persuasion. Even in that he was too optimistic. Prebisch had argued in the 1950s and 1960s that economic forces worked to the secular disadvantage of the poorer countries (identified as exporters of primary commodities) and to the advantage of the more advanced industrial countries (identified as exporters of manufactures) in international trade and investment, at least in the absence of specific countervailing policies and measures. On this view there is a secular tendency for the terms of trade of the developing countries to deteriorate. These views were seen as contradicting the optimistic belief that market forces tend towards results beneficial to all. On the contrary, it was argued, the operation of market forces, left to themselves, has damaging effects on the poor. Therefore the developed countries must be persuaded to take steps to countervail these unfortunate results of unadjusted market forces.

As it is the argument of this book that market forces cannot be relied on to work in ways that are necessarily of benefit to each country taken individually, or even to the benefit of all developed countries taken individually, it is no hardship to look sympathetically at a proposition that market forces do not necessarily work to the benefit of developing countries. Sympathy with that proposition does not require acceptance of the specific Prebisch thesis. There is little gain to developing countries to replace one kind of over-optimism, the over-optimism of classical economic views, with another kind of over-optimism, the over-optimism of the Prebisch view of the world. This over-optimism might lead one to believe first that developed countries can be easily persuaded to take the recommended steps to adjust the operation of market forces for the benefit of the poor;

secondly, that if they could be so persuaded, they could do much about it; and, thirdly, that if they could do much about it, it would in fact achieve very much by way of relieving the poverty of developing countries.

The reason why it is thought that developed countries can be persuaded is that if the secular disadvantage of developing countries was eradicated by measures that added to their prosperity, that would redound also to the benefit of developed country exporters. Addressing the Federal German Society for Foreign Policy in Bonn in June 1965, Prebisch said: 'Allow us to export that much [US$20 billion] more and we will be a ready market for an additional $20bn worth of your industrial products per year' (quoted Sidney Dell, 1984). Certainly, but if there are initial costs to developed countries in creating this happy state, they will not necessarily be compensated by an equal exchange of goods however large. Moreover the distribution of the costs may not correspond to the distribution of the benefits. Some developed countries may experience their share of the burdens while others march happily off with more than their share of the benefits.

Combined with the apparent optimism of Prebisch's expectations of developed countries goes a deep pessimism. In his Report to the first UNCTAD Conference he wrote:

> It is no good to preach the need for them [the developing countries] to develop by their own efforts and at the same time to limit their possibilities of giving practical expression to that effort in the international field through the expansion of their exports. . . . Hence a broad policy of international cooperation in trade, in financial resources and in the propagation of technology is unavoidable. Without it the economic and social cost of development will be enormous (UNCTAD, 1964, vol. 2, p. 64).

There could be no practical justification for relying on the level of cooperation for which Prebisch was calling. The cooperation between the developed countries, limited though it was, that had been established after the war was already beginning to erode.

Cooperation has been shown to be a commodity in limited supply and commanding a higher price than developing countries feel able to pay. Whatever his view of the costs, developing countries were going to have to rely on their own efforts rather than on charitable thoughts or even on the kind of far-sighted self-interest that Prebisch himself liked to preach in his sermons to the developed world.

MUTUALITY OF INTEREST: WORDS AND DEEDS

In any case the trade of the poorer developing countries is not so great that developed countries will be induced by the thought of beneficial effects on their economies to take steps which they see as having immediate significant costs. The argument for mutuality of interest between the developed and the developing world has never been accepted in practice by developed countries as a group. Developed country statesmen have frequently expatiated on the theme of a commonality of interests. Only action has been lacking. In part it has been lacking because the mutuality of interests is seen to lie in an hypothetical future, whereas the conflicts of interests and the costs are felt in the here and now. Only when developed countries see worthwhile political benefits from adjusting their policies to the advantage of developing countries, are they likely to give the matter much serious consideration.

EQUITY

There is also the argument from 'equity'. If the working of market forces is unfair, then in equity it should be corrected. Actions in equity can be the result of humanitarian feelings among those who benefit from the world as it is. Such humanitarianism is expressed in many of the actions of the developed world in its relations with the developing world. But such actions can also be the result of pressure. Alfred Maizels, a senior official of UNCTAD, puts the point thus:

> The underlying assumption of this approach is that the division of the benefits of economic interchange between rich and poor countries must be viewed as a consequence of the relative bargaining strengths of the two groups, rather than be left to the 'normal working of market forces'. Indeed the 'normal working' of these market forces must be seen as a

reflection of the powerful entrenched institutional position and bargaining power of developed countries (Maizels, 1984, p. 20).

But if the current state of international economic relations is simply the result of the exercise of power, and there is a desire to change that state, the first question is to assess the various sources of pressure and to calculate their likely influence on the actions of the developed world. Unfortunately, on this hypothesis, so unfavourable is the present position of the developing world that one must assume that heretofore all the cards have been in the hands of the developed world. OPEC succeeded for a time in changing that situation in its own interests, and may do so again, but it has certainly not succeeded in changing it for the benefit of the developing world as a whole. The depressing conclusion from such an analysis is that there is very little that the developing world can do to force concessions out of the developed world other than to plead poverty and threaten to open relations with the Russians. Discussion proceeds among developing countries on how far they can increase their collective bargaining power, and their economic strength, perhaps by establishing stronger economic linkages between their economies. They have not yet changed the realities of power in an unequal and unfair world.

CONCLUSION ON PREBISCH

There is, moreover, a deeper naïvety in the Prebisch approach. It would be most unlikely that the developed world and the developing world were such homogeneous groupings that the separate countries experienced, in equal measure, advantage and disadvantage from the operation of unadjusted market forces. If one once embarks on the thesis that unadjusted market forces do not confer universal benefit, then the probability must be that they also differentiate in their effects among developed countries and among developing countries. The world will then be found to be a much more complex organism than Prebisch allows, and it will be far more difficult to secure that harmony of action in either grouping, and especially in the developed world, that an attempt to relieve developing country problems along these lines would require.

THE EXAMPLE OF OPEC

OPEC in 1973 showed developing countries how a consortium of oil-producing developing countries could force a transfer of resources from the developed world by substantially increasing the price of oil and by depriving the major oil companies of a large part of their role in controlling the production and marketing of the western world's oil supplies. OPEC achieved this, for them very profitable, result by exercising power, by being prepared to commit the sin of the restrictive practice, one of the various kinds of sin in the liberal calendar. Contrary to the liberal rule that sins against the invisible hand are self-defeating, this sin appeared to confer grace only on the sinner.

OPEC had recognised the opportunity created by the large new American dependence on imports of oil, and the lack of any supranational power to prevent their exploiting it. Their motives were not philanthropic and, in any case, not all of them could afford philanthropy even with a quadrupled oil price. They were simply using their collective market power against the interests of the rest of the world and, if they stuck together, there was little that the rest of the world could then do about it. As usual in matters of this kind, some attempt was made to put the best face on a transparent act of exploitation. There was some talk at the time of the benefits they were conferring on consumers by making them aware of the coming scarcity of oil. Some consumer countries might have been prepared to deny themselves this particular benefit, in consideration of the high price put upon it. But they found they had no option. They found the virtue of conservation forced all untimely upon them.

This example activated the ambitions of developing countries. The question was whether the non-oil producing developing countries could emulate OPEC's example. OPEC's achievement had imposed on them a high cost which in other circumstances might have been expected to lead to an outcry in the United Nations, in UNCTAD, and in all those other fora in which developing countries meet to discuss their ills and the unfairness of the world in which they have to live. It had had a damaging effect on their current accounts and on the already exceedingly low standard of life of their people. In addition the recession had a particularly severe effect on commodity prices, and there had been an increase in the real burden of interest and debt service payments. Developing countries could bear the effects of the oil price hike much less well than could the developed countries for whom a reduction in standard of life did not mean, at least for the great majority of the population, a reduction to starvation levels. But the developing countries were resigned not to complain too loudly in public. Some of them were receiving from OPEC some private help designed to assist them in meeting their greatly enhanced current account liabilities. And they wished to find ways of exploiting for their own benefit the OPEC lesson on how to force the developed countries to pay up. They wanted OPEC to be their ally. OPEC having turned the screw for themselves might now be persuaded to turn it a little harder for the benefit of the rest of the developing world. No longer would it be a matter of their receiving, and the developed world dispensing, charity. At last they would have their rights.

The question was could OPEC assist, would OPEC assist? Would OPEC do much more than utter those routine words of sympathy heard so often from other sources of equally bad conscience? In any case were the lessons of the oil price hike relevant to any other commodity? OPEC proved, in practice, to be more interested in its own opportunities than in carrying a torch, or in making large sacrifices, or in attempting to exercise great influence, on behalf of the rest of the developing world. How far the developing countries really enjoyed OPEC's continuing successes on the stage of international economic relations must remain uncertain. Few were prepared to say in public what they must have felt in private.

THE NEW INTERNATIONAL ECONOMIC ORDER

One factor was in their favour. This was the guilt-ridden conscience of the developed world. There are even people in the developed world who believe that they are rich only because the developing world is poor. In giving such aid as they do, the developed countries have learnt over many years not to expect gratitude. This is perhaps fortunate as none has been forthcoming. Developed countries have merely been told by how much they are still failing in their duty. Indeed experience shows that they can be insulted with impunity. On the other hand the OPEC countries, which were also providing aid, and which had not yet learned the sophisticated forebearance of the developed world, or the sense of guilt which accompanies it, could certainly not be talked out of their price increases and might feel that those who criticised them in public were not as deserving of help as were their friends. The developing countries' clamour was not, therefore, to the effect that OPEC should reduce the price of oil, at least to them, but that the developed world, itself facing the costs of the oil price hike, should in addition agree to the reorganisation of the world's economic system at considerable cost to itself. This seemed the more likely gambit to play. The idea of the New International Economic Order was placed firmly on the agenda.

Under the New International Economic Order the developing world is to achieve greater economic security. It is to be done with the cooperation, forced if necessary, of the developed world. For example, developing countries have demanded the liquidation or rescheduling of debt. They have proposed the creation of a Common Fund with which to finance commodity agreements covering a number of the major internationally-traded commodities. They see this as a way of guaranteeing an acceptable price level and perhaps also as a way of transferring income from developed countries to developing countries. The developing countries have demanded the transfer of technology in ways which, they believe, would make them more independent of investment by multinational corporations. In making this demand they are not disturbed by the fact that, normally, the technology that they wish to see transferred does not belong to the governments of the developed world but to private companies, mainly in fact multinational companies. That is a complication that developed country governments should sort out in the course of doing their duty by those they have so cruelly impoverished.

THE DEVELOPED WORLD SEES THINGS DIFFERENTLY

Not surprisingly, these proposals, at least in the way they were originally stated, are ruled out by the developed countries. They reject any idea of compulsory transfers of resources under some kind of international jurisdiction in which the developing world would have much to say. It is not unnatural that the governments of the developed world should see some of these issues less urgently than do their impoverished contemporaries of the developing world. In their relaxed way, different countries, different governments, and different experts, take different attitudes to the problems of Third World development. In particular different attitudes are taken to the role of public money as compared with private money; and to the role of private investment as compared with public investment. Much that has been done since the Second World War to assist development through the instrumentality of governments is considered to have failed. Rather than encourage development it has helped to entrench in power governments which have wasted both their own people's resources, and also much of the aid that has been provided. It has been dissipated in corruption, in lavish and low priority schemes, and in the construction of new capital cities.

But above all the developed world considers many of the developing world's proposals impracticable and in any case is concerned to ensure the preservation of its own independent discretion in the grant of aid. Behind the attitude of developed country governments is a fundamental principle which, in itself, brings them into conflict with developing countries. That which is done, whatever the objective, is to be done entirely at the discretion of the donor nation and to the extent that it itself decides. It is not done because an unjust economic system confers rights of redress on developing countries. Though this toughly realistic attitude may be softened by humanitarian pressures among their own people and, as a consequence, more may be done to accommodate some minor points in the demands of the New International Economic Order than would otherwise be the case, there are here principles which the developed world is not prepared to relinquish. There will be no international sovereigns, doling out internationally conscripted aid, under the control of the developing world, or in which the developing world has too much influence. Economic security for the developing world will not be as of right. Equally it will not be based on plans conceived by the developing world if these appear inappropriate to the governments of the developed world. This does not mean that all the demands of the developing world will be rejected out of hand. In a world divided between East and West as well as between North and South, the North is conscious of the value of having friends. These particular friends may not be too valuable, and they are, in any case, rather unreliable. But concessions to developing country demands, within limits imposed by cost and philosophy, have been made from time to time, but under developed country control.

THE ALTERNATIVE ROAD

Some developing countries have chosen a road other than that of the New International Economic Order. They have chosen to do for themselves what they cannot rely on the developed world to do for them. To rely on one's own efforts rather than on the benefactions of the developed world is a choice made by peoples rather than by governments. But governments by their actions have encouraged or stultified the efforts of their peoples. To put the point another way, where a people is prepared and able to devote great vigour and intelligence to economic purposes, some governments have been able and have been prepared, not entirely but to some considerable extent, to stand aside, and the experience of such abstention from government intervention has been favourable. Around the world there are a number of developing countries which, lacking the stimulus of exportable oil, have nevertheless made great progress in development, agricultural as well as industrial. There are examples such as Hong Kong, Taiwan, South Korea, Singapore and Brazil. There are other countries such as Malaysia which, relying on their own efforts to exploit great natural riches, have also made progress despite the attitudes of the developed world. Some of this group of developing countries have seen value in opening their economies to international competition.

Action to open the domestic market has involved a departure from another aspect of the philosophic inheritance from the Prebisch era. It had been believed that so large were the unemployed resources of developing countries that virtually any production, at virtually any cost, that employed those resources would add to the national income. The countries that have rejected that philosophy in favour of greater liberalism have done it to varying degrees and without irrevocable commitment. Nevertheless they have perceived that there can be high costs in the protection of domestic industry. Those governments which have been prepared to expose domestic industry to some level of foreign competition might well have done more, did they not fear for their balance of payments. But they have done something. Those developing countries that have felt able to open the door have probably benefited from the experience. However, they have steadfastly refused to abandon their care for the balance of payments. Seeing the balance of payments as central to their security, they have been far less ready to accept the consolations of liberal religion in that regard. They keep their powder dry.

Nor, indeed, should the value of liberalisation be exaggerated. Little notes that 'liberalisation and reduced protection cannot achieve for all nations the miracles it has produced for the four Far Eastern countries' (Little, 1979, p. 271). This is an appropriate warning but its language suggests a gross overestimation of the effects of policy in the case of the Far Eastern nations. *Post hoc, ergo propter hoc.* Before it can be claimed that it was liberalisation and reduced protection that produced the miracle, it is necessary to know a great deal more about the miracle, and whether it would have been unattainable without the stimulus of more liberal policies. If it was just liberal policies, there is no reason to suppose that equivalent miracles are not available to all countries that adopt those policies. If equivalent miracles are not available to all countries that adopt those policies, it must be assumed that liberalisation and reduced protection are only part of the story.

NOT WAR BUT AN UNEASY PEACE

Fear of competition, fear in the developed world of loss of control, fear of the developing world's ambition to gain more influence over the international economic environment, makes for uneasy relations between North and South. As a result, the two worlds are in a constant state of negotiation in which, sometimes, economic war seems the inevitable result of breakdown. In fact there is no war because the developing world lacks sufficient guns. Instead, the negotiations rumble on, for years, sometimes for decades. Today there is among developing countries increasing disinclination for the 'rhetoric of confrontation' that gave rise to the concept of the New International Economic Order, and increasing preparedness to accept an incremental approach to North–South relations. The fact that the South cannot impose its own solutions does not mean that it should not even accept the crumbs that fall from the rich man's table.

9 The Common Fund

THE CONCEPT

The UNCTAD IV Conference in Nairobi in May 1976 saw the official unveiling of a proposal known as the 'Integrated Programme for Commodities', the key element in which was the Common Fund. The history of the Common Fund proposal tells a great deal about the politics of the developed and of the developing world, and how relations between them are managed.

THE OIL PRICE HIKE RAISES QUESTIONS

The oil price hikes of 1973 had place a heavy burden on the balance of payments of non-oil producing developing countries. Some favoured developing countries did receive special assistance from OPEC members to meet their greatly enhanced bills for oil imports. But the general effect on developing countries was severely unfavourable. On the other hand the actions of OPEC provoked a question. If collective action could produce such dramatic benefits for OPEC members, could the producers of other commodities achieve similar results by comparable actions? This was a question anxiously studied in both the developed and the undeveloped worlds. It appeared, after study, that oil, as a commodity, was in certain respects unique. In no other comparable case did the commodities considered share the particular properties of oil which had made OPEC's action possible. No other such commodity was as essential to civilised life and as difficult to substitute at competitive prices.

The ambitions of most developing country commodity producers were on a much more modest scale than the price hike that OPEC had achieved. They were concerned at the instability of commodity prices. The fluctuations had been particularly wild over the previous two or three years. Many countries were very dependent for their export income on the export of one, or perhaps two, commodities. They had found their export earnings varying drastically between one year and another for reasons entirely outside their control. They were

132

concerned that dependence on commodity sales left them subject to too many influences they could not control. This uncertainty about the level of export income had made the planning of economic development very difficult.

Commodity agreements had come to be regarded as an important part of the answer to these problems. That view was held not just in developing countries but in some developed countries as well. Unfortunately, despite the encouragement given by previous UNCTADs, very few commodity agreements had in fact been negotiated. Clearly there was a missing ingredient the absence of which was inhibiting the negotiation of commodity agreements. The operation of commodity agreements frequently required the creation of buffer stocks. Buffer stocks were seen as the instrument for controlling prices in the market. The buffer stock controller would buy from the market when prices fell below the agreed brackets, and would sell into the market when they rose above them. UNCTAD came to the conclusion that that missing ingredient was money to finance buffer stocks. It was out of that conclusion that the idea of the Common Fund was born.

THE INTEGRATED PROGRAMME FOR COMMODITIES

UNCTAD proposed what it called an 'Integrated Programme for Commodities'. This Programme was to be a major factor in the New International Economic Order. The key element was a Common Fund to finance commodity agreements. These agreements would encompass consumer countries as well as producer countries. The Programme identified eighteen commodities, or groups of commodities, that needed the benefit of commodity agreements. These were: bananas, bauxite, cocoa, coffee, copper, cotton and cotton yarns, hard fibres and products, iron ore, jute and products, manganese, meat, phosphates, rubber, sugar, tea, tropical timber, tin, and vegetable oils, including olive oil and oil seeds. UNCTAD discovered that of 104 countries about which it had data, 56 depended on the eighteen commodities for at least 50 per cent of their earnings from merchandise exports (*UNCTAD Bulletin* no. 192, April 1983).

To cover the costs of these buffer stocks and of the other costs of running the commodity agreements, there was to be a Common Fund of US$6 billion. The Fund would be the sole, or at least the principal, source of finance for buffer stock operations. It was estimated that US$3 billion would be required at once, the second US$3 billion later. It was further estimated that of each US$3 billion tranche, US$1 billion could be contributed by the member countries of the Common Fund and that the remaining US$2 billion could be borrowed on the open market. The US$1 billion contribution by member countries towards the first tranche of the Common Fund would be divided between them in accordance with their share in international commodity trade. It was, however, hoped that some OPEC countries would help by contributing significantly more than their share towards the initial US$1 billion. Saudi Arabia, Iran and Indonesia were particularly mentioned in this context. How realistic this idea was, was never really tested. Although at the Conference there was talk of US$250 million, or even US$300 million, coming from OPEC, the only country actually to put a figure on its contribution was Indonesia which pledged US$25 million.

HAROLD WILSON AT KINGSTON, JAMAICA

A year before UNCTAD IV, there was a Commonwealth Conference at Kingston, Jamaica. Harold Wilson, Prime Minister of the United Kingdom, had proposed a 'comprehensive' programme for commodities. He suggested that fresh impetus be given to identifying the scope for commodity agreements and seeking to conclude them. He urged the need for progress over export earnings stabilisation, and the development of producer/consumer forums for individual commodities. He wanted the establishment of better exchanges of information on supply and demand. Wilson's 'comprehensive' programme was based on a commodity by commodity approach, that is it was to be based on a series of commodity agreements negotiated separately, and financed by arrangements between their own members. It was emphatically not the Common Fund. All the British government departments most closely involved, the Treasury, the Department of Trade, and the

Ministry of Overseas Development, had exercised their influence
to ensure that what Wilson offered was not the Common Fund.
The Common Fund was then in course of being elaborated
at UNCTAD and in discussion with developing countries.
Developing Commonwealth countries at Kingston realised that
what they were hearing from the British Prime Minister was
definitely not the Common Fund. Some of them attacked him
for it. But Wilson's proposal of a 'comprehensive' approach to
commodity problems raised unjustified expectations as to the
British response when the Integrated Programme was at last
brought officially before UNCTAD IV at Nairobi.

CONFERENCE ON INTERNATIONAL ECONOMIC COOPERATION (CIEC)

Although the Integrated Programme on Commodities emerged
as the major issue before the UNCTAD IV Conference, it was
by no means the only issue. Two other issues, in particular,
commanded attention and debate. One was developing country
indebtedness. The other was technology transfer. It was, in
part, because so little positive could be done on these issues,
that developed countries generally tried to take a sympathetic
attitude on the commodities issue. Moreover another conference
deeply concerned with the problems of developing countries
was in progress in Paris. Following the oil price hikes of 1973,
and on the initiative of the French, the CIEC Conference had
been called to discuss how the changed world created by
OPEC's action could be regulated. The CIEC Conference was
making little progress. Developing countries found little comfort
from its proceedings. There was resentment among those who
had been excluded in order to give preference to OPEC
representatives within the limited group that made up the
Conference. There was suspicion that CIEC would attempt to
'steal' the commodities issue from UNCTAD which had handled
it for the previous ten years. Developing countries insisted in
CIEC that progress should be made on commodities in Nairobi.
Here, too, was reason for developed countries to take as
favourable a view as they could of the Common Fund proposal.

UNCTAD AND OECD

It was, however, very difficult to take a favourable view of the Common Fund. The developed countries of OECD had as little confidence in UNCTAD itself as in the schemes which UNCTAD elaborated. UNCTAD was a forum created to enable developing countries to state their grievances and command an audience among developed countries. It was not regarded by developed countries generally as a reliable repository of executive powers. In so far as there was executive power in international economic relations, the developed countries wished to keep it in safe hands. An institution with a large sum of money at its disposal could influence commodity markets without benefit of any commodity agreements. It could create a buffer stock without reference to either producers or consumers. It could decide its own price brackets and operate in the market between them. It could attempt to raise prices by operating in the futures markets in the way Pancafé did in the coffee market in the early 1980s. It could make profits and it could make losses. It would be ironic if the power which developed countries had always wished to deny to UNCTAD was at last achieved with money substantially granted by, or borrowed from, the developed world. To the developed world the Common Fund proposal looked like a bid by UNCTAD for power over world trade in commodities.

THE COMMON FUND ANALYSED

The Ministry of Overseas Development

It was widely assumed that as the British Ministry of Overseas Development was devoted to the interests of developing countries it must take a favourable view of the Common Fund. This was not the case. The Ministry foresaw that if resources were transferred to the developing world through the instrumentality of the Common Fund, and of higher commodity prices, less resources would be transferred through aid. It was convinced that if the UK made a contribution to the Common Fund, the Treasury would insist, however unjustly, that it come from the Aid Programme. The Ministry had as its policy the concentration of aid on the poorest developing countries and peoples. The Common Fund would, on the contrary, transfer the additional resources simply on the basis of commodity sales. The transfer would take place to those countries, often the relatively richer among developing countries, and to those people often the richest in their own countries, which produced marketable commodities. Instead of aid being directed to projects which had been properly appraised and which could be controlled, transfers resulting from the Common Fund would, in practice, amount to unconditional balance of payments support capable of use even to buy arms. Not only would the transfer of resources be in all these respects irrational, that is based not on need but on participation in commodity trade, but the poorest countries which were not involved in the commodity trade would actually lose from the Common Fund proposal because they would have to pay more for whatever commodities they had to import. Judith Hart was among my severest critics over the Common Fund proposal, while she was on the backbenches. In fairness to her it has to be said that once she had returned to the government as Minister of Overseas Development I heard little more from her on the Common Fund.

The cost

The proposal had clearly not been worked through. International organisations play a very special role in developing country relationships. They provide a secretariat of a quality which most developing countries cannot provide for themselves. They provide a means of communication between developing countries which is of particular importance given that most developing countries do not maintain embassies in one another's capitals. UNCTAD was preeminent among international organisations in fulfilling this role. UNCTAD should have worked the proposal through before committing developing countries to support it. US$6 billion seemed a considerable under-estimate of the cost. The inclusion of copper alone made it improbable that US$6 billion, large though it was, would be enough. A copper buffer stock would be extremely expensive. Indeed no one had really calculated how large a copper buffer stock would have to be to influence the market and what it would cost.

Developed countries were being asked to commit themselves to the principle of the Common Fund without the comfort, if comfort it turned out to be, of any reliable costing.

The objective: stabilisation or enhancement

Was the object of the proposal to stablise commodity prices around some long-term trend, or to increase them above the long-term trend? There seemed to be no agreed position on this fundamental question among the developing countries in UNCTAD. Stabilisation was certainly not an exact concept. However, to take stabilisation as the objective at least established that the purpose of the exercise was not deliberately to raise the trend of commodity prices above what was necessary to guarantee adequate investment. The Malaysian government, with its considerable experience of commodity trade, and the relatively high standard of living of its people, was content to argue that the objective should be stabilisation. Some developing country governments, among which Jamaica was prominent, believed that the objective of the Common Fund should be to enhance commodity prices. They wished there to be an automatic system by which resources were transferred to them from the developed world, and they saw the Common Fund as one method. They did not want to be dependent for the transfer on the budgetary decisions of the North.

Earnings stabilisation or price stabilisation?

The stabilisation of commodity prices does not necessarily solve the problem of stabilising commodity earnings. The Integrated Programme for Commodities as originally presented had some elements concerned with the need to stabilise earnings but the emphasis was on price stabilisation or enhancement. However other schemes did exist and were in operation. First there was the Compensatory Finance Facility of the IMF. This was criticised on a number of grounds. It was not related to the instability problem in specific commodity sectors but was based on total shortfalls in earnings, including those from manufactures. Thus a fall in one sector could, so far as the Facility was concerned, be offset by a rise in another. The compensation was in nominal terms, not in terms of import purchasing power.

It was provided only when the shortfall resulted in balance of payments deficit and was limited by the country's quota in the IMF. Another compensatory scheme was the EEC's Stabex scheme operated for the benefit of the associated developing countries. This compensated shortfalls in export earnings suffered by the specific commodities covered by it. In addition to these two compensatory schemes, there was access to the IMF ordinary credit tranches which had been temporarily increased. All these schemes were criticised for being inadequate, though both the compensatory schemes were being improved. But the real criticism was that all of them were under the control of developed countries.

Distribution of benefits

That the Common Fund would probably represent a cost, not a benefit, to some of the poorest developing countries was recognised in the final Nairobi resolution. Out of this realisation came proposals to rectify the anomaly. Precisely for this reason, some developing countries were less than enthusiastic about the Common Fund idea, even though many were reluctant to say so openly. A Bangladeshi Minister told me that his government saw no benefit in the Common Fund. Nevertheless he wished me to know that they felt they had to maintain solidarity with the Group of 77. Support for the Common Fund had become a shibboleth to separate the righteous from the unrighteous whether in the developed or developing worlds.

The potential transfer of resources was not just to the richer developing countries and to the richer people within them. The world is not divided between developing countries producing commodities and developed countries producing manufactured goods. Developed countries as a group are large producers of commodities. To enhance the prices of commodities above the trend level would give an uncovenanted benefit to commodity producers in developed countries at the expense of other developed countries as well as of other developing countries. The principal producers of copper were the USA and the USSR with Canada following behind. Then came some developing countries such as Zambia but including Chile which was not the most popular of developing countries with the development lobby. The example of copper illustrated most persuasively the irrationality of a Common Fund which had as its aim the raising of prices above the long-term trend.

Indexation

Developing country commodity producers were concerned also that the relative importance of commodities in international trade was declining. UNCTAD had encouraged the belief that there had been during the post-war years an unfavourable secular trend in the prices of commodities relative to those of manufactured goods. It was taking an ever larger export of commodities to pay for the same imports of manufactured goods and machinery. Thus life was being made even more difficult for developing countries. Some countries, therefore, wanted an arrangement whereby the prices of their commodities would be indexed to the prices of manufactured goods. Developed countries were not prepared to accept the validity of the argument or the practicality of the solution.

The dearth of commodity agreements: was finance the problem?

The Common Fund proposal was based on the assumption that lack of money to finance buffer stocks accounted for the scarcity of commodity agreements. An assumption more in accord with experience was that where there was the will on all sides to negotiate a commodity agreement it would be done. If it were a commodity agreement within which buffer stocks were appropriate and feasible, the money to finance the buffer stock would always be forthcoming.

The real problems arose out of the competitive interests of the proposed members of any commodity agreement. There was, for example, the problem of achieving agreement among supplying countries on the allocation of market shares. This problem was especially great where there could be no buffer stock, and where consequently the only control on prices would be by allocating quotas among suppliers. Supplying countries did not wish eternally to be locked into their existing share of the market if it was small. On the other hand, if it was large, they did not want their large share to be sacrificed to any agreement with their competitors.

In principle commodity agreements required only the participation of producers. But consuming countries might also place a high value on price stability. They might therefore be prepared to cooperate in price stabilisation. The UK regularly participated in commodity agreements even though not itself a significant producer of any of the eighteen UNCTAD commodities. Consuming countries might help with the provision of finance. There was, therefore, a wish to involve consumers. At its lowest, their participation might help to ensure that they did not seek ways to undermine any agreements. The participation of consumer governments did, however, increase the difficulty of negotiating the upper and lower brackets within which the price was to be controlled. It was important to consumer governments that there should be an acceptable upper price limit and that they could have confidence that it would be respected.

These reasons seemed to developed country governments to constitute a much more plausible explanation for the slow progress of commodity agreements than the lack of a Common Fund to finance them. It could even be that the existence of a Common Fund would be an obstacle rather than an aid to the negotiation of commodity agreements. If it was thought that the Common Fund would be free to use its resources to influence commodity trade, that could become a disincentive rather than an incentive to the conclusion of an agreement. But if the policy was to begin with individually negotiated commodity agreements, there could then be no certainty that such agreements would see any value in participation in the Fund. For what advantage would they surrender their own sovereignty to an institution that they themselves did not control?

How would the Common Fund remunerate borrowings?

The idea that the Common Fund would derive two-thirds of its resources by borrowing might prove unrealistic. It would depend on its policies and on who controlled the proposed US$4 billion of borrowings. The successful operation of buffer stocks was not easy. They had to be of a size appropriate to the size of the market. Otherwise they could not sell enough or buy enough to influence prices. It was easy to misread market signals and intervene in the wrong direction, selling when one should buy and buying when one should sell. Mistakes could be expensive. Unless the Common Fund had a prospect of making a return, it would be impossible to borrow. If the return was to be derived from speculation in commodities then, despite the ability of the Fund to influence markets, the prospect of loss was very real, as indeed Pancafé found out to its cost. At the very least it was not clear that the Common Fund could borrow US$2 billion or US$4 billion, unless there were guarantees of repayment from creditworthy governments. Therefore the calculations that suggested that, because two-thirds of the money would be borrowed, the contributions from countries such as the UK would be small were themselves questionable. It would have been equally extraordinary to imagine that developed countries, having made direct contributions to the Common Fund and then guaranteed its borrowings, would not require a high degree of control over its operations.

Why did developing countries support the Common Fund?

It was arguments such as these that influenced government opinion in developed countries, and not in developed countries alone, against the Common Fund. In the light of these arguments the question arises why the Common Fund had so much support among developing countries. One explanation is not available. The Common Fund was not a good idea. The developing countries had committed themselves to it at their Manila Conference which preceded Nairobi. Their leading spokesman at Nairobi was President Marcos who had been the host of the Manila Conference and presented at Nairobi the so-called Manila Declaration. Undoubtedly many developing countries were facing a crisis. UNCTAD resented the fact that after years of talk about commodity agreements, almost nothing had been achieved. The commodity problem had been discussed at every previous UNCTAD Conference. Resolutions had been passed by consensus among the different groupings at UNCTAD Conferences. Actual achievement remained minimal. A grandiose idea for which widespread developing country and development lobby support could be organised had a great deal going for it. The alternatives that were being proposed by developed countries had no such attraction. They depended on the goodwill of developed countries and that was not assured. They did not meet the required criteria, automaticity in the transfer of resources and a share in power over the world's economic system.

NAIROBI AND AFTER

Divergences within OECD

At the Conference in Nairobi no major developed country supported the Common Fund. Despite the very general wish to appear sensitive to developing country needs, and their clear appreciation of the great difficulties being faced by developing countries after the oil price hike, it was opposed by the USA (under President Ford), Germany, Japan, and the UK. Canada hesitated. It greatly valued its reputation as an arbiter of world affairs and its co-chairmanship of CIEC. Once relieved of its CIEC responsibilities it settled sensibly into the same camp as the other major OECD countries. Australia, itself a major commodity producer, did not expect to lose from the establishment of a Common Fund. The more conscious it became of that fact, the more its line moved towards support of the Common Fund. Apart from any economic benefits it saw from the Common Fund, Prime Minister Malcolm Fraser wished to consolidate Australia's relationships with the developing countries of Asia.

Domestic pressure could lead to expressions of regard for the idea of a Common Fund, and of a willingness seriously to discuss it, which the governments concerned did not in their hearts feel. There was a great deal of such pressure in the UK. Right-minded people both in politics and in the Churches were virtually unanimous in support of the Common Fund. Many who had thought a little more about the actual proposal nevertheless took the view expressed by some MPs: don't bother me with practicalities, show political will. Even the four 'hardline' countries – the USA, UK, Germany, and Japan – were only relatively hardline. They knew the proposal was nonsense but when they realised the opprobrium that saying so attracted, more accommodating phraseology was sought.

The Netherlands takes the lead

The Netherlands emerged as the Common Fund's principal supporter in the developed world, though its view was shared by countries such as Norway, Sweden and Denmark. Norway and Sweden choose carefully the issues on which they give support to the developing world. They are very restrictive on textile imports but they had little to lose in supporting the Common Fund. The Netherlands has always shown itself sympathetic to the ambitions of developing countries. Because of the attitude of the Netherlands and to a lesser extent of Denmark, it proved impossible to coordinate an EEC view for presentation at Nairobi by the then President of the European Community, Luxembourg's Gaston Thorn. This, as it turned out, was very convenient for the French. Thorn himself, when he came to address the Conference, could only tell it that there was no European position but that we all came in cooperative mood, ready to discuss.

The Labour Cabinet

One month before the Nairobi Conference, I had become Secretary of State for Trade and UNCTAD matters fell within my departmental remit. Before the reshuffle that brought me to Trade, my predecessor as Secretary of State for Trade, Peter Shore, had received Gamani Corea, the Secretary-General of UNCTAD, who was making a tour of the capitals of member states. I learnt that Peter Shore had listened sympathetically. I could only assume, from what I heard directly from Peter Shore, that he personally was indeed sympathetic to the Common Fund. Apart from Peter Shore it had support of a sentimental kind from other members of the Cabinet. Thus for a British Minister to treat the proposal with the brusque contempt that was all it really deserved was very difficult. My problem was that having just taken over the responsibilities of the Department of Trade, I had no time really to consult or to assess the atmosphere internationally. Only two points were clear to me. The first was that the proposal itself was absurd. The second was that nevertheless it might, for reasons of international politics, be necessary to concede some ground to it. I did not see, however, why we should concede that ground before we had to, and, if we could avoid it, so much the better.

There was some discussion as to whether the UK should be represented at Nairobi by me as Secretary of State for Trade or by Anthony Crosland as Foreign Secretary. There was some fear that I might not take a sufficiently conciliatory line. The Foreign Office, it was thought, would better understand the wider implications of the debate on the Common Fund and would phrase the British position with diplomatic care. However, it was my departmental business and it was decided that I should go. Over the next two years I was to have frequent exposure to developing country pressure on commodity issues. First there was the Nairobi Conference; then the annual Lomé Conference at which, during the British Presidency of 1977, I acted as President of the European Community; finally there was the 1978 Commonwealth Conference on the Common Fund which took place in London and at which I took the chair.

In my speech at Nairobi, unlike my American and French colleagues, I had nothing new to propose as an alternative to the Common Fund. After all, only the year before, Harold Wilson had outlined his 'comprehensive' plan for commodities. His ideas had been largely incorporated in the response to the Common Fund from the OECD countries, gathered together for UNCTAD purposes as Group B. The UK could not have bright new proposals for dealing with the commodity problem every day of the week, or indeed every year.

Henry Kissinger

Others were able to be more imaginative. For the first time an American Secretary of State attended an UNCTAD Conference. Henry Kissinger proposed the creation of an International Resources Bank. The idea apparently was to use this new Bank to channel private funds into investment in commodities. Its funds might be used to finance buffer stocks. One of its purposes was to reduce the political risks associated with investment in developing countries. There was considerable anxiety that the low level of investment in commodities, particularly in developing countries, might lead to another inflationary price explosion when the world economy recovered.

The evening before the Conference opened, Dr Kissinger gave a dinner in Nairobi to representatives of leading OECD countries. The dinner was attended by Dr Friderichs, the German Minister of Economy, and by myself, among others. At the dinner Dr Kissinger outlined his new proposal. It showed every sign of having been thought up at the last moment as a way of fending off the Common Fund. But at any rate, he did have something new to say to divert some attention from the USA's entirely negative stance on the Common Fund. His proposal did not actually serve that purpose particularly well. From the beginning it was rubbished by critics in the developing countries and by the French who felt that they had something better to propose. The proposal raised the hackles of all those who feared foreign investment in national raw materials. The anti-Americanism prevalent among some developing countries played its part in their decision to refuse the proposal even the honour of further study. In the end, it was voted down by the Conference by a majority of two votes. Having served its purpose, or having not served its purpose, it disappeared from history. Eight months later the Ford Administration also disappeared from history. Meanwhile, as to the Common Fund itself, Dr Kissinger at dinner that evening in Nairobi firmly stated the American position. They would not move an inch towards it. What he had to say the following day at the opening of the Conference would be America's last word. It did not in fact prove to be America's last word for long.

The wily French

Jean-Pierre Fourcade, the French Minister of Finance, came to Nairobi with a rather brighter proposal than that of Dr Kissinger, at any rate from a political point of view. The French idea was to create not a Common Fund but a Central Fund. Instead of setting up a Common Fund in advance in order to encourage the negotiation of commodity agreements, the Central Fund would come into existence when there were already enough commodity agreements to support it. After perhaps four or five commodity agreements had actually been negotiated and set up, they would be able to subscribe any surplus funds to this Central Fund. There might, as a result, be certain economies in the demand for finance for commodity agreements. Finance from one commodity agreement could, through the Central Fund, sometimes help to stabilise the prices of entirely different commodities. All this seemed unlikely, but it was a sufficient peg on which to hang a cynical proposal poor on merit but politically ingenious.

This idea gained the French great credit. True, it was not the Common Fund. It ignored the principal purpose of the Common Fund which was to encourage the establishment of commodity agreements by providing a large fund with which to finance buffer stocks. But it was sufficiently like the Common Fund to encourage the belief that the French were rallying to the side of the developing countries. Naturally, the French had not given their partners in OECD any notice of their intentions. They were delighted with the reception they received at Nairobi. The French proposal was an early sign of weakening among the OECD countries. In the end, it became the basis for the developed countries' acceptance of a Fund, but one which was a 'pool', not a 'source'.

The Germans play it straight

Dr Hans Friderichs was the least inhibited of the OECD Ministers attending at Nairobi. He made no concessions to courtesy. The proposal was inconsistent with free market principles and unacceptable to the German government. He warned against the creation of 'instruments for the regimentation of the world economy' (*The Financial Times*, 8 May 1976). No one was to be more scathing about the Common Fund proposal in the days ahead than Chancellor Helmut Schmidt. At the summit conference at Puerto Rico on 27–28 June 1976, Schmidt, who introduced the discussion on the topic of commodities, circulated figures to show that commodity price stabilisation would benefit a limited number of mainly middle-income countries, as well as commodity-exporting developed countries including the USA and the Soviet Union. It would be of no help to the poorest. Schmidt was not indifferent to the problems of developing countries. He was concerned about the commodity earnings stabilisation problem. A great deal had been done to improve the compensatory finance facility of the IMF. These improvements had led to a greatly increased usage of that facility by developing countries. Schmidt felt that more yet could be done through a Stabex facility comparable to that operated by the European Community.

Britain's name is mud

The British development lobby was well-represented in Nairobi. They soon began to circulate the justifiable conclusion that Britain was one of the hardliners. Journalists began to report back that Britain, unlike France, had seriously misjudged the atmosphere at Nairobi. Whether we had or had not misjudged the atmosphere became more important than the merits of the Common Fund proposal. For my part, I was sure that it was absolutely right to be among the hardliners, as long as any could in fact be found. That proved not to be very long. The hardline attitude raised an uproar among developing country representatives at Nairobi. The uproar there was paralleled, in the case of the UK, by an uproar at home. The development lobby, the Council of Churches, Judith Hart and friends in the Parliamentary Labour Party, and even some Tory MPs who I would have expected to have had more sense, attacked me for the stance I had taken at Nairobi.

The Americans capitulate

None of this would have had any effect if the USA had not suddenly weakened. Presidential elections were approaching and perhaps the administration's stance was not one which they felt able to carry into an electoral battle. The Ford administration came to the view that the Nairobi Conference must not be allowed to break down in disorder. More important considerations were involved than the fate of the Common Fund. Henry Kissinger sent his Deputy, Charles (Chuck) Robinson, to Nairobi to rescue the Conference. Frank Judd of the British Overseas Development Ministry and Egon Bahr, the German Minister of Economic Cooperation, went out as well. The European Commission pressed for a commitment by the European Community to begin negotiations on a Common Fund within six months with the objective of setting it up within two years.

The Conference is saved

The Conference was saved. It was settled that within an agreed timetable there would be negotiations about the Common Fund.

There would be preparatory discussions with a view to a negotiating conference to be called by March 1977 which would establish the Common Fund. Other preparatory talks on individual commodity agreements would take place between September 1976 and February 1978. The resolution even suggested the need for indexation by stating that the prices of manufactured goods would be 'taken into account' in fixing commodity prices. The developing countries took much credit from the fact that they had worked for consensus. But they knew perfectly well that confrontation would achieve nothing and that, in the end, they were dependent on the willingness of the developed world to cooperate. Explanatory statements were made on behalf of the USA, UK and Germany. These emphasised that we had undertaken only to study aspects of an integrated commodity programme, including a Common Fund to finance buffer stocks and other operations. We would decide later whether to participate in the setting up of a Common Fund itself.

Thus were officials of government launched by their political masters on months, and as it turned out, years, of negotiation the main point of which was not the welfare of the poor of the world but the preservation of good relations with their rulers, and, through their rulers, with development lobbies at home.

A period of uncertainty

Despite the existence of a timetable, officials of developed countries remained uncertain how far their political masters were really committed to the Common Fund. Many messages were coming from developing countries, for example in Latin America, indicating that enthusiasm for the proposal was a great deal less widespread than a visit to Nairobi in May 1976 might have suggested. Even at Nairobi, Colombia, while supporting the Common Fund resolution, had opposed any stockpiling of coffee on the ground that it could stimulate over-production. The more the proposal was examined, the less attractive it appeared even to developing countries. Perhaps, with time, it would go away. We had lived through UNCTAD IV. UNCTAD V was another four years off. If in the meantime we could show progress in negotiating commodity agreements, perhaps the Common Fund idea would be forgotten. We could work hard on the commodity agreement front and go slow on the Common Fund, despite the timetable. It was not a perfect strategy. Commodity agreements had always proved very difficult to negotiate. We could make no promises of success.

As a matter of prudence it seemed advisable to work out, as a contingency plan, the structure of an acceptable Common Fund. Such a Common Fund might prove a political necessity even if an economic absurdity. The question was what could be done to make the Common Fund proposal tolerable to the developed world if political considerations pushed us along that road. Three points stood out. First, the Common Fund should be based on individually-negotiated commodity agreements whose membership of the Fund should be voluntary. Secondly, the Fund should be controlled by the commodity agreements which became members of it. Thirdly, it should start at a level of funding well below the US$6 billion proposed by UNCTAD. Such changes would not make us enthusiastic but at any rate we could then live with it. On the side of the developing countries, too, further thought was being given to the Common Fund. African countries, particularly, had noticed how little benefit they would get from the proposal as it stood. Such countries were pressing for a 'second window', another Fund whose purpose would be linked to the production and marketing of commodities rather than to the trade in them.

Attitudes change

Little was achieved in the Common Fund negotiations during the remainder of 1976. Then, at the beginning of 1977, came a decisive political change. In January 1977, Jimmy Carter was inaugurated President of the USA. Almost at once Washington became a source of pressure for progress on the Common Fund. News of the change in attitude in Washington soon reached Europe. The European Council, meeting in Rome, did not waste much time in following the' American lead. It decided to support the negotiation of a common fund. Not *the* Common Fund, *a* common fund. The subtle distinction between *the* and *a* was, no doubt, intended to be a protection against the Common Fund proposal as it stood. But a further stage in OECD capitulation to the Common Fund had now been passed.

I was in Washington late in April 1977 on the way back to

London from the Lomé Conference at which I had acted as President of the European Community. At that Conference, in Fiji, there was discussion of extending the EEC's Stabex scheme to further products but the Common Fund was not on the agenda. Nevertheless the Conference gave me an opportunity of discussing the Common Fund proposal in the 'corridors' with some of its strongest advocates. I explained our objections but said we were prepared to make progress if some moderation was shown on the other side. While in Washington I received direct confirmation of the shift of opinion in the American Administration. I visited the members of the new Cabinet concerned with economic policy. At the State Department I saw Richard Cooper, the distinguished economist who had become Under-Secretary of State for Economic Affairs. He told me that the OECD countries must make progress on the Common Fund. I asked him whether he said that for political or for economic reasons. Was it a matter of better relations with the developing world or was it because the Common Fund was an idea that, as an economist, he could support? He assured me that he supported progress on both counts. It was necessary for better relations and the Common Fund could, he thought, actually achieve the benefits expected from it provided the object was simply to stabilise commodity prices. I told him that, for political reasons, the UK government was ready to make progress with a modified Common Fund. The London Summit of 6–8 May 1977 committed itself to the idea of a Common Fund. In the same month CIEC agreed 'in principle' to some form of Common Fund. What form was to be decided at the November 1977 UNCTAD Common Fund Conference. Thus all the original 'hardliners', Germany, Japan, the UK and the USA, were now on board. Politics had taken over, helped a little by the economic naïvety of the new Carter Administration.

Negotiations drag on, and on, and on

Negotiations continued throughout 1977. The parties remained far apart and progress was slow. In November 1977 there was a further negotiating conference in Geneva. That conference also collapsed in disarray even though the industrialised countries were now looking for agreement on some kind of Common

Fund. The developing countries still insisted on the key interventionist role of the Common Fund, while the developed countries still placed the emphasis on the individual commodity agreements. The developed countries continued to have doubts about the 'second window' which had appeared as a way of reconciling divergent interests among developing countries. There was the expected disagreement on who should have the larger voice in controlling the Fund, those who put up the money or those who had first put up the idea. Despite the evident modifications of attitude that had taken place, there was still talk about the hardline 'gang of four', the USA, UK, Germany and Japan.

A passage to India

Early in 1978 there was a regional Commonwealth Conference in Sydney, Australia, at the invitation of Malcolm Fraser. India was represented at the Conference by its Prime Minister, Morarji Desai. The resolution passed by the Conference gave support to the Common Fund. Shortly afterwards, in March 1978, I was in Delhi. I called on Morarji Desai, who had signed its communiqué supporting the Common Fund. I took the opportunity to say to him that the OECD countries were prepared to negotiate a reasonable Common Fund. But the developing countries must make concessions. Would he use his immense influence among developing countries to persuade them to moderate their demands?

Mr Desai treated me to the sceptical glance of an old man who had spent a life in politics and who had, no doubt, been pressed on many occasions to use his influence in some good or bad cause. 'What is the Common Fund?', he asked. I did not think it appropriate to remind him that, only weeks before, he had attached his name in Sydney to a resolution of support for the Common Fund. Instead I gave him an account of the Common Fund proposal in all its UNCTAD glory. 'Mr Dell', he said, 'I was once Minister of Finance here in India. You can image what I would think of a scheme like that.' I did not ask him to use his influence to get the scheme dropped. I turned to other subjects.

The Commonwealth Conference on the Common Fund

In April 1978, Shridath Ramphal, Secretary-General of the
Commonwealth, called a Commonwealth Conference in London
to discuss the Common Fund. Because the object of the
Conference was clearly to bring pressure on the British
government, Ramphal's initiative caused some resentment. As
the Conference was in London, the usual courtesies to the host
country prevailed and it was agreed that I should take the
chair. I detected some reluctance at this as it was feared that,
from my position in the chair, I might more easily be able to
defeat Ramphal's purpose. At least, however, the Conference
made possible a number of 'frank' exchanges within the
Commonwealth family.

According to his usual custom on these occasions, Ramphal
had commissioned a British expert, in this case Lord Campbell
of Eskan, to take the chair of a technical group charged to
prepare a report favourable to the Common Fund. Lord
Campbell who had a lifetime's experience of the sugar trade,
and therefore of Commonwealth sugar agreements, and who
was a well-known and generous supporter of the Labour Party,
obliged. He himself attended the Conference in order to present
his report, which was everything that Ramphal would have
wanted. This led to vigorous clashes between Lord Campbell
and myself when, apparently to his surprise, I made it clear
that the British government was not impressed by his report. I
explained to the assembled Ministers, not all of whom were
accustomed to such public clashes between a Minister and a
citizen, that Lord Campbell was a valued supporter of my party
and that the differences which had emerged between us on
the Common Fund in no way prejudiced the government's
appreciation of his great merits.

In my opening speech to the Conference I emphasised that,
so far as the UK was concerned, the issue of principle was
settled. We had agreed that the Common Fund should be
established. However I listed the three issues of major
importance not yet agreed: the Fund had to be based primarily
on financial commitments given by producers and consumers
through commodity agreements; the 'second window' would
have to be limited in scale so as to avoid duplication with other
international arrangements, and financed through voluntary

contributions; and all participants would need to be reassured as to the methods by which the Fund would be controlled and their interests safeguarded.

At the Conference I was virtually isolated. The temperature of the meeting was, perhaps, influenced by the fact that commodity prices had been falling for the previous two years. I had the support of the Canadian High Commissioner in London, Paul Martin, and of Eric H. Halstead, the New Zealand Ambassador to Rome, both representing their governments' trade ministers. But neither claimed to be an expert on the intricacies of the Common Fund and they gave me moral rather than oral support. From Australia came the special trade representative, Vic Garland, who did what he could as peacemaker but who was in the end bound to his Common Fund brief. But, though isolated, I was not presented with a united phalanx of developing countries. There was a distinct difference between the moderates, such as Datuk Taib Mahmud of Malaysia, and the extremists such as P. J. Patterson of Jamaica. This, to some extent, I could exploit. However solidarity prevailed among the developing countries when it came to drafting a resolution which committed the Conference to a Common Fund which took no account of British objections. I phoned James Callaghan, the British Prime Minister, and I asked him whether it would concern him if the Conference broke down in disagreement. He assured me that he would support my judgement. If I thought the resolution committed us too far, I could refuse to agree it even if that meant a breakdown.

Armed with that support I was able, after hours of debate, to get a resolution which, while giving some comfort to Common Fund devotees, did not commit the British government to the kind of Common Fund the developing world representatives wanted. My main concession to achieve agreement was to permit in the Final Communiqué a hint that direct government contributions might after all be acceptable. The final communiqué said:

Ministers recognised that there was now greater willingness to consider favourably at the appropriate stage in the UNCTAD negotiations proposals both for direct government contributions to the Fund's capital and also deposits by international commodity agreements and borrowing as possible sources of finance. While the precise mix of some or all of these elements would be a matter of negotiation, Ministers felt that the fund should be so structured as to ensure the most efficient operation of the Common Fund while recognising the special problems of developing countries.

Of such garbage is international agreement forged. It appeared to me better to let in a hint of direct government contributions than to allow the Conference to collapse, especially as Canada was beginning to weaken.

At the OECD Ministerial Council in Paris in May 1978, I attended a meeting called by the American Secretary of State, Cyrus Vance. He was accompanied by Richard Cooper. Representatives of other major OECD countries were also present. At Vance's invitation, Cooper introduced the discussion. The Common Fund, he said, was an economic nonsense but a political imperative. The question was, what were we going to give to get an agreement? Vance took over. We had, he said, to do something that the developing countries wanted. On everything else we were giving them nothing. They were getting nothing on debt and were likely to get nothing out of the Multilateral Trade Negotiations. Surely we could be more flexible on the Common Fund. I explained what I thought could be done to achieve an agreement acceptable to OECD countries which should also be acceptable to developing countries. Cooper endorsed what I said. The meeting broke up without any specific decision. Later Cooper thanked me for my help. I did not say that I thought we might be in a stronger position if the Carter Administration had not come into office flushed with enthusiasm for the Common Fund.

March 1979, success at last?

Eventually, in March 1979, agreement was reached on the elements of a Common Fund with further details finalised by June 1980. There were to be two 'windows'. The first would finance buffer stocks. The second would finance other measures which would help with the research and development and market promotion of commodities and, under exceptional circumstances, diversification of production. The initial paid-in capital for supporting buffer stocks would be US$400 million, not the US$1 billion originally proposed. The Fund could also receive deposits from commodity agreements associated with it up to one-third of their maximum financial requirements. The Fund could borrow up to US$4 billion, as in the original scheme, but the borrowing instruments would only be subscribed by the members of the commodity agreements concerned, not by all the members of the Fund.

Alfred Maizels summarised the outcome of the long negotiations thus:

> The agreement on the Common Fund for commodities, reached in 1980 after four years of intensive negotiations, is another landmark, since although it is considerably emasculated from the original proposals of the Group of 77, it is none the less of significance in so far as it will be – when it comes into operation – the first international non-aid financial institution not dominated by the developed countries. . . . However, it now seems unlikely that the Common Fund will be able to play the dynamic and catalyst role in strengthening world commodity markets that was originally envisaged, not only because it lacks its own substantial capital, but also because the developed market-economy countries have a 'blocking vote' which they can exercise in discussions with 'significant financial implications' and in 'other important' decisions. There is little doubt that the more powerful Western countries viewed the original Common Fund proposal as a potential threat to their present dominance of world commodity markets, and that this threat was successfully nullified by their skilful and determined negotiations in UNCTAD (Maizels, 1984, pp. 18, 21).

Agreement having been reached, there remained only to bring the Common Fund into operation. The target date for the coming into force of the Agreement had become 30 September 1983. At UNCTAD VI at Belgrade in June/July 1983, an effort was made to persuade the necessary number of countries to ratify in time for the Common Fund to being operating on 1 January 1984. This did not happen. The agreement was to enter into force when there were ratifications by 90 states accounting for two-thirds of the directly contributed capital of the Fund. On 14 January 1986, the Yemen Arab Republic became the 90th government to ratify the Common Fund. But the 90 countries still represented only 57.87 per cent of the Fund's capital. On the other hand, there were now possible combinations of countries, even excluding the USA, that by their adhesion could bring it into operation. However a Common Fund lacking the ratification of the USA was not likely to make much impact on commodity trade and although all other OECD countries had ratified, the USA had not.

Britain had ratified. The Commonwealth Conference held in October 1985 was still regretting 'the lack of progress . . . in establishing a common fund'. Equally, however, Whitehall was becoming increasingly confident that either the Common Fund would fall by the wayside for lack of sufficient ratifications; or, if it did come into operation, it would have little influence on the real world of commodity trading.

The years of unremitting, misdirected, effort would have found their appropriate culmination.

10 Hayek and the Illusion of a Federal World

THE NATURE OF THE DILEMMA

There are those who question the value of national sovereignty in an interdependent world. Is the state really these days in a position to protect its own citizens? Whatever protection it can give, powerful competitive forces will still exist. Before acting against such competition, it will always have to calculate the dangers of reprisal by its rivals. In the international arena there are heavyweights and bullies. The danger of reprisal may therefore be very real.

On the other hand, there are those who fear the illiberal power of some states. But what would they put in the place of national sovereignty? The several major powers of the post-war world have seen their economic interests and attitudes diverge. They have no desire to create an international authority so powerful that they would be unable to control it and which could then act with impunity against them. Any international authority intended to substitute for national sovereignty would need to be very powerful indeed. It would have to be able to guarantee the economic security of a state which had stripped itself of its own power to act. It would need sufficient authority to be able to ignore the representations of those states, some of them still very large, which felt their interests to have been damaged by its actions.

There would be other objections to the creation of a powerful international authority charged with the duty of standing guard over the economic security of each and every nation. One of those objections would be that no such international authority would have the knowledge or the insight to justify surrendering to it the powers of management it would need. Who could trust its wisdom or impartiality in matters so central to the political survival of national governments and the social peace of nations? In consequence no such international authority exists, is likely to exist, or would be other than a nightmare if it did.

There could be collective management of an interdependent

world by all or some states acting together. That idea appears more practical than the creation of an international sovereign. It still leaves undefined the guidelines by which such an entity would operate. To some it may appear that such management has a potentiality for great good. But the high probability must be that either it would prove an impossibility or it would be productive of interventions more damaging to world prosperity even than those of the separate states that would constitute it.

If both collective management and international sovereignty are rejected, we are left with national governments. National sovereignties actually exist. It is an advantage which they are evidently unwilling to relinquish. As they exist, they seek a hand in the business. Their objective will be to ensure, so far as they can, that they are in a position to protect themselves if need be. They will wish to increase their power of discretion rather than reduce it. They will want the power to deflect, even if they cannot ultimately control, those market forces seen as imperilling their own security and that of their people. They will not accept the role of onlooker.

IS THE EUROPEAN COMMUNITY A MODEL?

To find some intermediate way, according to taste, between weak or dangerous sovereign states on the one hand, and the impracticability of collective management on the other, various forms of association have been proposed. The European Community is a possible model. Such an association is intended to be more powerful than any of its constituent parts. Without pretending to the authority of a federal government, it is expected to safeguard the interests of its members. Its members are of comparable social and economic status. Its homogeneity can mean that it can be not merely strong but, in a certain sense, democratic. Certainly an association such as the European Community may have some role to play in solving the conundrum for national sovereignty created by the rise of interdependence. But it cannot fulfil that role more than partially. The existence of the European Community cannot totally answer the problems of its members in seeking economic security.

It would be another illusion to imagine that within such a

Community all conflicts of economic or political interest disappear and liberalism triumphs. All in the end depends on the cooperation of states which, while having many interests in common, also have interests in conflict. It is natural that member states, while they retain their political existence, will have interests in conflict. Certainly an attempt can be made to regulate conflict by means of European law. This is certainly a more practical alternative than any attempt actually to eliminate conflicts of interest. But even at this more modest level it raises problems. These problems are inherent in the fundamental dilemma that it attempts to solve, that the members are states, they have functions, they exist, and they intend to go on existing.

Moreover, the opportunities to create such organisms as the European Community are limited. Although there are some more or less effective free trade areas, the European Community remains unique. In many ways the existence of this economic super-power exacerbates the problems of nations outside it. It is so powerful, and its decision-making processes are so inflexible, that they have little chance of influencing its actions. Developing countries may be reduced to the hopeless task of trying to play off one protectionist economic super-power against another. If there is a need for some kind of international authority, the need is not answered by associations such as the European Community.

Here then is the dilemma. There is no credible international sovereign visible or foreseeable. Any proposal to create one would, on a variety of grounds, be rejected. There is no international institution of any kind able either to protect the general interests of the peoples of the world, or to ensure that the different protective actions of competing states do not cause ever more serious conflict. International management barely exists. It may be necessary, but not available. The European Community is only a partial answer for its members and no answer at all for others. Indeed it can be a menace to others. Summits of world leaders are useful but insufficient because when management is most needed, when the facts of recession appear to demand collective action, conflicts of interest and of understanding prevent the necessary agreement. If one powerful country, the USA, can dominate, it may provide the necessary management. If it can do so no longer, if there is no substitute, there may well be a retreat from interdependence into national laagers. That is the danger today.

Thus there is no effective alternative for national sovereignty with all its inadequacies and all its dangers. Nations may be prepared to cooperate for ends mutually agreed. But the forms of cooperation will have to respect different interests and different attitudes.

F. A. HAYEK AND *THE ROAD TO SERFDOM*

Professor Hayek, Nobel Laureate in Economics, has provided an answer to this conundrum. It is federalism. At the end of his famous book, *The Road to Serfdom*, he comes to the dilemma discussed in this chapter. Hayek's concern is directed towards the dangers of discretionary power in the hands of the state, a power which is bound in the end to be abused. In other words, at any rate at the time of the publication of *The Road to Serfdom*, he did not agree that the power of the state was, as some think, illusory. He is concerned that not every state will adopt a liberal economic policy, that some that have power, whether economic or political, may try to use it against their neighbours. He concludes that safeguards of some kind, preferably in the form of the Rule of Law, are necessary. As he looks to the Rule of Law as a safeguard against abuses of discretionary power, he has to confront the problem how to establish the Rule of Law in international affairs.

Unfortunately our hope for enlightenment is disappointed. We find only an illustration of the truth that it is easier to argue an impassioned case for economic liberalism at home than to make realistic proposals about how to resolve the problems of international relationships abroad. Hayek, writing in 1944, says: 'we cannot hope for order or lasting peace after this war if states, large or small, regain unfettered sovereignty in the economic sphere' (Hayek, 1979, p. 172).

In the field of polemic it is too much to expect precise statements. Perhaps, therefore, one must forgive the imprecision in the statement quoted. What states have, or ever have had, 'unfettered sovereignty'? Even Hayek will understand that states must have some discretion but it has never, in international relations, been unfettered. It has always been constrained by the existence of other states. Presumably the intention of the statement is to convey the impression that a high level of independent national decision-making power is inconsistent with order or lasting peace. But is the state, in the Hayek world, to have so little independent national decision-making power as to eliminate the practical discretions which governments wish to exercise in defence of their own citizens? We shall see as we go on.

> But this does not mean that a new super-state must be given powers which we have not learnt to use intelligently even on a national scale, that an international authority ought to be given power to direct individual nations how to use their resources. It means merely that there must be a power which can restrain the different nations from action harmful to their neighbours, a set of rules which defines what a state may do, and an authority capable of enforcing these rules. . . . The need is for an international political authority which, without power to direct the different people what they must do, must be able to restrain them from action which will damage others . . . it is essential that these powers of the international authority should be strictly circumscribed by the Rule of Law (Hayek, 1979, p. 172).

Hayek wisely argues against world government with power to plan the world's resources because of the difficult and discriminatory judgements that it would have to make and because what would have been delegated to that authority would not be merely a technical task, 'but the most comprehensive power over their very lives' (Hayek, 1979, p. 171). Yet having wisely ruled out one kind of super-state, we are back before the end of the chapter with this other kind of super-state, for the moment entitled an 'international political authority'. Certainly we have Hayek's word for it that his revised super-state is not to do some of those things which we have not learnt to do on a national scale. But it is to do other things that we have not yet learnt to do, such as enforcing the Rule of a Law yet to be written which will restrain nations from action which will damage others. Let us assume that this enormous, and as yet undefined, power will be exercised honestly, and that Hayek's supranational authority will have no motivation other than to serve the interests of the member states. This is an assumption very friendly to Hayek's proposal and one so unrealistic that Hayek himself would be the first to question it. But let us nevertheless assume, trying to be as friendly as possible, that Hayek's supranational authority is preternaturally selfless. It will nevertheless find in the course of its endeavours that it will be bound to make exactly those discriminatory judgements about the use of resources which, as Hayek has already correctly argued, no super-state or world government could possibly make without causing deep resentments and deep injustice.

> The form of international government under which certain strictly defined powers are transferred to an international authority, while in all other respects the individual countries remain responsible for their internal affairs, is, of course, that of federation . . . there can be no international law without a power to enforce it . . . the small can preserve their independence in the international as in the national sphere only within a true system of law which guarantees both that certain rules are invariably enforced and that the authority which has the power to enforce these cannot use it for any other purpose (Hayek, 1979, pp. 172, 173, 175).

We now see fully exposed the extraordinary nature of the system by which Hayek attempts to ensure that the laws of liberal economics are not evaded and that states are allowed to act only in ways consistent with a liberal approach to international peace and order. States are to be permitted, under this federation, to look after their internal affairs but presumably only that part of their internal affairs which does not impact on their international economic relations. The rules which are yet to be defined are to be 'invariably enforced', no doubt by force of arms if necessary. Only in such circumstances, he says, can the small states preserve their independence. Hayek himself has in other contexts pointed out that coercion is an inevitable accompaniment of socialism. He has written:

> The difficulty is that, in order to plan at all on an extensive scale, a much more extensive agreement among the members of the society about the relative importance of the various needs is required than will normally exist and that, in consequence, this agreement will have to be brought about

and a common scale of values will have to be imposed by force and propaganda (quoted Gissurarson, 1984, p. 13).

Hayek must realise that only by the use of coercion will his supranational authority be able to make its writ run. The members of the international community will disagree about the relative importance of various needs. To secure agreement, coercion will be necessary. Coercion cannot always be achieved with kid gloves. He may argue that his supranational authority is not to tell countries what to do but to tell them what not to do. But the 'invariable enforcement' of rules against the wishes of states will certainly require coercion and an apparatus by which that coercion can be achieved. It is indeed remarkable how far the imagination of one so deeply opposed to economic intervention on a domestic scale can take him when he comes to contemplate the problems of international economic relations. At home the state must hardly lift a finger unless it be to give minimum guarantees against the worst deprivation. Internationally we are to have the most extraordinary edifice of supranational power which will rapidly, in the fulfilment of its mission, take on all those additional tasks which Hayek himself has ruled as unacceptable. One of his concerns has been for the smaller states, but in this edifice of supranational coercion, the voice of the smaller states will be as nothing.

Hayek permits that in the first instance there should be a number of federations rather than just one world federation. He overlooks the fact that these federations, super-states in their own right, will certainly come into conflict with one another and will have to find some way, hopefully short of war, to reconcile their differences. We now have more experience of this than Hayek had when he was writing *The Road to Serfdom*. We can see the European Community in its relations with the USA, continual differences usually reconciled after intense negotiations, but seldom actually removed altogether, always waiting in the wings to be revived as some new grievance, one against the other. Many of these differences are relatively minor. Others often seem to threaten economic war. If Europe were not so dependent militarily on the USA, they would rapidly escalate both in quality and in number.

Yet if one contemplates a federation joining Europe and the USA to regulate such matters under the Rule of Law, what law is it that should rule? There is no law that so clearly reconciles conflicting interests, is so just and so reliable in its impact, that separate nations will accept it without question and without escape. The law is as lacking in foresight as any economist or any politician. Precisely because there is such ignorance, there is a need for the competition of different views. Precisely for this reason, there are some matters that have to be reconciled by negotiation, not enforced by law. Among the continuing problems between the USA and Europe is the use of American Law extraterritorially. Is Europe just to accept American law? How can the two, and the interests of the two, possibly be reconciled in a legal instrument when it is all that skilled negotiators can often do to reconcile the present conflicts of interest in a diplomatic document?

The European Community may be claimed as the realisation of Hayek's compromise of a federation more limited than a world federation. Within the Community there are enforceable rules and attempts are sometimes made to enforce them. But it would be an illusion to imagine that member countries never act in ways which damage their partners or that they can always, or even often, be prevented from doing so. The European Council appointed in December 1978 a Committee of Three to consider what adjustments might be made to the machinery and procedures of the Community in order to improve its working. I was a member of that Committee which was told to make its recommendations within the context of the need for progress towards European Union. Our view of the European Community was much more modest than would be implied for it if it indeed fell to be considered as a Hayekian federation. We referred to two unwritten Community rules which we held to express the 'profound solidarity' which united the Community's member states. The first of these rules we called 'the rule of active solidarity'. This rule stated that:

> if a Member State finds itself in serious difficulty, whether as a result of circumstances, or of the application of certain Community rules, or of its own mistakes, it is a question both of duty and of self-interest for the other Community countries to help it find a solution or to give assistance by all means in their power, within a programme aimed at correcting the situation (Report, 1979, p. 74).

The second rule was defined as the 'rule of passive solidarity'. It said that:

> Every Member State should refrain, so far as is at all possible, from any act which might directly or indirectly make life more difficult for other Member States and for the Community as a whole (Report, 1979, p. 75).

We then commented that:

> We are aware that it is not always practical to apply this rule. A state which sets out to reimpose financial discipline can rarely avoid a temporary slowing-down of activity which causes problems for its associates in the Community. But every Member State should bear in mind, in all its important decisions, the possible consequences of its actions for the Community and the other Member States (Report, 1979, p. 75).

These modest prescriptions were all that we considered practical even within so united an institution as the European Community, united by Treaty, by geography, by history and common experience, and by levels of economic development. But it is not just a matter of what is practical. It is not desirable to attempt to establish federal institutions to enforce rules which are believed to be against the interests of Member States and which they are not prepared voluntarily to accept. That would have been the route to the break-up of the Community. It has been found much better to accept that the Community is a Community of states possessing all the characteristics of states, to build on goodwill, and where interests conflict to find the best possible negotiated solution. That indeed is the way internationally to reconcile the protective nature of the state with the maximum of liberalism in economic and political behaviour.

Idealists have frequently argued for world government as the way to peace. Just a little thought would persuade them of the grave dangers that lie in what they propose. Hayek sees some but not all the dangers. He is prepared to ignore those dangers he recognises because he sees no reliable way to peace other than through his international political authority. He is gravely mistaken. Of course what Hayek proposes has not happened, nor, we must hope, will it happen. What did happen after the

Second World War is that for a period the political and economic dominance of the USA was such that it could get a good part of its way in ordering the affairs of the world. That period has passed. What Hayek offers is neither a practical nor a desirable alternative.

CONCLUSION: PROFESSOR HAYEK IS IGNORED BUT THE WORLD KEEPS ON COURSE

So the world struggles on, ignoring Hayek's wisdom, but somehow keeping on course. Hayek has proposed. The facts of international relations, the concerns of the state to preserve its discretion against the pressures of international regulation, have disposed. Yet, and this is a very important point, the postwar economic system continues to function. It does so presumably because, on balance, developed countries consider it to be in their interests, at least for the time being, even though few of them are totally satisfied with the behaviour of their economic partners. And governments have the continuing task of preserving that system through all the turbulences that are to come without any prospect that any supranational agency will actually come into being.

Apparently, for the time being, we can do without it and the enormous international bureaucracy that it would establish. It is a good thing we can do without it because it would cause more problems that it would solve. If the world ever did need it, it would be a sign that it was in real trouble. Unlucky is the world that needs heroes. While governments are waiting for that unhappy day they will just have to go on reconciling conflicts of interest by normal negotiating processes between opponents. The better way to preserve and promote the liberal society is for each state to negotiate its interests with its principal economic foes, to find some means to reconciliation, and thereby to avoid a call to arms, whether the arms be military or economic. If this can be done using some piece of international machinery, and thus reinforcing its authority, so much the better. In any case, the practical route is reconciliation through negotiation. Thus perhaps can both liberalism and security be maintained.

11 'Mercantilism'

THE MERCANTILISTS

The mercantilist view of the world is a Hobbesian view. It is a world in which there is no accepted law-giver or law enforcer, no authority capable of maintaining order, by force if necessary, and in which each nation has to look to itself for its own defence. Survival for the nation depends on whatever efforts, whatever power, and whatever diplomacy, it can deploy in its own defence.

The mercantilist era was the era in which the nation state was building. The nation state was built in conflict with other nation states. The claims of one state often entrenched on the interests of other states. For such reasons alone, one state would not wish to become dependent militarily, politically, or economically, on other states, even on other states with which it might find itself in temporary alliance. Many of the mercantilist writers were themselves merchants. The state would have the support of the merchant mercantilists because they, too, wanted their state to be strong. The merchant mercantilists were interested in the removal of *internal* as well as external barriers to their trade, and they looked to a strong state to perform those indispensable functions.

The merchant mercantilists understood that states were concerned with the use of economic policy to reinforce their own power and they saw it as in their interests to support that process. To that end both partners were prepared to make sacrifices of welfare. The Navigation Acts have always been regarded as a prime example of mercantilism in action. Francis Bacon spoke of Henry VII's Navigation Acts as 'bowing the ancient policy of this Estate from consideration of plenty to consideration of power' (quoted Pickthorn, 1934, pp. 145–6). This observation was perhaps informed more by the thinking of Bacon's time than that of Henry VII. Bacon observes the possible conflict between considerations of plenty and considerations of power, and that steps taken to enhance power may prejudice plenty. That would not, however, necessarily make such steps inappropriate.

The word 'mercantilism' is these days used by modern liberal economists simply as a term of abuse. In their vocabulary it is a synonym for protectionism. Apart from its association with protectionism, they attach to it no very specific meaning. The name 'mercantilism' exaggerates the commonality of the economic thinking of the two or three centuries before Adam Smith. Mercantilist writers built no consistent school of thought other than a few principles by which they thought statesmen should be guided. The first was the primacy of national economic security. The second was the primacy of the state in achieving national economic security.

DID ECONOMIC WISDOM BEGIN WITH ADAM SMITH?

First we need to dispose of a damaging prejudice, the prejudice that all economic thought before Adam Smith is to be at best neglected, at worst abused. Keynes says of his upbringing as a 'faithful pupil of the classical (i.e., free trade) school': 'As for earlier mercantilist theory, no intelligible account was available; and we were brought up to believe that it was little better than nonsense. So absolutely overwhelming and complete has been the domination of the classical school' (Keynes, 1947, pp. 334–5).

The situation is no better today. Sciences, and subjects which regard themselves as scientific, tend to disregard their own histories. After all, if knowledge can be accumulated through scientific investigation, if each generation can stand confidently on the shoulders of its predecessors, what need is there to look behind those immediate predecessors and in the search for truth to waste time on the study of history? There is a regrettable tendency, given any imagined advance in mankind's understanding of his social environment, to throw out the baby with the bath water. What is new must entirely displace what is old. In 1776 Adam Smith published *The Wealth of Nations* and the history of economics began again. No reference was henceforth thought necessary to such wisdom as his predecessors might have possessed, not even to check that Adam Smith had fairly represented the thinking of those he so eloquently condemned. There was some revival of interest at the end of the nineteenth century when the economic supremacy of Britain began to be visibly challenged by the rise of Germany. But for many years now only historians, and exceptional economists such as Keynes, have remembered and treated seriously the economic thinking of the generations before Adam Smith.

Adam Smith is regarded as having delivered an elegant *coup de grâce* to what he describes as 'the mercantile system'. Though governments might still operate it, they could no longer, after Adam Smith, think well of it. He argued not just on grounds of economics but on those of justice and equality before the law. He rejected in principle any 'selectivity', as it is called these days, in a government's support for its citizens, any action by government which discriminated against the interests of any other citizens. He set up an argument which since his time has strongly influenced the conduct of politicians and civil servants and which, until quite recently, was in the ascendant. As we will see, he was somewhat more divided in his mind where the discrimination was also against the foreigner, although the benefits he claimed for the international division of labour might have been expected to rule out such discrimination as well.

Modern consumerists can also look to him for support. In a classic observation he wrote:

> Consumption is the sole end and purpose of all production; and the interest of the producer ought to be attended to only so far as it may be necessary for promoting that of the consumer. The maxim is so perfectly self-evident that it would be absurd to attempt to prove it. But in the mercantile system the interest of the consumer is almost constantly sacrificed to that of the producer; and it seems to consider production, and not consumption, as the ultimate end and object of all industry and commerce (Smith, 1947, vol. 2, p. 155).

This supposedly self-evident observation led him to a vigorous denunciation of eighteenth-century British imperialism:

> In the system of laws which has been established for the management of our American and West Indian colonies, the interest of the home consumer has been sacrificed to that of the producer with a more extravagant profusion than in all

our other commercial regulations. A great empire has been established for the sole purpose of raising up a nation of consumers who should be obliged to buy from the shops of our different producers all the goods with which they could supply them. For the sake of that little enhancement of price which this monopoly might afford our producers, the home consumers have been burdened with the whole expense of maintaining and defending that empire (Smith, 1947, vol. 2, pp. 155–6).

It is no wonder that the reputation of the mercantilists has suffered under Smith's onslaught. And if they, and the governments supposedly influenced by them, were capable of such expensive absurdities, why bother to read them, why check whether perhaps Adam Smith had not told the whole story? It is one of the easiest errors open to the student of the history of thought to assume that predecessors with whom one disagrees were fools or knaves. That they were fools is the most obvious explanation of their folly. That they were knaves accords fully with experience of human history in which knavery has ruled more frequently than wisdom. Above all, to question these simple explanations would involve the difficult historical and intellectual task of actually working out whether there might not be other explanations for their views which would lead to their being taken rather more seriously.

The great surge of Adam Smith's eloquence carries the modern reader along and sometimes leads him to believe that Smith is saying something that in fact he is not saying, or at least not proving. It is perfectly true that consumption is the sole end and purpose of production. But that does not mean that it is self-evidently wrong to give some assistance to the producer. To consume is simple. To produce is difficult. Anyone can consume. Only those more or less skilled can produce. The people of the UK are very good at consuming. In recent years they have shown themselves less good at producing. That accounts for their so-called import propensity. Some assistance for developing the skills of production would seem to be a legitimate expense of governments.

The fact that some such expense is justified does not mean that any expense is justified. The general lesson is that in giving assistance to producers the costs and benefits should be weighed.

It does not teach that assistance should never be given. Indeed that is perhaps what Adam Smith himself meant when he said that the interest of the producer should be attended to only so far as it was necessary for promoting the interest of the consumer. But that is not a narrow limitation. On the contrary, it creates a window of opportunity for government intervention. If the interest of producers may be attended to provided that that tends to the interest of consumers (and we can be sure that Adam Smith would not have indicated the possibility if he had not intended it to be taken seriously), from whom should that attention come, if not from government, and from one's own government at that? And who was to pay for it other than the consumer through his taxes? Where British mercantilists would have taken a firm stand is in giving the interests of British consumers and British producers priority over those of foreigners. It is not absolutely clear that Adam Smith really took a different view on that point either.

Adam Smith was perfectly right to condemn imperialism as a means of assisting producers. He was right to indicate that eighteenth-century mercantilism degenerated into eighteenth-century imperialism. He was unable to foresee that nineteenth-century liberalism would degenerate into imperialism. In both cases it was not, perhaps, the writings of economic thinkers that were mainly responsible. Adam Smith was right to say that the cost of imperialism outweighed any possible benefit to the producers. It would be wrong to assume that governments were not aware of the fact, which may suggest that they had other objectives than benefit to producers. Those objectives may have involved 'considerations of power' rather than 'considerations of plenty'. Yet imperialism was no less wrong in the hands of liberal governments than it had been in the hands of mercantilist governments.

DEFENCE IS OF MUCH MORE IMPORTANCE THAN OPULENCE

Adam Smith was aware of the case for intervention and, indeed, defined the circumstances in which it was acceptable.

According to the system of natural liberty, the sovereign has only three duties to attend to: three duties of great importance indeed, but plain and intelligible to common understandings: first, the duty of protecting society from the violence and invasion of other independent societies; secondly, the duty of protecting, as far as possible, every member of the society from the injustice or oppression of every other member of it, or the duty of establishing an exact administration of justice; and, thirdly, the duty of erecting and maintaining certain public works and certain public institutions which it can never be for the interest of any individual or small number of individuals, though it may frequently do much more than repay it to a great society (Smith, 1947, vol. 1, pp. 180–1).

Under the head of this third duty, Adam Smith advocated publicly-financed education (Smith, 1947, vol. 2, p. 266). This third duty shows that Adam Smith himself did not believe in *laissez-faire*, a term which in fact he himself never used, as it is sometimes understood. The third duty is capable of such extension that this statement has caused Professor Milton Friedman great difficulty. Friedman has written that the third duty

describes a valid duty of a government directed to preserving and strengthening a free society; but it can also be interpreted to justify unlimited extensions of government power . . . at first blush [it may] appear to justify almost any proposed government measure.

Friedman concludes:

The lesson to be drawn from the misuse of Smith's third duty is not that government intervention is never justified, but rather that the burden of proof should be on its proponents. We should develop the practice of examining both the benefits and the costs of proposed government interventions and require a very clear balance of benefits over costs before adopting them (Friedman, 1980, pp. 22–4).

There is no evidence that a mercantilist, or indeed Adam Smith, would have thought any differently. The problem is that these cost-benefit calculations contain many elements of high uncertainty, and consequently lead to uncertain conclusions which leave the question in the end to the political judgement of governments. If the door is once opened to intervention, adjuration to enter into cost-benefit analyses is no certain way of closing it to economically ill-advised interventions. Where Adam Smith himself would have drawn the line is a question to which the answer can only be guessed from a study of *The Wealth of Nations*. *The Wealth of Nations* can as easily be read as the work of an intelligent mercantilist as of a free trader.

Adam Smith penned words that have become the classic statement of the case for freedom of trade:

> What is prudence in the conduct of every private family can scarce be folly in that of a great kingdom. If a foreign country can supply us with a commodity cheaper than we ourselves can make it, better buy it of them with some part of the produce of our own industry employed in a way in which we have some advantage (Smith, 1947, vol. 1, p. 401).

Yet for him, as for his mercantilist predecessors, there were exceptions because there were important objectives other than economic objectives. Political considerations had their place. For example, Adam Smith had a concern for agriculture that went beyond the dictates of his economics. He regarded support for English agriculture as the social basis of the independent English yeoman. 'The law of England', he noted, 'favours agriculture not only indirectly by the protection of commerce, but by several direct encouragements.' Although he regarded the encouragements as 'altogether illusory', he appeared to approve of 'the good intention of the legislature to favour agriculture'. The reason was that 'the yeomanry of England are rendered as secure, as independent, and as respectable as law can make them' (Smith, 1947, vol. 1, p. 372).

What European Commissioner or French Minister of Agriculture could have put the point better? Adam Smith did want to see freer trade in agricultural produce than prevailed in his own time. But this was because he believed that it would do no harm to the existing agricultural interest. He did not foresee the advances in agricultural technology that have so vastly increased agricultural productivity both per man and per hectare. For Adam Smith agriculture was one industry for which the division of labour had little to offer (Smith, 1947, vol. 1, p. 6). That view helped him to reconcile his free trade conscience with the special position he conceded to agriculture

(Smith, 1947, vol. 1, p. 403). It is the easier part of statesmanship to advocate free trade in those cases where it can do no harm to domestic vested interests. But how, in the late nineteenth century, with corn pouring into the UK from the great plains of North America, would Adam Smith have weighed the advantages of free trade against the security, the independence, and the respectability, of the yeomanry of England?

Adam Smith identified cases in which it was advantageous to lay some burden upon foreign for the encouragement of domestic industry. One was

> when some particular sort of industry is necessary for the defence of the country. The defence of Great Britain . . . depends very much upon the number of its sailors and shipping. The act of navigation, therefore, very properly endeavours to give the sailors and shipping of Great Britain the monopoly of the trade of their own country (Smith, 1947, vol. 1, pp. 406–7).

Adam Smith therefore supported the Navigation Acts with their very restrictive provisions regarding the carriage of British cargoes in British bottoms even though he believed that they represented a serious cost to the foreign commerce of England and 'to the growth of that opulence which can arise from it'. Despite that conviction he was ready to argue that:

> They [the Navigation Acts] are as wise . . . as if they had been dictated by the most deliberate wisdom. National animosity at that particular time aimed at the very same object which the most deliberate wisdom would have recommended, the diminution of the naval power of Holland, the only naval power which could endanger the security of England. . . . As defence . . . is of much more importance than opulence, the act of navigation is, perhaps, the wisest of all the commercial regulations of England (Smith, 1947, vol. 1, pp. 407–8).

His mercantilist predecessor, Josiah Child, had admitted that 'if the present profit of the generality be barely and singularly considered', the Navigation Acts could have harmful effects. But, he went on, 'this Kingdom being an Island, the defence whereof has always been our Shipping and our Seamen, it seems to be absolutely necessary that Profit and Power ought jointly to be considered' (quoted Luard, 1984, p. 72). It will be seen, therefore, that on this subject, there was a great deal in common between Adam Smith and Josiah Child, and that, if anything, Adam Smith went further in propounding the priority of defence over opulence.

Adam Smith was very hard on Colbert, whom he regarded as the prototype of the mercantilist in office. He spoke of Colbert's having 'unfortunately embraced all the prejudices of the mercantile system' (Smith, 1947, vol. 2, pp. 157–8). He claims that Colbert, in his policies, showed that he was 'imposed upon by the sophistry of merchants and manufacturers, who are always demanding a monopoly against their countrymen' (Smith, 1947, vol. 1, p. 411). If 'mercantilism' means anything, Colbert was certainly a mercantilist. He wished to promote the power of the state by achieving a surplus in France's balance of trade. To this end he wished to put the power of the state behind French commerce. Oddly, there is much in common between Adam Smith, the greatest theorist of free trade, and his *bête noire*, Colbert.

Adam Smith, as we have seen, based his support for the enactment of the seventeenth-century Navigation Acts on the power of the Dutch, on their threat to the security of England, and on the need to have a recruiting base for naval sailors at need. In the seventeenth century the Dutch were a great naval power capable of bringing their naval guns even into the Thames itself and of bombarding London. Writing in 1776, Smith does not withdraw his support in the light of the fact that the power of the Dutch had greatly diminished since 1651 when the Commonwealth Parliament passed the Navigation Act to which Smith is primarily referring, or since 1661 when Charles II's first Parliament re-enacted it. By 1776 Adam Smith's defence of the Navigation Acts as being necessary for the recruitment of sailors and shipping was also far-fetched and anachronistic. Perhaps he had fallen into the error he attributes to Colbert and had been imposed upon, in this case by the sophistry of the vested shipping interests. But to return good for evil, and to extend to Smith a courtesy and an understanding that he was not prepared to extend to Colbert, let us say that he was in fact more a man of his time, was more guided by the pragmatism of the mercantile system, than his admirers have allowed. When it comes to practical matters, Adam Smith turns out to be a Colbertian. Smith was not unaware of the fact that the original motivation behind the Navigation Acts, which he supported as 'having been dictated by the most deliberate wisdom', included their effect on Dutch commercial power and not just on their naval power. If some break the rules by using force to achieve commercial ends, then all must be prepared, if they can, to be equally forceful. Colbert had exactly the same concerns. He was insistent on the need to promote French prosperity and power by war against the Dutch.

That Colbert had such ideas is not unexpected. That Adam Smith was also prepared to concede that concern about the naval power of the Dutch, and the commercial advantages that gave them, justified countervailing naval action by England shows that he too was capable of believing that the state had a role in promoting the competitiveness of its nation's industry even by the use of military power, particularly where the competition was strong. But if he could believe it in cases where the strength of foreign competition was being enhanced by the use of military power, perhaps he would in the end bring himself to believe it in cases where the strength of foreign competition was being enhanced by subsidies or by protective measures of other kinds. Adam Smith is apparently to be found on the side of those who saw that in a world in which naval power was used by others to achieve commercial successes, the building of naval power for the same purpose was necessary for Britain. Adam Smith deserves every credit for seeing the value of the international division of labour based on 'natural advantages' (Smith, 1947, vol. 1, p. 402). But it would appear that he was as much a pragmatist and, even, mercantilist, as statesmen have been throughout the ages.

Adam Smith, perhaps, did not realise how wide a breach for protectionist incursions he was opening in the free trade case by making an exception of the 'particular sort of industry necessary for the defence of the country'. He was thinking specifically of the Navigation Acts but the breach is wide enough to permit any government to drive through it a broad spectrum of industries supposedly essential for the defence of the realm. The exception which governments these days do make for defence industries represents a major departure from free trade.

Consciousness of the need for naval forces suggests an awareness of a world of conflict rather than of harmony, conflicts that could not be reconciled simply by the liberating idea of the international division of labour. The conflicts of Adam Smith's time arose not simply from the manoeuvres of monarchs for territorial aggrandisement but from the exercise of economic power and the drive for it. Adam Smith himself wrote:

> The wealth of a neighbouring nation . . . though dangerous in war and politics, is certainly advantageous in trade. In a state of hostility it may enable our enemies to maintain fleets and armies superior to our own; but in a state of peace and commerce it must likewise enable them to exchange with us to a greater value, and to afford a better market (Smith, 1947, vol. 1, p. 437).

Statesmen might be forgiven in the eighteenth century, and indeed later, for not making the clear division which this statement implies, between the requirements of peace and those of 'hostility'.

I have given here an interpretation of *The Wealth of Nations* more sympathetic to Smith's commonsense than are most modern interpretations of his theories. There is more in common between the thinking of Adam Smith and that of the mercantilists than is generally appreciated by non-historians. That is not surprising. Revolutions in thought frequently turn out, on examination, to be less revolutionary than at first supposed. Smith's approving re-statement, of the great mercantilist principle, that 'defence comes before opulence', though less original than his arguments for the international division of labour, has in practice corresponded more closely with the actual policies of governments. That defence comes before opulence is a key insight of *The Wealth of Nations*.

MERCANTILISM AND THE CURRENT ACCOUNT

The mercantilists were concerned for the current account. Their concern arose from a desire to build power and preserve independence as well as because it was believed to be a measure of power and independence. Japan can be regarded as the modern exemplar of the mercantile state. Japan illustrates what can be achieved by a combination of twentieth-century industrial excellence and eighteenth-century economic thought. Mercantilists looked to a surplus in the current account of the balance of payments as a way of increasing their country's stock of money, i.e. gold and silver, and consequently its wealth. As one country's surplus is another's deficit, international trade was, in this sense at least, a zero-sum game, and hence a source of conflict. Josiah Child wrote that: 'all trade [is] a kind of warfare' (quoted Letwin, 1969, p. 44).

This idea of the zero-sum game, though they would not have put it that way, runs through a great deal of mercantilist thinking. Of power, of trade, of gold and silver, there were relatively fixed quantities. Therefore any benefit to one nation, or one trader, was a cost to another nation or trader. Of power, the zero-sum idea may well be true. But of trade it is now supposed not to be true. Colbert thought differently. There was, he believed, a limited amount of trade available and to increase France's share of it should be a major aim of the French state. At the time Colbert was almost certainly right. Trade was at that time a zero-sum game. It was growing very slowly.

> Until the nineteenth century, prosperity gained through trade usually involved a considerable beggar-my-neighbour element because of the limited size of the world market and its rather slow growth: national fortunes were largely gained at the expense of ousted rivals (Johns, 1985, p. 55).

Colbert told Louis XIV that he had 'already conquered Spain, Italy, Germany, England and some others, in which he had caused great misery and want, and by despoiling them he had enriched himself' (quoted Luard, 1984, pp. 9, 14). Here therefore is a fundamental difference between the mercantilists and the liberals. The idea that trade cannot be a zero-sum game is at the heart of the liberal belief in the existence of a natural harmony between nations interfered with only by the expensive and unjustifiable interventions of governments. The mercantilists rejected any such belief. For the mercantilists there is conflict, there is no invisible hand, no benign regulator which ensures that all is for the best in free international commerce. Today, even though there is mutual benefit in expanding international trade, mercantilists will still hold that there can be circumstances in which trade is a zero-sum game.

The mercantilists may sometimes have underestimated the practical problems of implementing policies conducive to a favourable current account balance. If so, they can be excused. Uncertainty as to the consequences of economic policy, however well designed, remains a principal preoccupation for governments even in the late twentieth century. It was no less a preoccupation for those in earlier centuries concerned to achieve the current account surplus beloved of mercantilism. Perhaps it was even more of a problem because of lack of experience and sophistication. As Keynes puts it:

> a policy of trade restrictions is a treacherous instrument even for the attainment of its ostensible object, since private interest, administrative incompetence and the intrinsic difficulty of the task may divert it into producing results directly opposite to those intended (Keynes, 1947, p. 339).

And again, to show that mercantilists did see some of the difficulties:

> It does not follow . . . that the maximum degree of restriction of imports will promote the maximum favourable balance of trade. The earlier mercantilists laid great emphasis on this and were often found to be opposing trade restrictions because on a long view they were liable to operate adversely to a favourable balance (Keynes, 1947, p. 338).

Heckscher said of the mercantilists that 'it was precisely this general mercantilist conception of society which led statesmen to even greater ruthlessness than would have been possible without the help of such a conception' (ed. Coleman, 1969, pp. 32–3). Indeed, the mercantilist era was one of war and of colonisation which deserves to be described as 'ruthless'. But war and colonisation were not limited to that era. Liberalism under pressure, liberalism which has discovered by experience the existence of conflict, liberalism which has failed to generate the expected harmony of interests, degenerates into mercantilism through its inevitable concern with the current account. Liberalism in the course of its degeneration into imperialism unleashed armies of conquest. Adam Smith would have been dismayed but there it was. In the nineteenth century, liberalism led to the seizure by military force of secure markets and supplies of raw materials. It was a free trading country, the

UK, which built the greatest empire of all and which compelled the Indians to become liberal importers of textiles which the producers among them might have preferred to make for themselves. For once the interest of Indian consumers was triumphing over that of producers, and it was triumphing through the use of external force. Indians remember that free trade was imposed on them by the British Empire. It was a failure of liberalism that, despite expanding international trade, it did not eliminate war and colonisation. In the seventeenth and eighteenth centuries, mercantilism appears as ruthlessness in international affairs. In the liberal age military power was also used, and not necessarily in a subtler and more civilised manner. The export of compulsory economic liberalism cannot be distinguished from mercantilism of the most predatory kind. Indeed in the mind of Joseph Chamberlain the building of a liberal empire, protected by tariffs against the powerful competition of Germany and the USA, became the preferred defence of British liberalism in decline.

KEYNES AND THE MERCANTILISTS

Keynes in his General Theory, Chapter 23, showed himself far more sympathetic to mercantilism than the great majority of modern economists. He even referred to what he called 'the element of scientific truth in mercantilist doctrine' (Keynes, 1947, p. 335). The mercantilists had 'hit upon maxims of practical wisdom without having had much cognisance of the underlying theoretical grounds' (Keynes, 1947, p. 340). Thus they saw that an unduly high rate of interest was the main obstacle to the growth of wealth, and were even aware that the rate of interest depended on liquidity preference and the quantity of money. They were aware of what Keynes calls the 'fallacy of cheapness' and the danger that excessive competitiveness can turn the terms of trade against a country. It was they who originally observed that the 'fear of goods' and the scarcity of money were causes of unemployment, an attitude 'which the classicals were to denounce two centuries later as an absurdity'. They 'were under no illusion as to the nationalistic character of their policies and their tendency to promote war.'

Keynes observes more than once how much at odds with the

'beliefs of the "natural man"' was so much of classical theory whereas mercantilist thinking approximated to it very closely, not thereby proving its theoretical soundness but at least raising question marks which economists had too long ignored (Keynes, 1947, pp. 340–51). It is a peculiar form of arrogance that rejects with contumely, longstanding and hard acquired experience simply on the uncertain basis of an economic 'science'. Keynes at least understood that lessons acquired from long experience, however lacking in a theoretical basis, might provide as penetrating an insight into the truth.

> As a contribution to statecraft, which is concerned with the economic system as a whole and with securing the optimum employment of the system's entire resources, the methods of the early pioneers of economic thinking in the sixteenth and seventeenth centuries may have attained to fragments of practical wisdom which the unrealistic abstractions of Ricardo first forgot and then obliterated (Keynes, 1947, p. 340).

A MODERN MEANING FOR MERCANTILISM

It may be easy enough to refute some of the specific prescriptions of mercantilism as it was propounded before Adam Smith. But it is unwise to miss out on its wider connotations and ignore its correspondence with deep national sentiment and with the most natural activities of the state both of which the theory of *laissez-faire* tried in vain to discourage.

If the practical wisdom of the mercantilists is to be reflected in the modern use of the word 'mercantilism', it should not be defined as necessarily hostile to imports or to increases in imports. Rather would it imply a calculating attitude instead of a committed attitude to the benefits of free international trade. It would reject the idea that all international trade is necessarily and in all circumstances of advantage to the nations that participate in it. It would not thereby deny that international trade brings benefits and it may well argue that in the given situation, and perhaps for political reasons rather than economic reasons, the open trading system should be preserved.

Modern mercantilism would accept that a current account deficit, which the early mercantilists would have regarded with horror, may in fact be supportable, need not in all circumstances be inconsistent with the requirements of economic security, and may bring increments of welfare to citizens of deficit countries. It would, however, be understanding of the anxieties of countries with weak or developing economies for whom a current account deficit can bring repercussions of an unacceptable kind. It would note that for a combination of historical and psychological reasons, Germany and Japan with two of the strongest economies in the world, strive for current account balance as a minimum, and preferably surplus. It would observe that France with its Colbertian intellectual inheritance cherishes and defends a current account surplus by such means as are open to it. It would not, therefore, expect that other nations that have come to feel themselves at least as exposed as a Germany, a Japan, or a France, would necessarily take a more relaxed attitude. It would insist that the economic interests of nations differ, and that therefore there is inevitably conflict, without thereby denying the desirability of seeking a reconciliation of such conflicts on the most acceptable terms. Indeed the idea that there are conflicts of interest but that it is the duty of governments to seek their reconciliation is a specifically mercantilist approach to international economic relations.

A mercantilist would bring considerations other than purely economic into his calculations regarding the future of international economic relationships. He would recognise the role of national economic and political power in determining the successive outcomes of international economic negotiations and the nature of international economic relationships. Moreover the mercantilist, though he would not accept as proven all the benefits argued by some economists for the open trading system, might consider that system as the one most conducive to the preservation of the Western Alliance, a purpose which he would see as deserving of support even at some domestic social and political cost. He might find the open trading system to be that system within which conflicts of interest between nations, whether within or without the Western Alliance, can most easily be reconciled. He might therefore find it the system of international trade which contributes most to the quality of international relationships.

He would not consider it wrong to take account of domestic political factors in determining policy. There is in mercantilism a sense that the people are entitled to hold their government responsible. In this sense too, mercantilism has a modern sound. It is recognised as one of the political problems of free trade that its benefits are dispersed whereas its costs are only too concentrated and too visible. The costs often take the form of redundancy at particular manufacturing plants. Unfortunately for the free trade case this is a consideration which no government, particularly no democratic government, can ignore especially at a time of high unemployment. It makes it yet more difficult for governments to ignore such considerations in that the benefits of free trade are not merely dispersed, they are to some degree speculative. They are won in competition with other producers from other countries. The competition may be quite tough. The benefits may not be won, at any rate in the short term, and without difficult readjustments. Even in the longer term and with the process of adjustment, by its nature a continuous process, in train, they may not appear to compensate for what has been lost. In the political world the visibility of benefits is important. Even in the economic world, the claim that benefits though dispersed do in fact exist may leave some residual scepticism which mere doctrine will not suffice to overcome.

The strength of the free trade argument is that the readjustment, however painful, is in the end inescapable. But the mercantilist would not need to deny that part of the free trade argument. He might simply feel that the readjustment can be better prepared and better cushioned than pure free trade would permit. And he would note the increasing enthusiasm of free trade economists for all methods of easing the adjustment other than barriers at the frontier. The mercantilist would not see why that particular method must always be ruled out.

Thus 'mercantilism' as it should be understood these days is hardly more protectionist than a great deal of liberal trade theory with its sanction for adjustment policies. Certainly mercantilism denies the existence of benign and automatic regulators which will ensure that all is for the best in the best of all possible worlds, and suggests that the state has a protective, but not necessarily protectionist, role in ensuring that life remains tolerable for its citizens. In other words, unlike *laissez-*

faire, a doctrine strange to human nature, it sees a role for the state in economic affairs, but not an easy role.

The mercantilist in Adam Smith accepted that political considerations could rightly influence economic policy. Nevertheless it was with him that there began the separation between political theory and economic theory which has been damaging to both but particularly to economic theory. This separation was the result of the belief first, that the economic system operates under natural laws; secondly, that these natural laws, if permitted, would create harmony between nations; thirdly, that as politics clearly does not operate under natural laws and does not necessarily tend to harmony, the more politics can be dissuaded from interference in the natural economic order the better it will function; and fourthly, that one could determine with some reliability what would happen if economic laws could be allowed to operate free from political interference. In short, economics could be studied separately from politics. The alternative view that no assumption can be made about a naturally arising harmony, and that it is impossible to separate out actions which are economic from actions which are political because most actions have both characteristics, lost influence in theoretical studies though never in the practical decision making of governments. The economic and political crises of the 1970s and 1980s should have the effect on academic disciplines of tending to the reunification of the study of politics and economics. That which academic disciplines have set asunder, practical commonsense should now once more bring together.

Part II
Arguments for Free Trade

12 Introduction

No attempt will be made here to prove or disprove arguments for free trade. The question will rather be of what value to governments, in deciding action, are the trade policy theories now current. It will be shown that it is not surprising that governments, who have to take responsibility for the consequences of their actions, do not find the arguments for free trade so persuasive as to commit themselves to them without thought of retreat. For the purposes of this book that is enough, though there are some who might feel that in adopting so moderate an objective I am throwing away a handful of aces. Trade theory is in bad repute, even among many economists. The attempted quantifications of the costs and benefits are among the least persuasive parts of the argument. It is the liberal economists themselves, starting with Adam Smith, who as much as anyone have mined their own arguments and muddied them with qualifications.

I begin Part II of this book by discussing the greatest qualification of all, the attempt by modern liberal economists to dissociate free trade from *laissez-faire*. I go on to examine some of the more important economic arguments for free trade, competition, comparative advantage, gains from trade. I question why, if the arguments are so persuasive, liberal economists are so ready to accept defeat at times of recession, and what is the significance of this capitulation to political pressures. I add that to question free trade theory is not the same thing as advocating protection. There are as many question marks against protectionist theories as there are against free trade theories. I examine the principle of non-discrimination and the practice of reciprocity, and review their place in the economic argument for free trade and in the hierarchy of political practicality. Certainly something is left after all the conditions and all the compromises that these days modify the free trade argument even in the mouths of liberal economists. But that residue is at least as much political as economic. And, as I show in an examination of the political arguments, even they depend very much on the circumstances and, while they can be important, have sometimes themselves been exaggerated and can cut both ways.

13 Free Trade and *Laissez-Faire*

THE INVISIBLE HAND

The liberal school claims to have established beyond reasonable doubt that a liberal world trade order conduces to economic prosperity and hence to the maximum of welfare. The freer the trade, the greater and more widespread the benefits. What is quite as important, the benefits are not just widely spread, they accrue to every nation. No nation can do itself as much good as by joining in the drive for freer and freer trade. Indeed what greater combination of benefits could be produced by one single act of policy? Nations would be more secure because the danger of war would recede. They would be more prosperous because competition would lead to all those benefits which Adam Smith had foreseen from the international division of labour based on natural advantages.

However, these claims prove, from the beginning, to have been conditional. From the beginning it was seen that there was a need for a further input which would achieve the chemical reaction of converting the selfish actions of entrepreneurs into the general good. For Adam Smith the additional input was that of 'the invisible hand'. Adam Smith wrote of the entrepreneur that:

> he intends only his own gain, and he is in this, as in many other cases, led by an invisible hand to promote an end which was not part of his intention. . . . By pursuing his own interest he frequently promotes that of the society more effectually than when he really intends to promote it (Smith, 1947, vol. 1, p. 400).

The same idea of an invisible hand appears in Smith's earlier work, *The Theory of Moral Sentiments*.

Some have thought that for Adam Smith the invisible hand was no more than a figure of speech, or that no more was intended by it than an expression of the fact that actions have unforeseen effects. This is to underestimate Adam Smith. He

189

saw that his theories left a problem unanswered. How was it that the self-regarding actions of entrepreneurs produced effects which were beneficial to society at large? The invisible hand was the best he could do by way of answer. The invisible hand was a benign and automatic regulator. Despite the nature and motivation of economic competition, it would ensure that, if only governments would stand aside, all would be for the best. It was also the view of Smith's successors that there was need for an active principle which would catalyse selfish actions into socially beneficial results. For example, Richard Whately, Archbishop of Dublin, wrote in the middle of the nineteenth century that 'through the wise and beneficent arrangement of Providence men thus do the greatest service to the public when they are thinking of nothing but their own gain' (quoted C. R. Fay, 1937, p. 15).

The invisible hand is not a chance, or minor, element in *The Wealth of Nations*. It is the *deus ex machina* of Adam Smith's economics. Whether it is the invisible hand or the interventions of Providence, Adam Smith and his successors were persuaded that something more was needed than *laissez-faire* to convert the self-seeking of individuals into the general good. The invisible hand is too metaphysical a concept for modern liberal economists. But their theories, too, require the assistance of catalysts. To achieve its purposes, free trade is today seen to require the support, if not of an invisible hand, then of adjustment policies and some measure of international economic policy coordination. The problem is that the adjustment policies are likely to be protectionist, and the economic policy coordination may not be practical.

FREE TRADE INTO PROTECTION

The conduct of trade policy, even of free trade policy, has seldom been inspired by *laissez-faire*. For much of the nineteenth century Britain had a competitive lead in manufactured goods. Britain not merely advocated free trade. It advanced boldly along the road towards it. It not merely opened up its own domestic markets but those of its foreign possessions also. This was not a soft, *laissez-faire*, policy. It early appeared that liberalism whether in the form of trade or of private overseas investment could degenerate into imperialism. The investments might be made by companies and individuals but they then often required military protection. Some overseas investors were prepared to accept the full logic of the *laissez-faire* position and provide their own military capability. Others were not able to provide for their own defence and it was not always acceptable to governments that they should do so. The activities of private military forces could lead to scandal. Governments which were prepared to allow their citizens freedom of choice in the location of their overseas investments, subsequently found themselves rallying to the defence of the investments if those choices resulted in trouble. In the nineteenth and early twentieth centuries, government commitment to the protection of its nationals' private investments overseas could and did lead to foreign military adventures if the likely opposition was sufficiently weak. Among the ways in which the world, and the conduct of nations, has improved over recent decades is that these days governments provide insurance against the risks of confiscation rather than an offer of military intervention.

Britain was prepared to fight wars to open up markets and for the purpose of securing payment. 'Unequal treaties' deprived China of its tariff autonomy and its right to regulate its own trade. Enforced free trade, destruction of the right of economic security, was for some countries the price of peace with Britain. Sometimes war, or the threat of war, seemed ill-advised owing to the strength of the opposition. Where this was the case, Britain was perfectly prepared to enter into agreements, for example with France and Germany, to create spheres of political and economic interest. Neither *laissez-faire* theory nor economic liberalism had proved a sufficient safeguard against the use of government power in international economic relations.

THE INVISIBLE HAND BECOMES VISIBLE

W. M. Corden has written that '*the link between the case for free trade and the case for laissez-faire has been broken*' (Corden, 1974, p. 4). In other words the link once existed but does so no longer. Presumably the link existed in the theories of economists because it never existed in the practice of governments. It is the theory that has changed and now permits interventions of some kind for some purposes in the market economy. Interventions can be of various kinds, not all of which would at any time have attracted the opprobrium of the purest free trader. There can certainly be interventions whose purpose is to preserve or strengthen competition. But interventions to preserve or promote competition do not represent the limit of the new thinking behind Corden's conclusion that the case for free trade can now be separated from the case for *laissez-faire*.

What this new case for free trade now permits is intervention by way of assisting 'adjustment' to the impact of market forces on the domestic economy. Along with this type of intervention goes a further permissible type of intervention the object of which is to iron out 'distortions' in the operation of the domestic economy. These distortions can arise out of the difference between the private costs and the public costs of certain kinds of economic activity. The entrepreneur sees his private costs and those are acceptable to him. But the community suffers other costs which do not fall on the entrepreneur, and it may be necessary to subsidise him so that he is persuaded not to inflict these public costs on the community. An example lies in regional policy. An entrepreneur may propose to invest in an area of high employment where, in the judgement of the government, there is some danger of 'over-heating' and hence of igniting inflation. He may be diverted by means of subsidy and planning controls to a development area. We thus get to the doctrine ascribed to Professor James Meade, the doctrine of 'modified free trade'. As its name suggests, modified free trade is not free trade at all. The best that can be said of it is that it is free trade inclination at the mercy of political convenience.

H. G. Johnson was not prepared to rule out the possibility that something more than adjustment assistance will be necessary. In a review of Corden, he wrote:

> given the existence of a situation requiring intervention of some kind, there are many policy options available and generally (but not always) the best policy does not involve intervention in the freedom of *international* trade as such. The general implications of this theme are obvious – a shift of attention from commercial policy and a focus on *laissez-faire* – versus intervention, to a focus on optimal policy-making as such, with trade-policy intervention issues appearing at a

secondary, tertiary, or still lower level of policy analysis (Johnson, 1976, p. 189).

In the same review Johnson adds:

> The current theory of protection leads to only one, rather aseptic, conclusion: that tariffs and similar devices are very unlikely to constitute first-best policies for anything that is thought to require a policy in the first place (Johnson, 1976, p. 198).

Four points shine out from these quite well-known quotations from H. G. Johnson. First, it is accepted that there are circumstances in which 'policies' may be necessary, policies which by their nature are inconsistent with *laissez-faire*. Secondly, although 'optimal policy-making' is recommended rather than '*laissez-faire*', one option, interventions in the freedom of *international* trade, is frowned on (though not entirely ruled out). It is frowned on before the process of optimal policy-making even begins. This seems ill-advised. Optimal policy-making should not begin with a mind prejudiced by one particular economic theory. Thirdly, the possibility must exist that the optimal policies adopted will affect foreign trade even if they do not act directly, at the frontier, to cut foreign imports. Subsidies which are intended to have only a domestic effect, will in fact also affect foreign trade. It is, indeed, very difficult to specify policies which have a significant domestic impact in curing distortions and yet do not affect foreign trade. Fourthly, and despite these first three points, interventions in the freedom of *international* trade are not always ruled out.

It is easily understandable that modern liberal economists should wish to separate the case for free trade from the case for *laissez-faire*. They understand that governments are confronted with problems from which they cannot turn aside. They therefore see it as their duty to provide solutions for such problems, or ways of ameliorating them, which leave intact the main structure of open international trade. But it is a misuse of language to describe the resultant of such interventions as free trade. It is not free trade because such interventions are bound to have their effect on the freedom of international trade. If that be the case, and the objective is no longer free trade but 'optimal' policy-making, no policy can *a priori* be eschewed.

There is in fact a hierarchy not of policies but of approaches to the problems of international trade. There is free trade which is inseparable from *laissez-faire*. Secondly, there is 'modified free trade'. Modified free trade permits interventions which inevitably affect the flow of international trade but it places barriers at the frontier at the bottom of a hierarchy of possible interventions. Modified free trade is an abuse of language. It is neither one thing nor the other, neither free trade nor optimal policy-making. Thirdly, there is pragmatism which attempts to calculate what is in the national interest, while keeping as free as possible from any burden of doctrinal preconceptions. This is the optimal policy approach. In any calculation of optimal policy, pragmatists will not place different types of intervention in any particular hierarchy. In making such calculations, an important consideration for pragmatists will be the likely international impact of any measures of intervention. Finally there are the protectionists. They are the direct opposite of the modified free traders. Whereas the modified free traders place barriers at the frontier at the bottom of their hierarchy of possible interventions, the protectionists place such barriers at the top.

Confronted with these four different approaches to international trade, governments will choose pragmatism. They will not be unduly disturbed if they are then described as mercantilists. This is an attitude from which they are not at all likely to be shifted.

14 The Political Case for Free Trade

INTRODUCTION

Free trade these days needs all the support it can get. If therefore it can be shown that freer trade has a beneficial effect on the quality of international relationships, the conclusion will be welcome to anyone who cherishes freedom in international commercial transactions. Henderson argues thus: 'contemporary trade interventionism has damaging consequences for the international system of states.' It creates endemic friction between governments. Exercises in the use of economic power, for example against developing countries and against Japan, treat the countries concerned as second class members of the international community and represent a departure from 'the principle of the equality of states'. Finally, trade interventionism can undermine attempts to bring order into international economic relationships by bringing into question the rules and procedures of the GATT (Henderson, 1983, p. 15).

The rules and procedures of the GATT provide for a wide range of government interventions in trade by way of escape clauses. The rules and procedures of the GATT are brought into question by the trade interventionism it permits, by the trade interventionism it does not permit, and by the trade interventionism to which it turns a blind but consenting eye. This is not the best time to make a great deal of fuss about it. Nevertheless there is a great deal of truth in the remainder of what Henderson says. But there is another facet to this truth.

'COMMERCE IS RENDERING WAR OBSOLETE'

Emphasis on the political benefits of freer trade is important but it is not new. Cobden saw 'in the Free Trade principle that which shall act on the moral world as the principle of gravitation in the universe – drawing men together, thrusting aside the antagonism of race and creed and language and uniting us in

195

the bonds of eternal peace' (quoted Capie, 1983, p. 20). There
was among some eighteenth- and nineteenth-century thinkers,
an exaggerated expectation of the beneficial political effects of
free trade. J. S. Mill wrote:

> It is commerce which is rapidly rendering war obsolete, by
> strengthening and multiplying the personal interests which
> are in natural opposition to it. And it may be said without
> exaggeration that the great extent and rapid increase of
> international trade, in being the principal guarantee of the
> peace of the world, is the great permanent security for the
> uninterrupted progress of the ideas, the institutions and the
> character of the human race (Mill, 1909, p. 582).

The expectation was not irrational. If governments were no
longer to be involved in trade competition on behalf of their
citizens, one major source of the frictions that lead to war
would have been eliminated. If, moreover, trading relationships
were to develop on an international scale between persons and
companies, the interdependence thus created would be a strong
disincentive to military conflict. Only understanding of the
realities of free trade would have led these politicians and
thinkers to foresee that their hopes exceeded probability. The
realities were, and are, that free trade was an unobtainable
ideal; that governments were not less involved in international
economic relations, they may have been more; that freer trade
required negotiation between governments; that the more trade
there was, the greater the potential for conflict would be; and
that freer trade has an inherent tendency to degenerate into
protectionism, to prevent which constant effort is needed. So
whereas the expectation was not irrational, it was at least
naïve.

'AN EXTENSION OF ALLIANCE POLITICS'

Shonfield described the international organisation of Western
capitalism as an extension of alliance politics (Shonfield, 1976,
p. 76). The key influence in this area of policy has been the
need to preserve the NATO Alliance. The NATO Alliance has
been of vital importance in preserving the open trading system
through a period of economic depression, and indeed before.

Even before the 1970s there were stresses in the system: 'the Kennedy Round had originally been envisaged as an important means of consolidating the Western Alliance' (Shonfield, 1976, p. 18). The Tokyo Round which was conducted amidst the economic turmoil of the 1970s achieved such success as it did largely because of the fear that failure, by exacerbating economic relations, would endanger political relations. The West has been held together not by economic interdependence but through its involvement in a policy of military deterrence. The open trading system is today preserved as the most hopeful way of minimising within the West economic conflict of a kind which might jeopardise the Alliance. It is the most hopeful way mainly because it is what we have, governments have experience of living with it and managing it, and because there would be grave political dangers in trying to change it fundamentally. A central purpose of economic policy since the Second World War has been to find ways of reconciling economic conflicts that have arisen between members of the NATO Alliance and between the OECD countries generally. To preserve the Alliance, economic conflicts have been resolved. Without the Alliance, and the military imperatives that led to its creation, they might well not have been resolved and the postwar international economic system would have collapsed. Freer trade, it was hoped, was one way to avoid disruptive disputes between Alliance members. It was not the only way but it was the way that had been adopted under American leadership.

THE AGRICULTURAL POLICY OF THE EUROPEAN COMMUNITY

The Common Agricultural Policy of the European Community is replete with ironies. To the extent that there is free trade in agricultural products within the Community, it has generated within the Community intense political resentments. To the very great extent that it is protectionist against the rest of the world, it has generated outside the Community resentments no less intense.

It could hardly be claimed that free trade in agricultural products within the European Community, so far as it exists, has served to improve relations between farmers of different nationalities within the Community, nor between their governments. On the contrary, each country's farmers continue to regard the national market as primarily their own and they oppose with any available weapon from riot to blockade any penetration which acts to their disadvantage. Nor are they dismayed by the illogicality of claiming rights to their 'own' market and to the markets of other countries. For who would not prefer both to have his cake and to eat it?

French farmers have been particularly forceful in demanding exclusive ownership of the French market for the products of their agriculture while in no way abandoning their claims to export to the markets of other Community countries. They own their own market on protectionist principles and they export to other member countries on the free trading principle that within Europe their agriculture has a comparative advantage. They return to protectionist principles when they wrap up the whole policy in 'Europeanism' in order to justify quotas and levies on the import of temperate zone agricultural products from countries which have a comparative advantage even against France. French governments have felt bound to listen to so powerful an electoral voice. The Germans have found it politically convenient to protect their agriculture through the intermediary of the European Community rather than to undertake directly a task so alien to the purposes they usually proclaim, the extension of free trade. But when it comes to the crunch they, too, have been willing to offend their Community partners in defence of their agricultural interest. If the British government with so small a percentage of its population working in agriculture listens so attentively to the voice of its farmers, often to the disadvantage of its consumers, there need be no surprise at the even greater sensitivity to these voices of the French government or indeed of the other Community countries, all of whom have a much higher percentage of their population in agriculture than have the British.

Henderson would be right to say that European agricultural protectionism creates endemic friction between governments. But so does 'free trade' in agricultural products within the Community.

THE PRINCIPLE OF THE EQUALITY OF STATES

As quoted above, Henderson has unearthed a 'principle of the equality of states'. This is one of those high-minded confections which find little reflection in the practical business of international relations. It has, no doubt, value in international law in the same way as the equality of citizens should be upheld in domestic law. Civilised behaviour between states demands restraint in the use of power. All should be treated with respect wherever possible. But it is a pointless pretence that states are equal or that an international system, whether political or economic, could be constructed on the basis of an assumption so far removed from reality.

The European Community and the International Monetary Fund belie in their constitutions this principle of the equality of states. The Charter of the United Nations is self-contradicatory, affirming at once the equality of states and the privileged position, and veto, of the five permanent members of the Security Council. The denial of this principle, partly as a result of experience with the League of Nations whose constitution did embody this absurdity, is the fact that alone has made it possible for international organisations to work successfully so far as they do. Perhaps it is the IMF, which denies it most completely, that functions best. It is of no value calling upon the 'principle of the equality of states' as an argument for free trade policies, when as a matter of fact states are not equal, when no such principle is recognised, and when there is no means of enforcement even if it were recognised. In the circumstances it is not surprising that the influence of the Henderson principle on international relations is imperceptible.

FREE TRADE AND THE DEVELOPING WORLD

In relations between the developed and developing worlds, the free trade idea has become a source of grievance rather than of friendship. This is not entirely because free trade does not in fact exist. Developing countries want preference, not freedom for all. Political relations with the developing world may be improved if developed countries open their markets to developing country exports. They will certainly be harmed if developed countries close their markets or demand too much by way of reciprocity.

Many developing countries vigorously rebut any requirement on them to open their own markets. They regard any such demand as an attack on their sovereignty and on their privileged position under Part IV of the GATT. They believed that their privileged access to international markets should not be questioned at any stage of their economic development, even if their industrial capacity comes to exceed that of many developed countries. Developing countries regard any demand from the developed world for reciprocity as a debating point intended to provide specious cover to a denial of their moral and economic right to freer entry into developed country markets, a right which they see as only partially recognised by the various generalised schemes of preferences. Beneficiaries of schemes of preference have objected when developed countries have reduced their own tariffs in the apparent interests of freer trade. Reductions in tariffs between developed countries erode developing country preferences, a source of grievance unashamedly advanced at international conferences. Developing countries have particularly objected to the American demand for free trade in services. Nothing, they think, could be better designed to deprive them of any remnant of financial self-determination. The demand is an arrow pointed at the heart of their sovereignty. And they note that there is no offer of reciprocity from developed countries in respect of the services that some developing countries can offer. American and British civil engineering projects are not yet to be constructed by Korean construction companies.

Any attempt by developed countries to control the impact of developing country imports on their industry or levels of employment is condemned as protectionism. The negotiation of successive Multi-Fibre Arrangements has caused considerable damage to relationships with the developing world. Hong Kong, as the freest market in the world, has some reason for complaint. Entry into its own market is entirely unimpeded. It has not, on that account, found itself exempted from developed country import restrictions. The USA, which is particularly exigent where questions of reciprocity are concerned, has not offered to match Hong Kong's unilaterally conceded freedom of entry to American goods.

Thus unedifying accusations of protectionism fly each way across the two worlds divide. There is a strong input of trade policy humbug in these exchanges. So far as developing countries are concerned, free trade is a political cement only if it is unilaterally conceded. So far as developed countries are concerned, freer trade is a concession to be measured out to mendicants in accordance with political calculation, not liberal principles. Relations between developed and developing countries might well be better if the free trade idea had never emerged, if relations were overtly built on self-interested calculation, and there was less room for humbug and name calling. But the opportunity for so simple an approach to economic relationships is long past. The contrariness of world affairs has chosen the free trade idea as another victim of its purposeful irony. That which was intended to join, instead sets asunder.

CONCLUSION ON THE POLITICAL ARGUMENTS FOR FREE TRADE

Freer trade has not proved a solvent of international friction nor has it had an unmixedly beneficial influence on international relations. Contrary to some expectations, interdependence generates international friction and conflict. There is a political argument for freer trade but it is not one which J. S. Mill or Richard Cobden would have recognised, any more than they could have foreseen that in the late twentieth century peace would be maintained far more because of nuclear deterrence than because of the existence of an open international trading system. There has been massive political support for the open trading system. This has been largely due to the need to preserve the NATO Alliance, and protect it against the disintegrating effect of national economic grievances, especially American economic grievances. Even in these circumstances, dangerous economic tensions have developed between members of the Alliance and within the EEC and OECD, and the system of international economic relationships constructed since the Second World War has been in constant peril.

The political argument is, today, the principal support of the post-war international economic system. But invaluable as is this support, it is a continual question whether it will be sufficient. Economic conflict can be very destructive of international relationships even between countries whose overwhelming political requirement is that they sustain their unity in face of a potential enemy. Economic conflict has not been avoided by freer trade. There is no reason for higher expectations of any likely future arrangements.

15 The Economic Case for Free Trade

INTRODUCTION

There are many economic arguments for free trade which have great intuitive force. It improves the international division of labour. It recognises and respects 'comparative advantage'. There is the maximum wealth creation internationally and a more efficient allocation of resources nationally and internationally. Whether these arguments are as heavily supported by evidence as they are by intuition is more doubtful.

MAXIMISING WORLD WELFARE

We can deal briefly and at once with the argument that unhindered trade flows maximise world welfare. As it has never been tried, no one knows. In any case it is, for governments, the wrong objective. Governments are interested in national welfare. No government in modern times has acted as though it believed that the maximisation of world welfare was a condition sufficient for the maximisation of national welfare. One reason for this lack of action is that a government would not know what to do if it did believe it.

THE IMPORTANCE OF COMPETITION

It is too frequently assumed that, without competition from foreign trade in the domestic market, domestically produced goods must necessarily be more expensive and of lower quality. It is true that competition may promote the production of cheaper and better quality goods (Scott, 1980, pp. 75–7). But it is perfectly possible for cheap and high quality goods to be produced without the benefit of foreign competition in the domestic market. Britain had its highest reputation for quality textiles when it faced little competition in international markets

203

or from imports. The USA produced some products of high repute when foreign trade represented 4 per cent of its GDP. But Japan is the present prime example of this point. Certainly Japanese products meet competition overseas but it would be an exaggeration to claim that the quality of their products was a function of this competition rather than of their national drive to command export markets and thereby achieve for themselves, despite isolation and high dependence on foreign raw materials, a position of relative security. Competition for a secure place in a world of conflicting interests is a likelier incentive to high quality production than competition between firms whether foreign or domestic. In any case the importance of international competition depends on the quality of domestic competition. There may be no foreign competition of a quality superior to that of domestic producers. The conclusion of this argument might be to admit foreign competition only when it adds something new to the domestic market place. This would be a friendly interpretation of Japanese practice.

There is another way in which competition could be combined with protection. Protection, or even the threat of protection, can promote inward investment. Domestic producers will then face competition from highly efficient foreign producers. This can do domestic producers a great deal of involuntary good, so much good, so involuntarily accepted, that they are often the first to complain about any government encouragement to inward investment. Even with protection of the home market, there could still be competition with foreign products in international markets. Whatever limits are placed by protection on competition in the domestic market, no government can limit the competition which its national firms will experience in international markets. This is not intended to be an argument for protection. It merely shows that the argument for free trade cannot depend on the benefits of foreign competition in the domestic market. Circumstances alter cases.

THE UNFORTUNATE CASE OF THE MISALIGNED EXCHANGE RATE

Market forces can operate in ways which, if not unexpected, are at least inconvenient. They can act in brute disregard of what enlightened liberal economists would consider to be the fundamentals of the economic conjuncture. In particular, they appear to show inadequate regard for the 'fundamentals' in moving exchange rates. As a result exchange rates, those subtle determinants of price signals and trade balances, can become 'misaligned'. Experience shows that exchange rates may be misaligned, if misalignment is the right term, for long periods. During those long periods, workforces may become employed or unemployed, countries may go into current account surplus or deficit. One of the problems with misaligned exchange rates is that actual business decisions, including major investments, are based on them. Once those major investments have been made, it is not the least surprising that the business leaders responsible will do everything they can to defend their viability in face of changes in exchange rates. Governments are more likely than not to help their business leaders to justify their investments decisions. One method that may then be used is protection. It may indeed be right to do so. Who knows when the exchange rate will overshoot or undershoot once again?

The misaligned exchange rate is therefore a hiccup in that free flow of resources to mutually beneficial ends upon which liberal economists rely for the accomplishment of their humane purposes. This may not distress some liberal economists. They may place the emphasis on competition from foreign trade irrespective of whether it derives from an exchange rate which has departed from the 'fundamentals'. Other liberal economists accept that if exchange rates are misaligned it can have unfortunate effects not merely on their arguments but on the countries that suffer from it. Misaligned exchange rates can have political consequences. An overvalued exchange rate weakens the constituency for free trade policies by reducing exports and increasing imports. An undervalued exchange rate promotes protectionist pressures abroad.

Yet what is a misaligned exchange rate? Exchange rates are determined by movements of currency in the market. Governments may intervene but it is widely accepted that they cannot intervene successfully contrary to the pressures of 'the fundamentals'. There are many such fundamentals. Some of the fundamentals may be political, for example the political stability and power of a country such as the USA. Another political fundamental may be uncertainty and the desire, so far as possible, to avoid risk in situations in which there are many risks to be avoided. Governments may know some of the fundamentals but not all. They may be able to evaluate some of the fundamentals but not all. They may intervene and then find that their intervention has, momentarily, moved their exchange rate in a direction contrary to that which others, more powerful, have assessed to be in accordance with the fundamentals. Even in this era of information technology, one fundamental may be ignorance. If knowledge was perfect, there would be no room for speculation. The evidence suggests that there is a great deal of room for speculation.

It has been asserted on high authority that 'exchange rate misalignment is a more potent cause of trade friction than overt and covert protection in Japan' (Bergsten *et al.*, 1982, p. 28). There may be some in government or in industry who, while contemplating the problems caused by another country's competitive advantage, may be consoled by the thought that all is due not to improper trade practices, nor to violations of the GATT, but to a misaligned exchange rate. Others may take the view that 'misalignment' is just another liberal economist's fiction or excuse, and that while no doubt a large mede of pity is due to the Japanese for suffering so long and so bravely the consequences of their own undervalued currency, it is up to governments to do what they can to protect their people against unfair competition.

COMPARATIVE ADVANTAGE

Intuition suggests that comparative advantage should be the basis of the international division of labour and should be allowed to be the decisive element in determining the structure of international trade. That is the free trade view. But it is not the view that determines policy. Comparative advantage is not the prime consideration of governments when they enter into international trade negotiations. They then have a combination of concerns, for reciprocity, for economic security and, indeed, for politically powerful vested interests. If the requirements of reciprocity, economic security, and vested interests can be met, comparative advantage may be allowed into the picture as a fourth candidate for consideration. High among the vested interests is the agricultural interest. Agriculture is the industry in which the force of the comparative advantage logic is most determinedly rejected by almost every government.

Governments are not without respectable support for their dismissive attitude. Ricardo's comparative advantage theory showed that, on certain assumptions, trade, by enabling a country to economise on the use of those resources which it employed least efficiently, helped to improve living standards by bringing about the yet more productive use of the same nation's other, and more efficiently employed, resources. The sheer simple delight of this theory is something in its favour. Unfortunately empirical evidence appears not to support it. J. Borkakoti speaks of the 'empirical refutation of the simplistic Ricardian hypothesis'. He then adds: 'Thus, the empirical corroboration which was attempted during the last thirty years and which mostly refuted the Ricardian hypothesis may clearly be taken, in our opinion, as completing the process of "sophisticated" falsification' (Borkakoti, 1983, p. 178). Stein speaks more mildly of the 'lack of any conclusive confirmation of the Ricardian hypothesis' though in a forgiving mood he goes on to comment that this 'may not be unduly disturbing considering the hypothesis' limited practical usefulness' (Stein, 1984, p. 25). Johns tells us that 'no well developed body of theory has yet emerged to provide a satisfactory dynamic theory of comparative advantage', and Dunning that 'The well known principle of comparative advantage holds good only under very restrictive conditions, e.g. the existence of perfect competition, full employment, and immobility of factor services, and is concerned only with efficiency goals' (Johns, 1985, p. 169; Dunning, October 1985, p. 6). Life is made impossibly difficult for governments which wish to be responsible free traders when they are told that the great principles upon which the argument for free trade is based apply only in conditions which will never occur.

None of this means that governments should ignore the idea of comparative advantage. Comparative advantage is a reality, even if a changing reality. Serious costs can be incurred by ignoring comparative advantage. It simply means that the idea of comparative advantage should not be allowed to dictate trade policies to governments. They should take account of it. They should not bow down before it.

COMPARATIVE ADVANTAGE IN ENERGY AND ITS IMPLICATIONS

If a country has cheap and abundant sources of energy, that gives it a comparative advantage in many industries, and not alone those such as aluminium smelting and chlorine production which are particularly energy intensive, or those such as primary chemicals for which natural gas can be a cheap feedstock. There is nothing its competitors can do about such a natural comparative advantage. They can search out areas of productive activity in which the cost of energy is less important. But the energy cheap country may enter those other fields of activity as well. They may actually gain a comparative advantage there as well. As their industrial production will be cheaper and will sell better in a free market, they are likely to have more resources to devote not just to chemicals or to the energy intensive industries but to energy unintensive activities as well. Are their competitors abroad just to curl up and die, or to emigrate? Emigration may indeed be the economic logic of comparative advantage, despite Ricardo's optimistic demonstration of the fact that there will always be *something* that it will be to the advantage of a supremely efficient country to import, even that is if its own efficiency in every industry is superior to that of its foreign supplier. It should be no surprise if emigration is the economic logic of comparative advantage. After all free trade should involve freedom for all the factors of production, including capital and labour. Emigration should always be freely available as an option both for the benefit of the individual and so that market processes can achieve their looked-for benefits. J. S. Mill was aware of this logical consequence of comparative advantage theories.

> The labour and capital which have been sunk in rendering Holland habitable would have produced a much greater return if transported to America or Ireland. The produce of the whole world would be greater than it is, or the labour less, if everything were produced where there is the greatest absolute facility for its production. But nations do not, at least in modern times, emigrate *en masse* (Mill, 1909, p. 578).

One reason why nations can stay at home is that comparative advantage does not rule unchallenged.

A GOVERNMENT ROLE IN CREATING COMPARATIVE ADVANTAGE

The Japanese have their own ways of reversing other countries' comparative advantage and have done so with some success. There is controversy as to the relative importance in Japanese success of government guidance and industrial ingenuity. Industrial ingenuity is not at the disposal of governments, nor, normally, of academic economists. Therefore concentration in jealous European political and economic debate has been on the role of Japanese government, rather than that of Japanese ingenuity. It is not absolutely clear that the Japanese government has been in any way decisive in creating Japanese economic success. The role of the Japanese Ministry of International Trade and Industry (MITI) has often been simply to warn Japanese industry not to push its luck too far in international trade, a valuable role in preserving the open trading system but not central to Japanese industrial performance. Nevertheless the Japanese achievement has encouraged other governments to attempt comparable miracles by means of their own interventionist policies. If in other countries, governments feel that they can improve comparative performance in some wealth-creating area of national activity, and propose to take steps to that end which do not commit them to an unending flow of subsidy, it is not easy on principle to claim that they are wrong. All one can say is that there is now a great deal of evidence to the effect that, however successful the Japanese may have been, government intervention in these matters in the UK has often been exceedingly wasteful.

COMPARATIVE ADVANTAGE WILL NOT RULE UNCHALLENGED

Governments would like their citizens to benefit from cheaper supplies, and cheaper supplies may often be available only from countries with a comparative advantage in their production. But that can be only one consideration. Comparative advantage cannot be the determining factor in international trade negotiations. Governments will not surrender to comparative advantage their right to determine under what conditions they

should permit even the most efficient producer a right to
invade their markets.

GAINS FROM TRADE

The purpose of international trade is national gain. The
question is whether the gains are assured or speculative.

PARETIAN WELFARE ECONOMICS AND THE 'OPTIMUM TARIFF' ARGUMENT

In summarising their conclusions about international trade,
Milner and Greenaway say:

> We have seen then some of the more important international
> and intranational effects of free trade. What kind of comments
> can we make by way of conclusion on the welfare implications
> of free trade? We have already seen how free trade increases
> the welfare of the world as a whole, and of the individual
> country. It is this proposition, that free trade leads to a
> maximisation of world welfare, which provides the classic case
> for unrestricted trade flows. This however is far from being
> the be-all and the end-all of trade and welfare theory, for two
> related reasons. First, countries may gain from free trade in
> unequal proportions. When this is the case, given the tenets
> of Paretian welfare economics, it becomes difficult to comment
> meaningfully on gains and losses. Furthermore . . . the 'best'
> policy for any trading nation *acting in isolation* might not in
> fact be to engage in free trade but rather to impose an
> 'optimum tariff' on its trading partner. The second
> complication in considering the welfare effects of trade is that
> different income groups within a country gain unequally from
> free trade. The relatively abundant factor will generally gain
> from free trade at the expense of the relatively scarce factor.
> Again, given the foundation of Paretian welfare economics, it
> is difficult (though not impossible) to comment on the net
> effects of trade. As Samuelson (1962) showed though, in a
> situation where some gain and some lose, it is still possible to
> show that *everyone* can be better off as a result of free trade,

providing the gainers can compensate the losers (Milner *et al.*, 1979, p. 43, authors' emphases).

How large a gap is opened up in free trade theory by the 'optimum tariff' argument? In accordance with this argument countries with sufficient purchasing power to manipulate world prices can steal welfare by improving their terms of trade by means of some level of tariff protection. If such a country, acting in isolation, might gain more by imposing an 'optimum tariff', it has lost by participating in free trade and thus condemning itself only to those gains which will accrue to it under a free trade system. If free trade can result, as most evidently it can, in losers as well as gainers *within* a country, it is difficult to conceive that it cannot result in losers as well as gainers among countries. Within a country social policy may well be designed so that the gainers compensate the losers. Everyone may then gain. As between countries no transfers large enough to cancel out the losses can be expected. International generosity is not the most prolific form of that admirable human characteristic. Many gainers will, in their pride, condemn the losers as having got exactly what they deserved.

RETURNS TO SCALE

The argument which is perhaps most telling in favour of gains from trade is the argument from returns to scale. Returns to scale may yield very large gains. But the argument from increasing returns to scale implies both reduced competition, and hence conflict with national competition laws and policies, and a national vulnerability to the power of major foreign corporations which itself would introduce unacceptable uncertainties into policy. There is usually room for debate whether the returns to scale justify the loss of competition.

In discussing returns to scale in the European context, one set of authorities comes to the conclusion that 'if a case is to be made for an open and liberal trading environment, then a necessary concomitant of this must be a willingness not to bar European firms from effectively competing in world markets on the basis of inappropriate "domestic" criteria' (Pearce *et al.*,

1985, pp. 154–5). These same authorities direct severe criticism against the German Cartel Office for not appreciating that within a quite open trading environment, 'competition must be seen in the setting of the world market' (Pearce *et al.*, 1985, p. 164). This is a favourite argument of industrialists who wish to achieve, by a policy of merger, market power in their 'own' part of the world market, that is in the domestic or, possibly, European market. They know that the world market is not so open as to deny them considerable advantage from their market power in their domestic market, provided only that they have the technology, quality and productivity. The German Cartel Office, and other national administrators of competition policy, have good reason to insist on determining the existence of effective competition not on the basis of theories about returns to scale or open world markets but on the actual facts about the actual competitive position that they see before them. It is ironic that this line of argument leads to such severe criticism of the competition policy of the most successful industrial country in Europe.

Trade can reduce as well as increase opportunities for economies of scale. Exporters of capital sometimes appear to have it as their object to reduce the opportunity to achieve economies of scale in a recipient country. The incursion of IBM into European markets as a producer of computer hardware has made it more difficult to achieve economies of scale in computer manufacture in Europe. Of course IBM has a comparative advantage in computer manufacture. Therefore European countries benefit from having IBM operating manufacturing plants on their soil. But there is no reason to assume that IBM's comparative advantage is god-given and permanent. It might be easier for Europe to compete with IBM if Europeans could exploit the whole of the opportunities for economies of scale which a European market could provide. Equally, and understandably, IBM does not wish to encourage any such development even if it should prove to be the case that their market leadership is actually slowing down the pace of technological progress.

The returns to scale argument leads to conclusions that are paradoxical from the point of view of anyone conscious of the continuing power of considerations of national economic security and the key role within those considerations of the current account. To achieve the maximum returns to scale, and hence the strongest possible *domestic* producer, massive mergers are necessary. But if there are massive mergers, competition is prejudiced unless there are also massive imports from foreign producers. The effect, therefore, of seeking maximum returns to scale consistent with the maintenance of competition is to prejudice the current account of the balance of payments unless in practice the world market is so open, so uncommitted to sourcing supplies from some earlier entrant, as to make it likely that additional imports will be rapidly counterbalanced, or more, by new exports. Given the actual state of the world market, it is understandable that governments may treat arguments based on returns to scale with the same scepticism as they bring to the free trade arguments generally.

ADJUSTMENT COSTS

Against any gains from trade have to be set, among other costs, the adjustment costs. The adjustment costs will often be paid before the gains are reaped, sometimes long before. It is therefore necessary, before claiming overall gains, to reduce both the gains and the costs to a present value. This again would be a calculation in which the contributions of faith, judgement, and wishfulfilment, would be much more visible than those of any laws of economics. Nevertheless, it is authoritatively claimed that the gains from trade very greatly exceed the adjustment costs. Yet if the gains do so greatly exceed the adjustment costs, it is difficult to see why this is not as apparent to governments as to economists, and why the economists who make these claims feel it so necessary to place emphasis on the importance of adjustment assistance, even to the extent of requiring that it be an international obligation on governments to adopt effective national adjustment policies (Bergsten *et al.*, 1982, pp. 12, 76). The truth is that the emphasis on adjustment policies arises rather from the uncertainty of benefits than from any conviction that liberalisation has as its manifest destiny a major increment of economic welfare. An international obligation to adopt effective national adjustment policies is as likely to lead to an escalation of protection as to a new phase of liberalisation.

HECKSCHER-OHLIN AND ASSOCIATED SUBJECTS

What generates international trade? The leading trade determination theory is that ascribed to Heckscher and Ohlin. Their theory's most significant prediction is that a country will export the good that is relatively intensive in the use of its relatively abundant factor. This theory has failed to gain anything like unanimous support. Indeed it emerges that the trouble, not unexpected, with trade determination theories is that in an attempt to incorporate within their scope the whole of international trade experience, either they demand assumptions that are unrealistic such as perfect competition and full employment, or they descend to such banalities as that the same forces that give rise to trade within countries creates trade between them or that the generation of international trade has something to do with differences in technological levels.

Stein having noted among economists a 'budding awareness of the need to evaluate new hypotheses' goes on to say:

> By persistently maintaining it [Heckscher-Ohlin] in the *foreground*, the economic profession brazenly displays an inertia and conservatism which appears to flout the open mindedness and impartiality which they would have us believe they profess. . . . Considering that in manufactured goods alone, there is such a diversity of product characteristics, it is not surprising that various alternative hypothesis each have a glimmer of truth. Given that so many factors (of which some may be vague yet important. e.g. promptness, reliability, reputation for quality, after sales service, cultural-political ties, etc.) influence export performance, it would seem that the search for *the* solitary yet comprehensive theory is a chimera which should be abandoned. The pragmatic and eclectic approach, although not aesthetically satisfying to our mathematical and general equilibrium purists, is the only means by which we are likely to gain any practical and meaningful insights into the nature of contemporary trade flows (Stein, 1984, pp. 33, 49).

This is wisdom indeed.

Borkakoti asks: 'Is the theorem on gains from trade empirically corroborated?' He answers: 'There are certain economic propositions which do not really yield testable hypotheses . . .

and the general theorem on gains from trade falls largely in this category.' He adds:

> Economic policies are supposed to be based on the currently accepted economic theories. A great amount of confusion is created by the fact that economists have the propensity to cling to the empirically refuted hypothesis. They also have a good deal of inability to sort out their differences of opinion. These observed phenomena about the economists exist not because of a unique academic sociology but primarily because of the nature of the subject.

As a final expression of this gathering pragmatism, he warns: 'Careful attention should be given to the economy's specific characteristics before free trade policy is recommended' (Borkakoti, 1983, pp. 192, 194). The only trouble is that 'conscience doth make cowards of us all; and thus the native hue of resolution is sicklied o'er with the pale cast of thought, and enterprises of great pith and moment with this regard their currents turn awry, and lose the name of action.' If once one is allowed to think about it, it is unlikely that any progress towards free trade will occur, except under the impulse of an overmighty power like the USA acting as much on the basis of political calculation and of its own perceived economic advantage as from devotion to the interests of the world as a whole.

The reason, no doubt, why economists cling to the empirically-refuted hypothesis is that there are in economics rather few empirically-verified hypotheses. It is not to the discredit of economics that it is not a science. Discredit arises only when the insights of economics are raised to the dignity of natural laws without the evidential basis to justify it.

WHY WEAK ECONOMIES NEED FREE TRADE AND WHY THEY DO NOT ALWAYS GET IT

One can mount an argument to the effect that those developed countries which are least competitive, least flexible in their working practices, economically weakest, need free trade most as the most hopeful way of dissolving out restrictive practices of all kinds. There are two problems. One lies in the judgement

which governments have to make as to the social acceptability
of policy. The short term is the enemy of the long term. The
short term is highly valued in any discounted present-day
valuation of future benefits. Great as are the costs of inflexibility,
the costs of social discontent can be much higher, certainly in
the short term. The second problem is that it can make the task
of managers more difficult if they are having to persuade
collaboration out of their workforce at a time when the market
is declining and forcing compulsory redundancy. For this
purpose it does not much signify if the redundancies are brought
about by recession or by imports. On the other hand some
recent experience has shown that this second problem can be
overcome. Due to fear of unemployment at a time of high
unemployment, collaboration in modern technology and modern
production methods can sometimes be compelled by strong or
ruthless management. Governments should not be too easily
dismayed. Freer trade may be the best weapon they have to
hand.

THE BL EXAMLE

During the battle for BL, there was a great deal of pressure to
shut out foreign imports in order, supposedly, to assist in the
company's rebirth. To submit to such pressure would have
been absurd. It would simply have strengthened the resistance
of the BL trade unions to the necessary changes. A ban on
imports, or even a substantial reduction of imports, would have
handed the consumer over to British manufacturers. It would
have made BL appear fireproof, and the task of exacting the
necessary level of cooperation from the workforce would have
been made impossible. Sir Michael Edwardes, former Chairman
of BL, gives in his book *Back from the Brink* his account of how,
like Atlas, he held BL aloft. Unlike Atlas, he had the assistance
of princely sums of public money. He is, therefore, predictably
generous in his appraisal of Ministers at the Department of
Industry through whom was funnelled these hundreds of
millions of taxpayers' money.

   Predictably also he is ungenerous to those Ministers at the
Department of Trade who wished to accommodate, at least to
some extent, the British consumers' evident wish to buy

imported cars. There was the usual unholy protectionist alliance between manager and trade union leader. The author has been criticised by both Sir Michael Edwardes and by Frank Chapple, formerly General Secretary of the Electricians' Union, for his failure, when Secretary of State for Trade, to take stronger action to limit imports of cars. Both, with untypical timidity, deny that they are protectionists. Of course they are protectionists. Their denial merely serves to show how that word frightens strong men. Both would have been delighted by a total ban, particularly of Japanese and Spanish imports. A rather more liberal policy towards imports than that advocated by the protectionist collective of Michael Edwardes and Frank Chapple was an essential component in the salvation of BL from the restrictive practices that had so badly damaged it. For Sir Michael protection by subsidy was not enough. He wanted protection by higher barriers against foreign imports as well.

WHY SHOULD PERIODS OF RECESSION ERODE SUPPORT FOR FREE TRADE?

'Periods of rising unemployment always erode support for liberal trade policies' (Blackhurst etc., 1977, p. 1). This seems odd given the claimed benefits of freer trade and the alleged inappropriateness of import restrictions as a way of relieving unemployment. The medicine of free trade is increasingly rejected under the very circumstances in which its advocates see it as having particular curative properties, that is under circumstances of economic recession. This is the more remarkable in that some economists do not simply regard free trade as a cure for recession. They think that the lack of free trade, and the consequent failure of economies to adjust, is a principal cause of recession and will inhibit recovery to more satisfactory rates of growth. In other words, if governments wait for a higher rate of growth before advancing further towards free trade, they will wait in vain. This is a powerful argument if it can be believed. Governments have to decide whether to believe it or not. And economists have to decide how strongly they will advocate it.

Free trade is not a new and untried medicine. Britain had decades of experience of it before it abandoned it under the pressure of recession in 1931 – the very condition to which in the view of liberal economists, but not of Keynes, its medicinal properties would have been most appropriate. Best of all, there is the post-war experience of freer trade associated with a period of an unparalleled economic growth. Thus there is considerable experience of free trade under conditions which should have enabled it to demonstrate its curative or stimulatory potential. It has been tried and in the view of the doctors, the liberal economists, it has been a great success. Admittedly it has certain side effects but none of them have been grave enough to lead the doctors to withdraw the prescription. But governments have not been moved. Never has so much persuasion and so much negotiation been required to get governments to act in their own clear best interests. For there is nothing so clearly in the interests of a government than that it should be able to present to its people the statistics of economic success and claim responsibility for them. If free trade is the best answer to recession, surely governments will see it and act on it.

If it is under threat today, despite a long period since the Second World War of increasingly liberalised international trade, it must be that the economic arguments for free trade have been found in practice less powerful than liberal economists believe them to be, and certainly less powerful that the desire of governments for some control over national destinies. 'Autonomy should not be viewed as an end in itself; the freedom to act against one's underlying interests is not worth much' (Henderson, 1983, p. 18). In fact, autonomy of national decision making, especially at times of recession, is a more important consideration than Henderson is yet prepared to admit, even though it does mean freedom to act mistakenly and against underlying interests. The freedom to act is so important that governments are prepared to risk the possibility that they will sometimes act unwisely.

Blackhurst, Marian and Tumlir attempt an explanation of the phenomenon that recession erodes support for free trade although it is the very circumstance under which, in their view, free trade policies should be most in demand. Free trade, they point out, can produce a permanent redistribution of income between the various domestic groupings. The loss of employment due to imports may be regarded as the responsibility of governments that have failed to provide the necessary protection. The gains in employment due to additional exports are attributed to the efforts of those industries. Job losses are likely to be concentrated and visible. Job gains may be highly dispersed. Much the same is true for owners of capital. Those whose ownership of capital is concentrated in failing import-competing industries see clearly what is happening, blame the government, and form a powerful pressure group to secure better protection. Those who gain from the new export opportunities see their successes, and the better incomes they derive, as the reward for their own entrepreneurial drive (Blackhurst *et al.*, 1977, pp. 30–4).

'This asymmetry in the perception of the results of the policy decision only reflects a lack of understanding which it is the first function of the politicians themselves to remedy' (Blackhurst *et al.*, 1977, p. 50). But if so, it is the first function of the economist to provide the politician with the necessary persuasive arguments. If there is high and persistent unemployment representing in the public mind a failure in policy prescription both by politicians and by economists collectively, the task of persuading the redundant worker to see the national benefits arising from his redundancy is likely to prove beyond human skills. Faced by such an impossible task the politician may well try a little selective protection as a way of showing that he is doing something to help to avoid the distress of redundancy. He may also, thereby, deflect pressures for more serious and widespread restrictions of imports.

Yet the courage of governments is also undermined by the discovery that it is not just they who are doubtful about the virtues of freer trade at times of recession. Many economists lose their free trading courage when faced by recession. Even liberal economists accept rather easily that recession brings about a retreat from free trade. Henderson is himself somewhat ambivalent in his attitude to the current economic conjuncture. On the one hand he does not wish to surrender the great liberal point that progress to free trade would actually help with our present problems. On the other hand he wishes to show himself the practical man of affairs conscious of the difficulties of making progress with free trade under present economic conditions. He says: 'Much will depend on whether a sustained economic recovery is achieved. At the same time, however, a more liberal trading system would itself contribute to recovery' (Henderson, 1983, p. 18). The practical man of affairs knows that free trade is a medicine which is likely to be administered only when the world is not ill, and which will not work, or is not available for work, when the world gets sick.

Henderson's ambivalent view seems to have been shared in his time by M. Olivier Long, then Director-General of the GATT. He saw a successful conclusion of the Tokyo Round as providing a key to economic progress. Yet it was Long who, in a subsequent lecture calling for the progressive opening up of trade, said: 'This is no plea though for free trade which is clearly impracticable in present circumstances' (*The World Economy*, June 1978, p. 255). Once again we have the paradox of the medicine that allegedly cures but which cannot be administered. To what is this paradox to be attributed, to the qualities of the medicine, or to the doctors' lack of faith in it? It is difficult to escape the conclusion that the doctors retreat into pessimism because they are not sure of their analysis or of their remedies. They have very good reason to be unsure because there is little evidence for either their analysis or their remedies.

The caution of the free trade doctors can therefore only be respected. Nothing is more dangerous in economics than to have remedies actually tested. The march of the post-war world towards free trade has not prevented recession. If a free trading system is insufficient to prevent a decline into recession, it is not immediately self-evident why an extension of the system should encourage emergence from it. Its influence for good is clearly not great, or at least not decisive. This important lesson is illustrated by the failure of the Tokyo Round of multilateral trade negotiations to achieve the economic purposes claimed for it. The Tokyo Round was successfully completed in 1979. The success failed to give the boost which Long anticipated. Though it may, temporarily, have taken some pressure off the American President, the Tokyo Round failed, despite its claimed success, to serve as an effective constraint on gathering protectionism. Any hope of such a boost was drowned by the second oil shock. The world economic recession deepened. It was shown once again that more or less free trade is of marginal significance to the progress of the world economy as compared with other more powerful factors. Only when the USA began to run its enormous current account deficit did the clouds begin to lift, just a little.

None of this means that protection is as an economic remedy any better. To be fair to protectionism, it is not an increase in the general level of protection that has in recent years slowed down the expansion of world trade. To the extent that protectionism has escalated, it is an effect rather than a cause. The slowdown has been due to the recession. This is an epoch in which the quality of international economic cooperation has deteriorated. Yet there has continued a remarkable level of international cooperation in the general resistance to any major escalation of protectionism. The battle to preserve the open trading system has been assisted by the pragmatism of governments. They have been willing to implement some selective protection in areas of particular sensitivity. They have shown sufficient understanding of the actions of their trading partners in sometimes acting likewise. Tribute is overdue to the good sense with which so far these problems have been handled.

HOW IMPORTANT ARE THE ECONOMIC ARGUMENTS FOR FREE TRADE?

However intuitively attractive the arguments for free trade, their actual influence on governments is necessarily marginal at best, and practical men are likely to think that now is not the time for much progress towards freer trade. The problem lies in actually evaluating the arguments for free trade. Persuasive as they sound, what do they in practice amount to? How do they compare in importance with the social factors making for faster or slower growth in a particular country? Would it now be argued that the world's rate of economic growth during the first twenty-five years after the Second World War would have been even faster had progress towards freer trade been more rapid? Would Britain's rate of economic growth have been comparable with that of Japan if it had been more open to foreign imports? Has Japan suffered in its rate of economic growth from its protectionism? Such assertions, if made, could only be made as a matter of faith, not of evidence.

One does not have to be a protectionist to be sceptical about the strength of the economic case for free trade or a liberal to be sceptical about the economic case for protection. Under both systems trade will move and the differences are unlikely to have major economic effects. After an historical examination of the economic value of tariff protection, Capie comes to the magisterial conclusion that 'In international trade theory, neither the argument for free trade nor for protection seems very strong' (Capie 1893, p. 1). Given the social forces that determine economic progress, what seems clear is that trade policy, as it is in practice found operating in the world, cannot be a major factor. To the extent that it can be a factor, it will be used in a calculating way. In making those calculations, governments will not be greatly influenced by the economic textbooks. There is a danger that liberal economics will be far more influential in providing the rhetoric than in deciding the policies.

16 Non-Discrimination

NON-DISCRIMINATION FUNDAMENTAL TO THE LIBERAL APPROACH

Non-discrimination is fundamental to the liberal approach to international economic relations. Liberal economists have support for their views from summit meetings of heads of government. For example in the Downing Street Declaration which concluded the Summit Meeting held in London in May 1977, it was resoundingly stated: 'Policies of protectionism foster unemployment, increase inflation and undermine the welfare of our peoples. We are therefore agreed on the need to maintain our political commitment to an open and non-discriminatory world trading system.' Yet, on this evidence, all the governments represented at the summit were engaged in fostering unemployment, increasing inflation, and undermining the welfare of their peoples, because each one of them was in greater or lesser degree, and none of them in small degree, protectionist. Each one of them was to a greater or lesser degree, and none of them to a small degree, conducting discriminatory trade policies of one kind or another.

NON-DISCRIMINATION AND THE DOMESTIC MARKET

When liberal economists speak of non-discrimination, they are not only speaking of non-discrimination as between foreign countries. They are speaking also of non-discrimination as between the home market and foreign markets. Liberals condemn not just tariffs and import quotas as departures from the liberal norm but any instruments which impinge directly and significantly on trade, whether they be export subsidies, domestic subsidies or the tieing of aid. In short, governments are not to seek out types of intervention which favour, or attempt to favour, their own country because to do so would be discriminatory.

223

There is no experience of such total commitment to the principle of non-discrimination. A high level of faith is therefore necessary in anyone who advocates it as a policy, and an even higher level of courage in any government that actually adopted it. The nearest example is Hong Kong and that example may be taken as encouraging. But governments might hesitate to commit themselves to an economic policy founded only on the experience of Hong Kong. At least they would want some possibility of retreat if so exposed a position was found to be untenable. Additionally they might wonder whether they were not entitled to countervail, by discriminatory action in favour of their own countrymen, the discrimination in favour of theirs that they perceived in the actions of foreign governments. Despite liberal enthusiasm for non-discrimination, there is no Queen's Award for imports.

NON-DISCRIMINATION AND THE GATT

Discrimination in favour of one's own countrymen is understandable if not, in liberal eyes, forgivable. Is the GATT principle of non-discrimination between foreign states any more practical in international trade? The United States after the war at first wished to eliminate British imperial preference. But the USA had to wait for quite a time before imperial preference disappeared, and even then it was not because of any GATT rule. British imperial preference was at first protected within the GATT by the 'grandfather clause' which permitted the retention of pre-existing preferential arrangements. After many years, imperial preference was phased out. This began when the newly independent members of the Commonwealth decided that it was no longer in their interests to be tied in this way to a declining political and economic power. The final blow to imperial preference came with British entry into the European Community. British adherence to the common external tariff of the Community deprived member states of the Commonwealth of their preference in the British market. Even the older independent members of the Commonwealth then saw no further benefit in conceding preferential advantages to Britain in their markets.

The GATT has from the beginning permitted preferential

arrangements within free trade areas and common markets. This can be regarded simply as the acceptance of political necessity. Throughout the post-war period, the principle of non-discrimination has had to fight against the priority the signatories of GATT have given to political considerations and political relationships. Various international groupings have been formed. The reasons have been mainly political even where they have had a strong economic element. These groupings have regarded discrimination against non-members as a component in the cement that binds them together. The European Community is the major example. The USA was interested in the construction of a politically and economically sound Western Europe. This was an objective which it believed would be aided by the formation of the European Community, and it considered it more important than its other economic objective of ending discrimination against its exports. Even at the time of the Marshall Plan, the USA was pressing its European allies to ignore Article 1 of the GATT, the Article dealing with general most favoured nation treatment. Like the Stuart monarchs in a different context, the USA has always regarded itself as entitled to a dispensing power where the laws of international trade are concerned. This claim has at any rate this justification, that, as the prime instigator of the legislation, there could be no more suitable depositary for a right of unilateral repeal.

DISCRIMINATION IN FAVOUR OF LESS DEVELOPED COUNTRIES

Part IV of the GATT, introduced in 1963, specifically permits discrimination and preferences for the benefit of developing countries. Developing countries have long campaigned for a privileged position in international trade and it was considered politically wiser to concede the demand within the context of the GATT rather than to allow UNCTAD a significant role in the regulation of international trade. This is not the limit of the privileges developing countries enjoy in international trade. Their principal privilege is the right to protect without exposure to anything like the pressure and criticism a developed country would attract in comparable circumstances. Many economic arguments are available particularly from liberal sources to the effect that developing countries have been ill-advised in exercising these privileges. They have thereby been encouraged to protect uneconomic industries and to transfer resources from already very poor rural populations to possibly less poor urban populations. They have provided industrial countries with an additional excuse to discriminate against them whenever it is politically convenient to do so.

The developing countries do not merely fight to retain the privileges they have. Under the slogan of the New International Economic Order, they have since 1974 demanded even more. They have stepped up their demands for free or preferential access to the markets of the west for their manufactured exports. As Henderson puts it: all this 'is based on the idea that the adoption of liberal trade policies is a duty that the rich countries owe unilaterally to the poor, for whom such policies will in general be inappropriate' (Henderson, 1983, p. 10). It may be that developing countries are entirely mistaken in their rejection of the non-discrimination principle. But there can be no doubt that this is what they, or most of them, want. It is a demand made for a combination of political and economic reasons.

The political reasons include the belief that there is a strong public opinion in some developed countries willing to grant them some privileges. More important, they include the desire shared with developed countries to retain the maximum possible control over their own destiny. For them, interdependence is just one more risk they are asked to face in a world careless of their interests, and in which the only unconditional support they can rely on in an emergency is that derived from such strength and such independence as they can secure for themselves. The economic reasons include a non-liberal approach to the problems of economic development. Many developing countries believe in a high degree of government intervention, and in planning and control as a means to the promotion of economic development. This non-liberal approach is clearly in the political interest of certain political and economic elites. It puts power in their hands, and in those of development economists, even though seldom is there an administrative structure capable of exercising that power efficiently or even honestly. But the non-liberal approach continues to persuade development economists.

A VESTED INTEREST IN DISCRIMINATION

Once some discriminatory preferential advantage has been conceded whether to developing countries as a whole or to a group of particular developing countries, they become a vested interest striving against any dilution of their preference. When the scheme of general preferences was introduced, developing countries became an enemy of further tariff reductions between developed countries unless action was taken to avoid any erosion of the preference they had been granted. When preferences were granted within the Lomé Convention to the associated African, Caribbean and Pacific countries associated with the European Community, they became a vested interest against any improvements in the general scheme of preferences because such a general improvement would erode their own particular advantages.

The principle of non-discrimination invites developing countries to abandon their preferences. But who is to say with the degree of certainty that a government normally requires before it voluntarily abandons a trick it has won in international trade, that the countries beneficiary of these arrangements would be better advised to abandon them and open themselves to a non-discrimatory trading system? Such unilateral gestures are rare. At least the developing countries beneficiary of these arrangements would want something of comparable value in return. It is not easy to see what it could be.

FREE TRADE AREAS AND COMMON MARKETS

We have seen that the principle of non-discrimination is inconsistent with the creation of free trade areas and common markets. Yet in the post-war world these have been considered helpful in their time, economically as well as politically, and some of them continue to command the loyalty of member states. Henderson, somewhat naïvely, regards the formation of the European Community as a part of the 'liberalising aspect of western trade policies' (Henderson, 1983, p. 9). But if non-discrimination is the highest objective of liberal economics, he is premature in his enthusiasm. Preferential arrangements once created tend to become entrenched, among developed countries as much as among developing countries. Common markets are not a step in the direction of non-discrimination. They are a further guarantee that it will never be achieved.

COMMUNITY PREFERENCE WITHIN THE EUROPEAN COMMUNITY

The formation of the European Community depended on an act of discrimination entitled 'Community preference'. The common external tariff is one expression of Community preference. Discrimination is implied whenever there is talk of creating a 'European' technology protected by the purchasing power of European governments, whenever there is action to support a European aerospace industry with orders from European airlines, airlines whose deficits are financed directly or indirectly by European Governments, and whose ordering policy is subject to intense political pressure. There is discrimination whenever the Community as a whole acts to protect industries in member countries whether as in the Multi-Fibre Arrangement or in voluntary export restraint agreements. There is discrimination in the Community's trade relations with the African, Caribbean and Pacific countries, relations which are regulated under the Lomé Convention. There are preferential arrangements with some Mediterranean countries and with the countries of the European Free Trade Area. The highest expression of Community preference is the Common Agricultural Policy, a policy which commits the further aggression against liberal economics of defying the principle of comparative advantage and which has proved largely inviolable against the pressures both of commonsense and of multilateral trade negotiations.

It might be argued that none of these discriminatory features of the European Economic Community, other than the free internal market itself, is essential to its existence. That would be an idle pretence. It is a matter of history that France would have refused to grant preference to the industrial products of other members of a European Economic Community, notably the Federal Republic of Germany, had there not been a Community preference for agriculture, notably French agriculture. The Community exists out of a spirit of common purpose in which 'Europeanism', and Community preference, are key elements. The European political unit has found its initial expression in a Common Market. But at the end of the road there is to be something called 'European Union', a description both obscure and meaningful: obscure as to the proposed structure and content of European Union, meaningful in its foreboding of discrimination against non-members for ever and ever.

Whatever the meaning to be attached to the idea of 'European Union', the European Community is not, even today, simply a free trade area. One argument raised against greater reductions in tariffs during the Tokyo Round was precisely that each reduction in the common external tariff diluted the cohesion of the Community. If the tariff disappeared altogether and the Community conceded other demands such as an end to discrimination in public purchasing policy, what would be left of the Community other than the Common Agricultural Policy? If that went too, the whole economic basis of European political unity would have been abandoned at least until the road could be opened to a common currency, an ambition well beyond the present political and economic horizon.

It is of the essence of the Community that it is a powerful trading bloc negotiating as one. The motivation for this unity of action is the fear that if the individual members depended only on their own strength, they might well find themselves powerless to extract from the USA and Japan reciprocal advantages in return for concessions granted. They do not find 'the principle of the equality of states' to be an active ingredient of their own experience. The fact that strength is felt to be needed in such negotiations is evidence that the negotiations concerned are of a kind in which, without the necessary power, interests in peril will not be defensible. The USA has never hesitated to use its economic power when it calculated that it would be a more useful instrument of persuasion than diplomacy. The member countries of the European Community wished to be in a position to resist the pressure of American economic power, and also to bring their own collective economic power to bear on recalcitrant foreigners of all kinds. The European Community is an expression of mercantilism in its historic sense. Mercantilism was in part concerned with reinforcing the authority of the state. European Community trade policy is in part concerned with reinforcing the authority of Community institutions.

NON-DISCRIMINATION AND INTERNATIONAL FRIENDSHIP

It may be claimed as a political plus for non-discrimination that it makes for more friendly relations between different states. Although presented as a liberal *economic* objective, non-discrimination can perhaps more reasonably be thought of as a *political* objective related to Henderson's principle of the equality of states. However it is not invariably the case that non-discrimination makes for more friendly international relations. Frequently, a sense of justice or even a difference in economic theory, suggests discrimination in protective measures as politically more acceptable. When, for example, in 1978, Canada took non-discriminatory action under GATT Article 19 it caused great annoyance in the UK. The UK was not the cause of Canada's difficulties at that time. Canada had a considerable trade surplus with the UK. Why, it was asked, other than the dogmatic requirements of Article 19, should Canada act against UK trade? Why should it cause the UK, which had problems enough, further problems?

CONCLUSION

The principle of non-discrimination is at war with political realities. It is inconsistent with every instinct and with every policy of national governments. Even the Americans, who are understandably keen on non-discrimination abroad, regard that wish as subsidiary to many of their political objectives, and certainly have no intention of operating in accordance with a principle that would deny them the right to discriminate in favour of their own citizens. If non-discrimination is the key to better international relationships, there seems to be considerable evidence that God does not wish international friendship to advance too far too quickly, at any rate by that particular road. The advocacy of non-discrimination provides deeper insights into the abstract nature of liberal economics than into the problems of economic policy-making.

17 Reciprocity

There is free trade and there is reciprocity.

The principle of reciprocity emerges whenever real business is to be transacted in trade negotiations. While the disciples of Adam Smith have claimed intellectual and moral victory over the errors of mercantilism, the real power has remained in the hands of the practical men who play the mercantilist game of reciprocity.

Reciprocity has different objectives from those of free trade. Its objectives are political rather than economic, to absorb international pressures rather than to advance liberal utopias. Reciprocity does not create free trade. It may create freer trade, a more open international trading system. On the other hand, in different circumstances, it may result in withdrawals from freer trade. Reciprocity allocates only a relative importance to comparative advantage and the international division of labour. Reciprocity has never been more than protection to some degree disarmed. Reciprocity is concerned with all those matters wrapped up in the concept of 'economic security', that is that governments should not voluntarily give more than they think they are getting in international negotiations, and, above all, should, if at all possible, retain the discretion to put things right if they go wrong. Reciprocity is mercantilism in action. It is not free trade.

Reciprocity is not good enough for the true liberal, and on his own grounds, with good reason. A liberal should not accept that if there is no other way of making progress towards the desirable objective of freer trade, then there is nothing wrong in paying this tribute to the false gods of mercantilism. It may be suggested to him that if the objectives can be the objectives of economic liberalism, there is no reason why the methods should not be the methods of mercantilism. The true liberal will see through that argument. The methods, in fact, mirror the reality. The principle of reciprocity conditions not just the procedures but the outcome. If, in a trade negotiation, what has been exchanged is believed to be an equal quantum of advantage, and subsequently it is found that more has been conceded than has been gained, defensive mechanisms will at once be brought into play. What is more, the governments concerned will be ensuring that no concession made during the course of negotiation prevents the subsequent use of defensive mechanisms if experience proves it necessary. If defensive mechanisms do not exist they will be created. If they cannot be created, the concessions will not be made, or if they are made, only under great pressure. Governments will not simply be employing the rhetoric of reciprocity, they will be drying out their powder in case a return to reciprocity has in some way to be enforced. The road of reciprocity can also be the road to protection.

FREE TRADE

A brief recapitulation of the doctrine of free trade will underline the difference between free trade and reciprocity. The doctrine of free trade dictates free access for foreign products *irrespective* of what other countries may do. The logic of free trade is, therefore, unilateral government action against obstacles to imports. The benefits may increase if other countries also open their markets but they are not dependent on it. The current account can be left to look after itself.

The free trade position is therefore clear enough. Apart from the control of restrictive business practices, all governments, and if necessary each government separately, should get out of the regulation, promotion, and restriction of trade by any means whatever, whether it be by tariff, quota, public purchasing policy, enforcement of national standards, subsidy, tax arrangements, Queen's Awards for export achievement, or any other of the multifarious devices by which governments attempt to promote exports and reduce imports. Action to open the domestic market should not await or be dependent on action by foreign governments. If those foreign governments desire to subsidise their exports, so be it. They will thereby impose on themselves a cost, and on their customers a benefit. If goods are dumped, so be it. Customers will get the advantage of a cheaper supply. If they act to restrict imports, so be it. They will thereby do some harm to the trade opportunities of more enlightened countries but, above all, they will deny themselves the incentive of foreign competition in their domestic market. Negotiations to achieve tariff reductions and the removal of other impediments to international trade by reciprocal concessions are not merely beside the point. They are counter-productive because they encourage governments to believe that they are dealing in 'concessions' to and from opponents whereas in fact, their opponents are their friends and, by their supposed concessions, they are directly conferring benefit on themselves.

On this view there should be little to be done by way of negotiation at government level with trading partners. Trading partners can be left to learn by example. If they have sufficient good sense, they will themselves act unilaterally to open their own markets. They will thereby add to the freedom of trade in the world and that will be good. But that is a matter for them, not one for negotiation with us. Indeed it is difficult on this view to see what could possibly be thrown into a negotiation. The retention of trade barriers is on the free trade view harmful. To eliminate trade barriers is not a concession to others but a benefit to oneself. It therefore cannot make a sense to retain trade barriers as a bargaining counter, or to threaten to retain them. To make such threats or to retain trade barriers on such grounds would be simply to cut off one's nose to spite one's face except in the rare case where the threat or the bluff may yield rapid results. The only possible negotiation would lie in the use of economic power or political coercion to extract a forced liberalisation from reluctant trading partners.

Some economists develop arguments for reciprocity which attempt to place it within the bounds of liberal economic respectability. The terms-of-trade argument notes that mutual tariff reductions will not shift the global terms of trade one way or other to the disadvantage of a partner in the negotiations. Unilateral tariff reductions might improve the allocation of resources but any benefit resulting might well be cancelled out by an adverse shift in the terms of trade. There is the employment argument that reciprocity balances increased exports against increased imports and therefore compensates by new employment on exports for any employment lost through imports. There is the balance of payments argument which notes, first, the deficit that might arise in the current account from unreciprocated concessions and, secondly, that correction by means of depreciation in the exchange rate is not without cost (Curzon and Curzon, 1976, p. 158). Though all of them seem sensibly pragmatic, there is no need here to evaluate these arguments. They have one thing in common. By making its benefits dependent on reciprocity, they necessarily place a lower value on free trade. If reciprocity is not in practice achieved, and that must of necessity be uncertain, then the advantages of freer trade to any individual country are eroded and perhaps negatived. These arguments, by justifying the search for reciprocity, lead on to all those shifts and devices by which governments protect themselves against those consequences of freer trade which are most embarrassing politically, and which make them feel most insecure economically.

MERCANTILISM AND RECIPROCITY

The mercantilist will probably take the view that the economic benefits of free trade are in any case greatly exaggerated. He will certainly hold that such advantages as are to be derived from a more open trading system depend in an important degree on reciprocity. The mercantilist view requires governments to seek to retain the option to withdraw from commitments if the effect of an agreement is significantly different from that estimated when the agreement was made. Sidney Golt wrote during the course of the Tokyo Round of multilateral trade negotiations that it was important that the Japanese should demonstrate that their 'internal market did not present such natural and structural impenetrability that the rest of the world could not hope to achieve a fair balance of mutual trading advantage' (Golt, 1978, p. 13). Presumably then, if the Japanese cannot demonstrate that their internal market is penetrable and that there would be a fair balance of mutual trading advantage, they should be denied concessions available to those whose markets are demonstrably open. Or if they promise but do not perform, the option must, on this logic, be open to rescind what has been conceded. Indeed the implication goes wider than exacting revenge on the unpopular Japanese. The implication must be that if trade negotiations do not achieve a 'fair balance of mutual trading advantage', those countries that feel themselves disadvantaged should be entitled to withdraw from the commitments which they only made on the assumption that 'fairness' would result.

Reciprocity is at odds with comparative advantage. In their

negotiations, negotiators will try to combine reciprocity with some recognition of comparative advantage, thus maximising the benefits from the kind of freer trade being achieved. But they will be well aware that too manifest a dedication to comparative advantage is inconsistent with reciprocity and may, as a matter of fact, bring squalls around their heads. Negotiators may well decide that because they are required to achieve reciprocity, they have to sacrifice some advantage which might otherwise be gained for their own most competitive industries. The threats will always be easier to perceive than the opportunities. Reciprocity measures what they can hope to gain against what they dare not lose.

FREE TRADE IN NINETEENTH-CENTURY BRITAIN

Apart from the special case of Hong Kong, there is only one example of a government being prepared to follow free trade policies. During the first half of the nineteenth century, Britain attempted to establish free trade on the basis of reciprocity. As a means of arriving at free trade, the policy was found not to work. The problem was that foreign countries which found benefit in their own protectionist policies saw no reason to pay for concessions which Britain's free trade policy would in due course let them have without charge. This provides a lesson in negotiating tactics which some modern economists still need to learn. As a result of this experience, free trading Britain changed its earlier practice, and did not demand reciprocity before opening its own markets.

This position was somewhat compromised by the Anglo-French commercial treaty, signed in January 1860, and negotiated on the French side by Michel Chevalier and on the British side by Richard Cobden. Richard Cobden had himself always argued that the benefits of free trade were not dependent on the policies of other nations. Cobden was much criticised for his pains precisely because the Anglo-French treaty departed from the pure faith. Palmerston, whose pragmatic mind was not diverted from realism by the mystique of *laissez-faire*, criticised Cobden on mercantilist grounds. He alleged that Cobden had given away more than he got. Palmerston's doubts did not prevent British ratification. Tariffs were reduced and trade between the two countries expanded. The treaty was also an attempt to improve political relations between France and Britain, and could be defended on those grounds.

However, at that time, British governments for the most part took the classical view that free trade was a good thing in itself even if not reciprocated. By the normal standards of conduct in international economic relations, Britain's conduct was highly principled. The policy was not of course disinterested. Britain as the most advanced industrial country, and the most competitive, could expect to benefit from the widest possible extension of free trade. There was the expectation that the unilateral renunciation of tariffs, possible because the introduction of income tax in 1842 had made government revenues less dependent on duties on imports, would reduce the cost of living and hence, no doubt, the cost of wages. Another expectation was that when the benefits of free trade to the UK were appreciated by its trading partners there would be reciprocity in the form of unilateral action by foreign governments to remove trade barriers. The hope may have been that when that reciprocity did arrive, it would add to the benefits to the UK itself. Keynes noted: 'It is, indeed, arguable that in the special circumstances of mid-nineteenth-century Great Britain an almost complete freedom of trade was the policy most conducive to the development of a favourable balance [of trade]' (Keynes, 1947, p. 338).

Unfortunately the benefits to the UK economy of unreciprocated free trade never seemed sufficiently evident to its trading partners to prompt them into a comparably principled self-denial. Though influenced by the prevailing intellectual climate, they were even more influenced by calculations of their own advantage. They acted when it seemed sensible to act, and for a variety of reasons of which benefit to their commerce and their economy was only one. Moreover whatever the benefits to the UK from its unreciprocated advance into economic liberalism and free trade, they appear to have been insufficient to countervail other tendencies which were taking the USA and Germany ahead of Britain in industrial performance and capacity. The jury is still out on the question whether Britain's unreciprocated free trade stance was or was not beneficial to its economic performance. True, Britain under unreciprocated free trade lagged. But without free trade it might have lagged even more. It may be, therefore, that Britain's experience in the nineteenth century is irrelevant to the question whether *laissez-faire* in trade works to the benefit of the unilateral economic disarmer, or whether reciprocity is the key not just to the creation of a more open international trading system but to the attainment of the benefits, or some of them, normally attributed to free trade. The judgement by successive British governments of the free trade experiment was clear enough. Free trade was abandoned as a policy in favour of imperial preference and Britain ended up in the years after the Second World War deeply imbedded in the ranks of the mercantilists.

RECIPROCITY AND THE PROBLEM OF NON-TARIFF BARRIERS

Reciprocal negotiations require some kind of valuation of the mutual concessions on offer. It is, therefore, virtually impossible to deal with non-tariff barriers, other than quotas or other quantitative restrictions, on a reciprocal basis. This is a further reason why policies of reciprocity cannot lead to free trade, though they may lead to freer trade. In a world in which tariffs have been very substantially reduced, non-tariff barriers of various kinds have become the predominant means of protection. During the Tokyo Round of multilateral trade negotiations, an attempt was made to elaborate various codes which would govern the international commercial behaviour of governments in areas other than tariffs. One example was in the matter of subsidies. It was found that to agree a definition of 'subsidy' was very difficult. Yet a definition was necessary before the negotiators could proceed to an agreement on how to control them. The longer the negotiation, the vaguer the wording became. Certain countries were very keen on codes that would exercise significant influence over international trade practices with protectionist overtones. In the end even those countries became content to get what they could. They decided to console themselves with the hope that they could build in the future on whatever they could achieve as a first attempt. It was recognised in the code on subsidies that subsidies intended for domestic purposes could damage other countries. Therefore a complaints procedure was established. Countries with reason to complain could hope to get relief. The code negotiated on public purchasing opened up some of these purchases to competitive bidding from abroad. Much, including defence purchasing, was excluded. The difficulty in negotiating this code was enhanced by the fact that in different countries different proportions of the national product are produced by public agencies. Federal systems of government caused difficulties in cases where the states were not subject to federal control.

What these codes will amount to is, perhaps, a matter for future judgement. But hope for their effectiveness is not high. The procedures for enforcement and the settling of disputes were not exactly credible. There are those who have felt confident enough not to wait for the future but to pronounce at once. The codes have been variously condemned for their vagueness, their lack of specificity, for encouraging discrimination, for being ineffective and even for being counterproductive.

If non-tariff barriers are to be reduced, and thereby greater openness achieved, two methods are available. Either there must be law enforceable by an international authority with its own powers to act, or it must be the result of the unilateral action of governments that see benefit from it. Within the European Community there is an authority, the European Commission, which, subject to the jurisdiction of the Luxembourg Court, can compel action against non-tariff barriers. But the Commission operates on the basis of the Treaty of Rome, that is on the basis of law, not of reciprocity. In the world as a whole there is no comparable law or authority. On the other hand, if much is to depend on the unilateral action of governments, there will have to be a substantial change in the international economic climate.

Tariffs are transparent, and may be quantifiable in their effects. They can therefore be dealt with on a reciprocal basis. Quotas are also transparent and susceptible to reciprocal bargaining. Many non-tariff barriers are not transparent and these are seldom quantifiable. They may even be publicly defensible. If everything is made to depend on reciprocity, there will be little progress. It would depend too much on trust in an area of policy in which trust is not a commodity in prolific supply. No government likes being discovered for a trusting fool. Governments are likely to act only if they truly believe that, even if their trust is abused, their action will be beneficial to their economy.

Of what value then are negotiations for the removal of non-tariff barriers other than quotas? Such negotiations can be thought of as confidence building measures. In favourable circumstances, they may assist governments politically in taking limited risks in the removal of non-tariff barriers. A more likely benefit from such negotiations is that they will serve as a warning to offenders. Excessive creativity with non-tariff barriers can provoke retaliation. If countries go too far in depriving their trading partners of benefits reasonably expected from tariff reductions, there will be a reaction. Though we are sinners all, we should not become hooked on sin.

THE PRACTICE OF RECIPROCITY

What does 'reciprocity' actually mean and how is it to be calculated? What it means is obscure, subjective, and may in the end be determined simply by what is politically acceptable. Although reciprocity is a key concept in GATT negotiations, there is no definition in the GATT. There are various ways in which reciprocity could be calculated. The calculation could relate to the depth in the tariff cut offered, whether on average or across the board. It could be related to volumes of trade affected. It is up to each participating government to decide what definition is appropriate in its own case (Curzon and Curzon, 1976, p. 159).

Despite the absence of any agreed formula for assessing reciprocity, it has become practice to negotiate reciprocal agreements in accordance with two common principles. First the negotiations are on a most favoured nation basis, that is on the basis that a concession to one trading partner will also be allowed multilaterally. This can be regarded as an expression of the non-discrimination principle of the GATT. Secondly, reciprocal agreements are not calculated specifically on a bilateral or sectoral basis. Reciprocity based on these two principles may, for convenience, be called 'general reciprocity'. General reciprocity is a far more powerful instrument for freeing trade than the old-time reciprocity based on bilateral treaties.

If freer trade is to be based on reciprocity, this is probably the only kind of reciprocity on which it can be based. If it were necessary to achieve both bilateral and sectoral balances in every important trading relationship, the difficulties would be insurmountable. Nevertheless negotiators cannot neglect the bilateral and sectoral consequences of any agreement for their own country. However difficult it is to foresee all such effects it is essential that the attempt be made if negotiators are to be able to rebut criticism from sectoral interests that may consider themselves disadvantaged by the overall deal.

In the first five rounds of multilateral trade negotiations conducted after 1947, it was easier to be aware of the bilateral and sectoral consequences because negotiations were conducted on an item-by-item basis. Agreements were negotiated between principal suppliers and then extended multilaterally through the operation of the most favoured nation principle. In the sixth round, the Kennedy Round, it was decided to proceed by means of linear cuts in tariffs. This procedure speeded the process of liberalisation though, in practice, the Kennedy Round negotiators continued to be very conscious of bilateral and sectoral effects.

In any but a rapidly expanding international economy, it would have been very difficult to achieve by this means results acceptable as representing reciprocity. Reciprocity was a matter of government calculation, often of rather crude calculation, in which considerations of politics and economics were intermixed in varying proportions. Inevitably countries strove to mould agreement to their own requirements. Their purpose has been to reconcile two rather contradicatory objectives. On the one hand they wished to protect their weaker industries from an import onslaught. On the other hand they were striving to gain for their stronger industries additional export opportunities. It was a conundrum that could not find a perfect resolution.

It could not be foreseen how far different countries would succeed in exploiting the new opportunities open to them. The result could be a long way from the guess on which the original concessions had been based. Calculations assuming fixed exchange rates could be undermined if relative exchange rates changed significantly. A floating rate world was bound to make such forecasts even more hazardous. When to all this is added the need to calculate the trade effect of a concession in a multilateral trading situation, with the most favoured nation clause operating, it will be appreciated that the problem is likely to defeat the most expert study and the most subtle computers.

In these calculations there has been little of the spirit of economic liberalism. A suggestion that tariff concessions were good in themselves has been seldom heard. On the contrary, the whole spirit has been cabined, cribbed, confined, by a desperate fear that something might be given without an adequate return. Carefully watching the progress of these negotiations have stood the trade associations and industrial confederations. Their function has been to ensure that nothing was given away without adequate reciprocity. The consumer has been the least of their concerns. Any government officials engaged in these negotiations, who allowed themselves to be influenced for one moment by the rhetoric of economic liberalism, were taking a grave risk. They could expect only to be denounced by the interest groups, and in national parliaments, as betrayers of their country's industrial interests and therefore of the welfare of its people. Ministers have had a ready ear for such complaints. On the post-war battlefields of trade negotiations they have displayed their heroism in resisting incursions of foreign goods unless an equal and opposite opportunity could be persuasively shown to have been conceded on the other side. And sometimes even then. The chambers of our parliament buildings have resounded to the cheers which such heroism deserves as its reward.

UNILATERAL DISARMAMENT

Those who hold the general reciprocity view will regard the pure free trade view as arguing for a kind of 'unilateral disarmament'. They will not want 'to go naked' into the negotiating chamber. Those who hold these views will be bound to argue that as the benefits of free trade depend in an essential measure on reciprocity, no sacrifice is being made by withholding from trading partners, concessions which they are refusing to match; or even *in extremis* creating new barriers in order to reinforce a bargaining position providing only that they are not too damaging to oneself, a calculation which is itself not a matter of science but of judgement. But its very nature, therefore, the general reciprocity view must put a lower value on free trade as an economic objective than does the pure free trade view.

THE USA AND THE POLITICS OF RECIPROCITY

Why, given the mercantilist preconceptions of governments, has the cause of freer trade prospered since the Second World War? We have seen that the principal impetus, without which progress would have been impossible, has come from the USA. The USA has striven through successive negotiating rounds to reduce the discrimination against its exports constituted by preferential trading areas, first the area of British imperial preference, and then succeeding preferential areas of which by far the most important have been the European Community and, if it can be so described, Japan. As the whole motive force behind American action was to gain more than they gave, it is ironic that the Americans have insisted on reciprocity. It was the express American intention in the Kennedy Round to increase their export surplus. President Kennedy, in presenting his trade bill to Congress, said: 'we must reduce our own tariffs if we hope to reduce tariffs abroad and thereby increase our exports and our export surplus' (Curzon and Curzon, 1976, p. 177). In fact things turned out rather differently for the USA. The completion of the Kennedy Round was rapidly followed by the Nixon measures of 15 August 1971. The USA temporarily absented itself from the international economic community of nations while it strove, with only moderate success, to bully its trading partners into submission to its own requirements.

Reciprocity constitutes the only politically acceptable mode of advance towards freer trade. In the case of the United States, this fact is explicit. The United States Congress insists on reciprocity in trade negotiations between the USA and the rest of the world. The demand for reciprocity is embodied in the successive Reciprocal Trade Agreements Acts. Presumably the USA has relied on the principle of reciprocity as an insurance against losing out in trade negotiations but with the hope that its enormous economic and political power would gain it a negotiating victory over its partners. As there has to be reciprocity, other countries have to have obstacles to trade with the USA or they can get no concessions from the USA. The introduction of obstacles to trade for the purpose of bartering them away against concessions is no new postwar idea. Of course countries would have them even without this encouragement from American legislation. The principle of reciprocity has provided countries on the receiving end of American pressure with an instrument of defence, the more effective because the USA itself has always insisted on reciprocity. Reciprocity has not merely been the road to freer trade, it has been an important defence against too rapid a progress towards freer trade.

Yet the purity of the liberal ideal no longer has much practical attraction even among those for whom it is an intellectual option. Free trade economists have become dealers in political realism. For example, Henderson would prefer free trade but is prepared to settle for reciprocity. His political realism leads him to say that 'it is easier for each government to contain the pressures on it if all of them are acting in concert' (Henderson, 1983, p. 18). He knows all about the pressures that can influence the behaviour of even the most liberal governments if their trading partners do not themselves behave in a liberal way.

> Once a trend towards ad hoc interventionism and breaking the rules has set in, it is hard for any country to stand aside. To fail to match the mercantilist devices of others would be generally regarded as sheer ineptitude. Nor is this just a matter of each government being seen to be as resourceful and responsive as the next: a deeper issue of national autonomy is also involved. By eschewing the right to adopt discriminatory trade measures, governments limit their freedom of action. Not only is this perceived as irksome in itself, but it carries with it the apparent risk that the way in which a country's economy develops is made subject to the trade policies of more opportunist countries. Unilateral trade liberalism, like unilateral disarmament, is thus seen as restricting the ability of states to decide their own destinies (Henderson, 1983, p. 16).

There is no doubt, then, that Henderson sees the practice of demanding reciprocity as politically advisable. He accepts without comment the paradox that so unpersuasive have the arguments for free trade been found that a government will actually be considered 'resourceful and responsive' if it replies to protectionist actions by its trading partners by equally damaging protectionist measures of its own. Most liberal economists are these days too practical to allow their eyes to be misted over by distant perceptions of a free trade ideal. They are no longer men of the ideal but of the practical. They are mercantilists all. They will give their loyalties to the real tasks, and those tasks are the practice of reciprocity.

THE 'NEW' OR 'AGGRESSIVE' RECIPROCITY

A harder approach to the concept of reciprocity is now visible, an approach emanating from the USA and described by William R. Cline as the 'new' or 'aggressive' reciprocity view (Cline, 1982). Cline defines the difference between the general and the new reciprocity positions as follows:

> US reciprocity objectives in the past meant seeking reciprocal *changes* in protection in trade negotiations; the new approach seeks reciprocity in the *level* of protection *bilaterally* and over a *certain range of goods* (Cline, 1982, p. 7).

He also says:

> The new reciprocity movement has appropriated the term to a narrow usage focusing on equivalent market treatment, in some cases even for limited ranges of goods. In the more traditional conception of the term, reciprocity has meant broad balance between the reduction in trade barriers offered by the United States and the liberalisation secured from other major trading partners in negotiations, or reciprocity 'at the margin' on a basis of all products considered together (Cline, 1982, pp. 7–8).

There has been a feeling in the USA that in many cases, whatever the intention of American negotiators, reciprocity has not in fact been achieved. Trading partners have been found to have had the better of the bargain. This is particularly thought to be the case in the USA's relations with Japan. Cline says:

'The immediate cause of the conflict is Japan's large bilateral surplus with the United States', and he quotes Senator Robert Dole [Rep.-Kan.], once majority leader in the Senate, as arguing: 'reciprocity should be assessed not by what agreements promise but by actual results – by changes in the balance of trade and investment between ourselves and our major economic partners' (quoted Cline, 1982, pp. 11–12). There is pressure, therefore, that the USA should withdraw something of what it has conceded, largely though not entirely in its relations with Japan.

Such action would be likely to be damaging to the world trading system. Any unilateral American action against Japan which diverted Japanese exports to the European Community would cause grave trouble in the relations between Europe and the USA. It might perhaps not be too damaging to the USA. At any rate that might be the view of those whose approach to free trade is through the reciprocity principle. The USA can get away with a great deal without too much risk. Comparable freedom may not be available at comparably low risk to other members of the international community. Even in the case of the USA the risks might be greater than foreseen by those who argue for unilateral action in accordance with the principles of aggressive reciprocity. That is one reason why the USA, which is often threatening in its relations with Japan, so often draws back, having perhaps squeezed some concession from the Japanese. The Europeans tend to do the same in their relations with Japan, but they lack the political muscle that sometimes achieves results for the USA.

Cline describes this approach as 'aggressive' reciprocity in part because of its tendency to use negotiating weapons, such as the withdrawl of concessions, aggressively. 'The danger of aggressive reciprocity is that foreign countries may respond in kind. Imposition of a retaliatory trade barrier may provoke the foreign country to impose counterretaliatory barriers of its own' (Cline, 1982, p. 21). He cites the Hawley-Smoot Act of 1930 as an example of the counterproductive nature of policies based on aggressive reciprocity. Cline is right to point out the rise of what he calls the 'new' approach, precisely because of the dangers it represents to the world trading system.

The world trading system could never have been built on the basis of bilateral and sectoral balances. Widespread insistence on them would inevitably destroy it. Cline nevertheless overestimates the degree to which even the general reciprocity approach could ignore bilateral and sectoral imbalances. 'General' reciprocity and 'aggressive' reciprocity have more in common than Cline is prepared to allow. There are two points worth making in this context. The first is that reciprocity of both kinds is a matter of negotiation. Although the result of negotiation may be a fair balance, each party is in fact striving for its own advantage. The balance, if it is achieved, results from each party striving for its own advantage. In fact balance may not be achieved. One side may win out either by mistake, or through superior negotiating tactics, or through the use of superior economic and political power.

The second point is that one weapon of negotiation must be the threat to withdraw concessions. Such threats have indeed been the normal currency in successive multilateral trade negotiations. If such a threat is used there must be a real readiness to implement it. The result may indeed be a reduction in world trade which free trade economists, including Cline, would regard as deplorable. On the other hand the threat may work and the dimensions of free trade be thereby increased. How much then is to be risked in order to achieve the possible benefits? The USA is particularly well equipped by reasons of its vast resources to fight an aggressive retaliatory battle if it feels that the situation justifies it. It has the money with which to subsidise export credit. It has the agricultural supplies and the money with which to threaten quite seriously the prospects for the European Community's subsidised agricultural exports, and thereby to impose very high costs on the European budget. If the USA cannot achieve its objectives by influence, it might easily decide to achieve them by aggressive retaliation. It might conclude that in such a battle the USA was unlikely to be the loser. Cline is, apparently, not prepared to risk anything but that may not be the attitude of governments under pressure, and particularly of the American government under pressure. And they may succeed by aggressive retaliation and by the quality of their negotiating tactics in opening up a new quantum of international free trade which would otherwise not have been realised.

The USA and other developed countries have for the most part used their power, and their power to issue such threats, with discretion. They have so far shown full regard to the dangers to the open trading system posed by aggressive retaliation or by aggressive demands for bilateral or sectoral reciprocity. Whether the USA, with its large current account deficit, will continue to show the restraint it has so far exercised is now a worrying question in international trade relations. The USA is threatening the increasing use of bilateral arrangements outside the GATT. It may be that it will be satisfied only by major concessions by its trading partners, concessions for which there will be no reciprocal return. With each American threat, with each American bilateral arrangement, the risks to the open trading system increase. American policy will be the main determinant of its future. But there is no value in complaining that the techniques of aggressive reciprocity are illegitimate because they involve risks to the open trading system. Willingness to take the risks inherent in their use is part of the game play of trade negotiations and is also just one more piece of evidence that governments, and particularly the American government, place only a relative value on the economic benefits of free trade.

THE GATT AND RECIPROCITY

The Preamble of the GATT speaks of 'reciprocal and mutually advantageous arrangements'. Those who drafted the GATT will have seen this as the merest political realism. But how does the GATT see it today? Where is their priority, in free trade or in reciprocity? The answer to this question is very important to the future of the GATT. Institutions acquire vested interests. Supposedly liberal but actually mercantilist institutions like GATT are no different in this respect from the generality of institutions. It is under the auspices of the GATT that multilateral trade negotiations take place. If unreciprocated free trade is beneficial to those who open their markets, then the whole costly farce of the trade round can be abandoned. If the truth is that those countries will benefit most who open up most, they can act unilaterally. They do not need the GATT. The GATT can be abandoned as the product of a mercantilist philosophy.

The GATT is an institution blessed with an objective – free

trade reciprocally negotiated – that can never be achieved. It is, nevertheless, uncertain whether it will show the same capacity for survival as the early Church whose object, the perfectibility of mankind, has proved at least equally difficult of achievement.

RETROSPECTIVE JUDGEMENT AND HOW TO ENFORCE IT

If a reciprocal agreement turns out less favourably than anticipated, if more industries are contracting and fewer expanding, is a government then entitled to withdraw any of the concessions it has made? So complex is a reciprocal negotiation that errors must be made and, apart from actual errors, there is as is usual in any economic calculation great uncertainty. In these circumstances it can be an important question whether retrospective regard may be had to the actual outcome of a reciprocal negotiation. The answer must certainly be that in principle it can. Indeed the GATT offers procedures by which it legitimately can. Whether a government is well advised to use these procedures must be a matter for its own judgement. They have not been frequently used. There are number of reasons for this. In the first place, during much of the period the general prosperity and the rate of increase of international trade tended to conceal the effect of any such errors in forecasting. Calculations of benefits in terms of increased export opportunities against costs in the form of increased imports no doubt frequently turned out to be wrong. But the errors might well prove to be self-cancelling. If they were not, resort could be had to protective actions outside the GATT which had the advantage of avoiding the need to offer compensation. In the last resort changes in the exchange rate remained as an ultimate recourse for dealing with, and hopefully correcting, current account deficits.

The fact that reciprocity is seen as the key to advances in free trade does raise some questions about the logic of the GATT in requiring compensation where a country reacts under the GATT to an unfavourable out-turn, either for employment or for its current account, attributable to trade negotiations. If the object is to restore balance where the outcome of a trade negotiation is worse than anticipated, the only questions should be whether the lack of balance is being correctly attributed and whether it is likely to be restored by whatever action is proposed. To suggest compensation where the proposed action is merely likely to restore balance is to suggest a return to imbalance. Indeed so far from being contrary to the GATT, a voluntary export restraint which restores the originally intended balance follows precisely the logic of reciprocity and hence the logic of the GATT. The real problem is not the logic of the case but the politics. The compensation requirement acts as a restraint on hasty, unjustified and politically motivated action. If it were removed the danger that new restraints on trade would be unilaterally introduced on the pretence of thereby restoring balance would be very great.

CONCLUSION

The development since the war of an open trading system has created a constituency for free trade among companies with successful export records. The integration of the world economy has made protective action by any nation potentially costly both economically and politically. But all this has been achieved by negotiation among mercantilists, not on the basis of free trade principles but on the basis of reciprocity. The danger is that the ground won under the flag of reciprocity can be surrendered under cover of the very same flag.

No government, with the enticing exception of Hong Kong, is sufficiently persuaded of the merits of the free trade argument to commit itself to it. Governments fear the hostility of their industries, and of trade unions. They fear the accusation of naïvety. It is always a better posture to be tough with foreigners. In all this, indeed, they surrender to vested interests. But they do have more respectable arguments on their side. They regard the whole free trade case as insufficiently proven voluntarily to take many risks on its behalf. They fear the risks to the current account of the balance of payments. They fear the social unrest that can result from concentrated areas of unemployment even where it is arguable that the economy as a whole will benefit. Governments are entitled to see reciprocity as not just a political requirement. In a situation in which the economic benefits of free trade are insufficiently obvious even to most liberal economists to justify their following the true liberal faith, it can reasonably be held by governments that they *are* making concessions when they permit freer access to their own market and that therefore such concessions need to be compensated by freer access to other markets. And however much they may bind themselves in such reciprocal agreements the option will remain of building barriers of new kinds if the need arises.

This combination of political constraints and economic doubts will ensure that reciprocity will continue to be the key to progress towards freer trade. But if this be the case, two consequences follow. The first is that a world of free trade remains inaccessible in the future as it has been in the past. The second is that the unilateral free trade gesture is likely to be as fruitless in trade negotiations as it would be in the case of nuclear disarmament. Unilateral measures, if good reason is seen for them, may of course be taken. They can always be withdrawn. But if the unilateral gesture becomes a commitment, it is simply one more negotiating point given away. Negotiating partners will tuck it under their belt seeing it simply as a quixotic gesture that, by its very nature, does not need to be reciprocated. They will then consider what they have to concede against further concessions from the other side. Trade negotiators are hard men. They have to be. They negotiate under the eye of powerful vested interests. However convinced they themselves may be of the benefits of progress, they know that what they must bring home is a deal, a deal defensible not in terms of liberal economics but in terms of a hard bargain well and truly made. Governments whose principal responsibility is to protect their people, and not to take incalculable risks, will stand behind their tough negotiators. They will have to be very sure of the benefits before they take unilateral action based on free trade principles.

Despite Adam Smith, reciprocity has won. There will be no unilateral disarmament. As the mercantilist scripture would put it: 'I will do unto others as they do unto me, within limits, and provided only that I cannot get away with some trick on the side. Moreover I will jealously husband every restriction until I have achieved some return for its abandonment. I will then invent some new ones. I will never go naked to the conference chamber.'

The paradox of reciprocity is that it is both the sand on which free trade as we know it is constructed, and the rock on which it might most easily founder.

Part III

Conclusion

18 Conclusion

Adam Smith's final recommendation was that Great Britain should 'endeavour to accommodate her future views and designs to the real mediocrity of her circumstances' (Smith, 1947, vol. 2, p. 430). His recommendation proved a little premature. Yet, having between 1776 and the present day conquered and relinquished half a world, the UK now has little choice but to do precisely what Smith recommended. The transition from Empire to mediocrity has been troubled and the troubles are certainly not at an end. Too much can be made of the relative stability of recent years. With the end of American tutelage came the breakdown of the Bretton Woods system which provided some protection for Britain's lagging economy. Since then, the UK has been relatively fortunate. It has been shielded from the full impact of the change. It has been shielded by North Sea oil. Before it was shielded by the reality of North Sea oil, it was shielded by the prospect of North Sea oil. That shield can no longer be confidently relied upon.

Other, even more deceptive, sources of comfort are on offer. The coordination of economic policy is proposed as a means of achieving a higher level of economic activity internationally, with consequent benefit to all, and especially the weaker, member states of the international community. For the reasons discussed in this book, this coordination will under present circumstances be very difficult to achieve. It will prove particularly difficult to implement any of those numerous policy propoals, or 'solutions' for economic discontents, which require from key governments some sacrifice of a defensive posture now in return for benefits in the years to come. The benefits from such policies to the 'locomotive' economies would be uncertain and small. They would perceive the risks as rather great. They would conclude that it is not for them, the economic achievers, to change their stance. In the absence of some power of coercion, they will continue to make their own decisions. The resistance of Germany and Japan to calls for more internationally oriented policies, gives the lie to those who proclaim the death of national sovereignty.

Failure to achieve economic policy coordination, or the

benefits expected to be derived from it, will sap resistance to protectionism. But, essentially, the prospects for an open world economy depend on the USA. If American domestic pressures overwhelm the resistance of the White House to extending protectionism, the system as it now is cannot survive. But if the system does collapse, there will still be a job to be done in international economic relations. It will still be desirable to live together with fewer disputes rather than with more, and that will present a continuing task for international economic diplomacy. The world has moved into an era when the settlement of disputes will necessarily take precedence over the coordination of economic policy. That will be the urgent practical requirement. In satisfying that requirement, the experience of international cooperation in the years after the Second World War should be a help in preserving a tradition of international discussion and reconciliation.

In this book I have argued three related theses. The first is that the instinct for national economic security has always been an important, sometimes decisive, element in economic policy-making. It continues to be an influence even within an interdependent world though the extent of that influence depends on the independent discretion that governments have been able to retain and the basic strength of the national economy. Policy today must always be seen in an international context. It cannot make sense to formulate policy, particularly within middle-ranking and smaller countries, as though their affairs could be isolated from the influence of market forces and of other governments. Equally, however, it is a mistake to claim that even well conducted governments are so powerless that they can no longer discharge their duties to their citizens and that nothing remains other than to obey. Interdependence is as much about the exercise of state power as about the operation of market forces. National sovereignty is still there as a thorn in the flesh of those who demand that the power of the market, often their power in the market, should dominate. The second thesis has been that no economic theory provides a reliable a basis for action. Economic theories of whatever kind are for pragmatic assessment in the light of particular economic conjunctures. None of them convey eternal truths. All of them leave political judgement as the final arbiter of action. The third has been that it is inevitable that nations will deploy their power in an attempt to secure for themselves that accommodation with their partners that most nearly serves their interests. The distribution of benefits from an interdependent world will recognise the distribution of power within it.

What is required is pragmatism, preferably with a liberal tinge. Considerations of personal freedom and welfare are involved as well as considerations of national economic security. In the hands of the pragmatist, economic liberalism becomes a potent critical weapon. Under all governments, whatever their rhetoric, the bias of our time is in favour of government intervention in the economic life of the community. Economic liberalism poses critical questions about what governments do and for what benefit. It probes every sort of vested interest, not just those of the professions and trade unions, but all those constituted by alliances between government and powerful pressure groups. No significant cost should go unscrutinised. The costs concerned are not just money costs. They are costs in loss of freedom however small, freedom to choose, freedom to spend, freedom to invest, freedom to join or not to join. If the costs are measured not in money terms but in terms of freedoms reduced, they will be seen to be a great deal less acceptable than if the argument is posed in terms of economic benefits foregone. The one will be visible and persuasive. The other is distant, doubtful, certainly controversial.

There is no likelihood that the exponents of international economic diplomacy will find themselves underemployed. They will continue to discharge two roles which can be in conflict. First, they have the national role summed up in the concept of national economic security. Secondly, they should be in the business of reconciliation. Reconciliation can add to economic security, but it can sometimes be at some sacrifice of economic security. Nothing will be perfect and nothing permanent. The terms of reconciliation will reflect the changing balance of power. Not everyone can be satisfied except that the alternative may be even less attractive. The gains of each negotiation will erode until restored by some new negotiation.

Nations that require some of their ablest servants to discharge two roles, so contradictory in character, so requiring of restraint in language and action, so dependent on precise calculation and careful judgement, have some reason for anxiety. They also have some reason for satisfaction with the expertise with which these same servants have thus far implemented the techniques of liberal pragmatism.

References and Short Bibliography

VINOD K. AGGARWAL, *Liberal Protectionism: The International Politics of Organized Textile Trade* (University of California Press, 1985).

FRANS A. M. ALTING, VON GEUSAU and JACQUES PELKMANS (eds), *National Economic Security: Perceptions, Threats, and Policies* (John F. Kennedy Institute, Tilburg, Netherlands, 1982).

RYAN C. AMACHER, GOTTFRIED HABERLER and THOMAS D. WILLETT (eds), *Challenges to a Liberal Economic Order* (American Enterprise Institute for Public Policy Research, Washington DC, 1979).

BELA BALASSA, *The New Protectionism: An evaluation and proposals for reform*, in Ryan C. Amacher, Gottfried Haberler and Thomas D. Willett (eds), *Challenges to a Liberal Economic Order* (American Enterprise Institute for Public Policy Research, Washington DC, 1979).

ROBERT E. BALDWIN, *Beyond the Tokyo Round Negotiations* (Thames Essay no. 22, Trade Policy Research Centre, London, 1979).

C. FRED BERGSTEN and WILLIAM R. CLINE, *Trade Policy in the 1980s* (Institute for International Economics, Washington DC, 1983).

C. FRED BERGSTEN and JOHN WILLIAMSON, 'Exchange rates and trade policy', in William R. Cline (ed.), *Trade Policy in the 1980s* (Institute for International Economics, Washington DC, 1983).

JOHN BLACK and BRIAN HINDLEY (eds), *Current Issues in Commercial Policy and Diplomacy* (Papers at the Third Annual Conference of the International Economics Study Group, Macmillan, for the Trade Policy Research Centre, London, 1980).

JOHN BLACK and L. ALAN WINTERS, *Policy and Performance in International Trade* (Papers of the Sixth Annual Conference of the International Economics Study Group, Macmillan, London, 1983).

RICHARD BLACKHURST, NICOLAS MARIAN and JAN TUMLIR, *Trade Liberalization, Protectionism and Interdependence*, GATT Studies in International Trade (GATT, Geneva, November 1977).

JITENDRALAL BORKAKOTI, 'Economic methodology, trade theory and policy', in John Black and L. Alan Winters, *Policy and Performance in International Trade* (Papers of the Sixth Annual Conference of the International Economics Study Group, Macmillan, London, 1983).

SAMUEL BRITTAN, *Steering the Economy* (Penguin, Harmondsworth, 1971).

WILLIAM A. BROCK and STEPHEN P. MAGEE, 'Tariff formation in a democracy', in John Black and Brian Hindley (eds), *Current Issues in Commercial Policy and Diplomacy* (Papers at the Third Annual Conference of the International Economics Study Group, Macmillan, for the Trade Policy Research Centre, London, 1980).

WILLEM BUITER, 'The future of economic management', in *Catalyst, A Journal of Policy Debate*, vol. 1, no. 1, Spring 1985.

FORREST CAPIE, 'Tariff protection and economic performance in the nineteenth century', in John Black and L. Alan Winters, *Policy and Performance in International Trade* (Papers of the Sixth Annual Conference of the International Economics Study Group, Macmillan, London, 1983).

YINK-PIK CHOI, HWA SOO CHUNG and NICOLAS MARIAN, *The Multi-Fibre Arrangement in Theory and Practice, Programme of Cooperation among Developing Countries* (Frances Pinter (Publishers), London, 1984).

WILLIAM R. CLINE, *Reciprocity – A New Approach to World Trade Policy?* (Institute for International Economics, Washington DC, September 1982).

WILLIAM R. CLINE (ed.), *Trade Policy in the 1980s* (Institute for International Economics, Washington DC, 1983).

D. C. COLEMAN (ed.), *Revisions in Mercantilism* (Methuen & Co., London, 1969).

W. M. CORDEN, *Trade Policy and Economic Welfare* (Oxford University Press, 1974).

GERARD and VICTORIA CURZON, *The Multilateral Trading System of the 1960s*, vol. 1, *International Economic Relations of the Western World* (Oxford University Press for the Royal Institute of International Affairs, London, 1976).

EDMUND DELL, *Political Responsibility and Industry* (Allen & Unwin, London, 1973).

EDMUND DELL, *The Politics of Economic Interdependence* (Fifth Rita Hinden Memorial Lecture, London, February 1977).

EDMUND DELL, 'The wistful liberalism of Deepak Lal', in *The World Economy*, vol. 2, no. 2, May 1979.

EDMUND DELL, 'Trade policy: retrospect and prospect', in *International Affairs*, vol. 60, no. 2, Spring 1984.

EDMUND DELL, 'Economic relationships between states', in *International Affairs*, vol. 61, no. 1, Winter 1984–5.

EDMUND DELL, 'Interdependence and the judges: civil aviation and antitrust', in *International Affairs*, vol. 61, no. 3, Summer 1985.

EDMUND DELL, 'Of free trade and reciprocity', in *The World Economy* (Basil Blackwell, for the Trade Policy Research Centre, Oxford, vol. 9, no. 2, June 1986.

SIDNEY DELL, 'The emergence of UNCTAD', in *UNCTAD: the first twenty years*, IDS Bulletin, vol. 15, no. 3, July 1984.

JOHN H. DUNNING, 'Multinational enterprises and industrial restructuring in the UK', *Lloyds Review*, no. 158, October 1985.

C. R. FAY, *Great Britain from Adam Smith to the Present Day* (Longmans, Green & Co., London, 1937).

MILTON and ROSE FRIEDMAN, *Free to Choose* (Avon, New York, 1980).

HANNES H. GISSURARSON, 'The only truly progressive policy', in *Hayek's 'Serfdom' Revisited* (Hobart Paperback no. 18, Institute of Economic Affairs, 1984).

SIDNEY GOLT, *The GATT negotiations 1973–79: The closing stage* (British–North American Committee, May 1978).

ROY HARROD, *The Life of John Maynard Keynes* (Macmillan, London, 1951).

F. A. HAYEK, *The Road to Serfdom* (Routledge & Kegan Paul, London, 1979).

P. D. HENDERSON, 'Trade policies: trends, issues and influences', *Midland Bank Review*, Winter 1983.

THOMAS HOBBES, *The Leviathan* (Dent 'Everyman', London, 1947).

ROBERT E. HUDEC, 'The GATT legal system', in *Journal of World Trade*, September–October 1970.

ROBERT E. HUDEC, *The GATT Legal System and World Trade Diplomacy* (Praeger, New York, 1975).

ROBERT E. HUDEC, *Adjudication of International Trade Disputes*, Thames Essay no. 16 (Trade Policy Research Centre, 1978).

DAVID HUME, 'Jealousy of trade', 1758, in Eugene Rotwein (ed.), *Writings on Economics* (Nelson, Edinburgh, 1955).

R. A. JOHNS, *International Trade Theories and the Evolving International Economy* (Frances Pinter (Publishers) Ltd., London, 1985).

H. G. JOHNSON, 'Protection and welfare in modern perspective', a review of W. M. Corden's *Trade Policy and Economic Welfare*, in *Journal of World Trade Law*, March–April 1976.

ROBERT O. KEOHANE, *After Hegemony: Cooperation and discord in the world political economy* (Princeton University Press, 1984).

ROBERT O. KEOHANE and JOSEPH S. NYE, *Power and Interdependence; World politics in transition* (Little, Brown, New York, 1977).

J. M. KEYNES, 'National self-sufficiency', in *The Yale Review*, June 1933.

J. M. KEYNES, *The General Theory of Employment, Interest and Money* (Macmillan, London, 1947).

DEEPAK LAL, 'The wistful mercantilism of Mr. Dell', in *The World Economy*, vol. 1, no. 3, June 1978.

DEEPAK LAL, 'Politicians, economists and protection – the deaf meet the blind', in *The World Economy* (Basil Blackwell, for the Trade Policy Research Centre, Oxford, vol. 3, no. 2, September 1980.

DEEPAK LAL, *The Poverty of 'Development Economics'* (Hobart Paperback no. 16, Institute of Economic Affairs, 1983).

W. LETWIN, *The Origin of Scientific Economics: English Economic Thought, 1660–1776* (Methuen, London, 1963).

W. ARTHUR LEWIS, *The Theory of Economic Growth* (Allen & Unwin, London, 1961).

I. M. D. LITTLE, 'The developing countries and the international order', in Ryan C. Amacher, Gottfried Haberler and Thomas D. Willett (eds), *Challenges to a Liberal Economic Order* (American Enterprise Institute for Public Policy Research, Washington DC, 1979).

I. M. D. LITTLE, *Economic Development: 'Theory, policy and international relations* (Basic Books, New York, 1982).

OLIVIER LONG, 'International trade under threat: a constructive response', in *The World Economy*, vol. 1, no. 3, June 1978.

EVAN LUARD, *Economic Relationships Among States: A further study in international sociology* (Macmillan, London, 1984).

JOHN STUART MILL, *The Principles of Political Economy, with some of their applications to Social Philosophy*, W. J. Ashley (ed.), (Longmans, Green & Co., London, 1909).

CHRIS MILNER and DAVID GREENAWAY, *An Introduction to International Economics* (Longman, London, 1979).

TOMMASSO PADOA-SCHIOPPA, 'Squaring the circle, or the conundrum of international monetary reform', in *Catalyst, A Journal of Policy Debate*, vol. 1, no. 1, Spring 1985.

JOAN PEARCE and JOHN SUTTON with ROY BATCHELOR, *Protection and Industrial Policy in Europe* (Routledge & Kegan Paul, for the Royal Institute of International Affairs, London, 1985).

SOL PICCIOTTO, 'Political economy and international law', in Susan Strange (ed.), *Paths to International Political Economy* (Allen & Unwin, London, 1984).

KENNETH PICKTHORN, *Early Tudor Government: Henry VII* (Cambridge University Press, 1934).

JOHN PINDER, TAKASHI HOSOMI and WILLIAM DIEBOLD, *Industrial Policy and the International Economy* (Trilateral Commission, Task Force Report No. 19, New York University Press, 1981).

SIR LEO PLIATZKY, *Paying and Choosing, The Intelligent Person's Guide to the Mixed Economy* (Basil Blackwell, for the Policy Studies Institute, Oxford, 1985).

E. H. PREEG, *Traders and Diplomats* (Washington DC, 1970).

ROBERT D. PUTNAM and NICHOLAS BAYNE, *Hanging Together, The Seven-Power Summits* (Heinemann, for the Royal Institute of International Affairs, London, 1984).

W. B. REDDAWAY, in collaboration with J. O. N. PERKINS, S. J. POTTER, and C. T. TAYLOR, *Effects of UK Direct Investment Overseas* (Cambridge University Press, Interim and Final Reports, University of Cambridge Department of Applied Economics Occasional papers, no. 12, 1967, and no. 15, 1968).

THE REPORT ON EUROPEAN INSTITUTIONS, Report to the European Council by Barend Biesheuvel, Edmund Dell and Robert Marjolin (Council of the European Communities, Brussels, 1980).

DOUGLAS E. ROSENTHAL and WILLIAM M. KNIGHTON, *National Laws and International Commerce, The Problem of Extraterritoriality* (Chatham House Paper no. 17, Royal Institute of International Affairs and Routledge & Kegan Paul, London, 1982).

BERTRAND RUSSELL, *Power, A New Social Analysis* (Allen & Unwin, London, 1938).

SIR ARTHUR SALTER, *World Trade and Its Future* (University of Pennsylvania Press, 1936).

M. FG. SCOTT, W. M. CORDEN and I. M. D. LITTLE, *The Case against General Import Controls* (Thames Essay no. 24, Trade Policy Research Centre, London, 1980).

ANDREW SHONFIELD, 'International economic relations', in *Washington Papers*, vol. 4, no. 42, 1976.

ANDREW SHONFIELD, *The Use of Public Power* (Oxford University Press, 1982).

ADAM SMITH, *The Wealth of Nations* (Dent 'Everyman', London, 1947).

JOAN EDELMAN SPERO, *The Politics of International Economic Relations* (2nd ed.) (Allen & Unwin, London, 1982).

LESLIE STEIN, *Trade and Structural Change* (Croom Helm, London, 1984).

SUSAN STRANGE (ed.), *Paths to International Political Economy* (Allen & Unwin, London, 1984).

ANTHONY TROLLOPE, *Orley Farm* (Oxford University Press, The World's Classics, 1985).

LOUKAS TSOUKALIS (ed.), *The Political Economy of International Money: In search of a new order* (Royal Institute of International Affairs, London, 1985).

LOUKAS TSOUKALIS (ed.), *Europe, America and the World Economy* (Basil Blackwell, for the College of Europe, Oxford, 1986).

JAN TUMLIR, 'The new protectionism, cartels and the international order', in Ryan C. Amacher, Gottfried Haberler and Thomas D. Willett (eds), *Challenges to a Liberal Economic Order* (American Enterprise Institute for Public Policy Research, Washington DC, 1979).

JAN TUMLIR, *Economic Policy as a Constitutional Problem* (Fifteenth Wincott Memorial Lecture, Institute of Economic Affairs Occasional Paper no. 70, 1984).

UNITED NATIONS CONFERENCE ON TRADE AND DEVELOPMENT (UNCTAD), Proceedings of the Conference, Geneva, 23 March–16 June 1964.

UNCTAD Bulletin, monthly series.

WILLIAM WALLACE, 'What price independence? Sovereignty and interdependence in British politics', in *International Affairs*, vol. 62, no. 3, Summer 1986.

Index

263

264

Index